UX Strategy

How to Devise Innovative Digital Products That People Want

Jaime Levy

O'REILLY®   Beijing · Boston · Farnham · Köln · Sebastopol · Tokyo

UX Strategy
by Jaimy Levy

Copyright © 2015 Jaime Levy. All rights reserved.

Printed in the United States of America.

Published by O'Reilly Media, Inc., 1005 Gravenstein Highway North, Sebastopol, CA 95472.

O'Reilly books may be purchased for educational, business, or sales promotional use. Online editions are also available for most titles (*safaribooksonline.com*). For more information, contact our corporate/institutional sales department: (800) 998-9938 or *corporate@oreilly.com*.

Acquisitions Editor: Mary Treseler
Editor: Angela Rufino
Developmental Editor: Angela Rufino
Production Editor: Melanie Yarbrough
Copyeditor: Octal Publishing
Proofreader: Eileen Cohen

Indexer: Bob Pfahler
Cover Designer: Ellie Volkhausen
Interior Designers: Ron Bilodeau and Monica Kamsvaag
Illustrators: Rebecca Demarest
Compositor: Melanie Yarbrough

May 2015: First Edition.

Revision History for the First Edition:

  2015-05-12   First release

  2015-07-10   Second release

See *http://oreilly.com/catalog/errata.csp?isbn=0636920032090* for release details.

The O'Reilly logo is a registered trademark of O'Reilly Media, Inc. *UX Strategy* and related trade dress are trademarks of O'Reilly Media, Inc.

Many of the designations used by manufacturers and sellers to distinguish their products are claimed as trademarks. Where those designations appear in this book, and O'Reilly Media, Inc., was aware of a trademark claim, the designations have been printed in caps or initial caps.

Although the publisher and author have used reasonable care in preparing this book, the information it contains is distributed "as is" and without warranties of any kind. This book is not intended as legal or financial advice, and not all of the recommendations may be suitable for your situation. Professional legal and financial advisors should be consulted, as needed. Neither the publisher nor the author shall be liable for any costs, expenses, or damages resulting from use of or reliance on the information contained in this book.

978-1-449-37286-6

[LSI]

[contents]

[*Foreword*]

When I was 21 years old and taking the train into Manhattan from Brooklyn to fix laser printers and dream of a career in "multimedia," I would read about Jaime Levy's work hoping that one day I would get to meet her.

In the early 90s, we didn't have the Web, but we did have bulletin board systems (BBS), and new media was evolving fast. Computers had just begun offering built-in modems and CD-ROM drives, but we were a couple of years away from web browsers and broadband.

Jaime got to the digital revolution before all of us, having made a floppy-disk magazine series from 1990 to 1992—*WIRED* debuted its print magazine in 1993. That same year, she did this crazy interactive press kit for Billy Idol that he distributed with his album *Cyberpunk*.

At that time, I started a "zine" called *CyberSurfer*, my screenname online, and published five issues. The folks at *PAPER* Magazine gave me a gig writing a column for them called "CyberSurfer's Sillycon Alley," and I would cover Jaime's work often—primarily because she was the only person actually doing work!

She never got rich, but she made great art and followed her vision of what the interactive world should be. In fact, she turned down her chance at being a billionaire as the third co-founder of Razorfish.

In 1996, I hosted a pitching contest called "Ready, Set... Pitch!" at Josh Harris' famous loft for Pseudo.com. Jaime pitched Electronic Hollywood, a studio that would make cartoons and interactive experiences for the Web.

She saw casual games and YouTube a decade before they hit, and before anyone used the terms "UX" and "IA," she was teaching all of us about "experience" and "flows."

I've been lucky enough to build or invest in over 100 Internet businesses, from Uber to Engadget, and I can tell you that if you want to build a product that changes the world, the first place you should begin is where you are right now—in Jaime's hands.

Listen and consider what she says in this book deeply. This is the "missing manual" for the Lean Startup and Lean UX techniques that you've always wanted.

Nondesigners especially should continue reading, because Jaime takes the time to explain the oftentimes intimidating jargon and processes that designers throw around, effortlessly and clearly for you, the reader.

Late one night, when we were kids in our 20s dreaming about the Internet and what it might become and how to be successful with it, Jaime explained it to me concisely: "It's all about the experience."

There is not better advice for building product, or living your life. It's all about the experience.

JASON MCCABE CALACANIS
APRIL 2015

[*Preface*]

STRATEGY IS ABOUT CONNECTING THE DOTS. IT REQUIRES YOU TO LOOK at what's happened in the past and what's going on in the present to make better guesses about the future. People who do strategy need to be inquisitive, objective, and fearless. They need to be risk takers who stalk and kill their prey by going for the throat.

User experience (UX) strategy lies at the intersection of UX design and business strategy. It is a practice that, when done empirically, provides a much better chance of a successful digital product than just crossing your fingers, designing some wireframes, and then writing a bunch of code.

This book presents a solid framework on the practice of UX strategy. It is geared specifically for crafting innovative products and takes you through numerous lightweight techniques that you can use regardless of your work environment. The basic principles of business strategy do not need to be a mystery requiring somebody with an MBA to understand. Strategy, just like design, is something that you can master only by practicing it.

Who Should Read This Book?

This book addresses the large knowledge gap between UX design and business strategy. It was written with the following types of product makers in mind:

Entrepreneurs, digital product managers, and intrapreneurial teams
> You want to lead your team—visual and UX designers, developers, marketers, and so on—to craft a successful product with a killer UX. However, there are limitations on your time, cash, and other resources, and that means focusing your team's efforts on techniques of *applied simplicity*, or putting the most essential and affordable tools into practice. You understand Lean Startup principles and

want to cut corners on research and evaluation, but you also know that you need to make decisions based on a sound strategy. This book will provide you and your team with the necessary lightweight tools for testing value propositions, finding opportunities for creating value in the marketplace, and designing for conversion.

UX/Interaction/UI Designers

You're frustrated. You feel like you are a cog in the wheel making design deliverables. You want your work to be more innovative and strategically sound, but you aren't involved with product definition at a strategic level. You fear that you are hitting a career wall because you don't have a business degree or marketing expertise. This book will teach you how to push back when you find yourself in the following situations:

- You're assigned to create a site map and wireframes for a product that you believe is just a rip-off of an existing one. You don't want to spend the next six months reinventing the wheel. This book will show you how to be innovative by systematically cherry-picking from your competitors.

- You have a stakeholder who is 100 percent certain that his product vision is right, and you are told to implement it as is. You want to do user research to help him deviate from his original vision, but he won't give you the budget. This book will demonstrate different options for being *intrapreneurial* with or without buy-in.

- You get handed a massive requirements document for a transactional product and are told to come up with a design that will increase conversion. This book will show you how to break down the stages of engagement and map desired actions to metrics.

Why I Wrote This Book

What has kept me on my toes while being a software designer and practitioner is being a part-time teacher of the evolving discipline of user interface (UI) design and product strategy. Since 1993, I have taught everything from graduate-level courses for engineering students to adult education courses for working professionals who wanted to reposition their career tracks with more marketable skill sets. But there was never a perfect book in any of those situations that gave my students everything they needed. Instead, I was constantly hounded to share my presentation decks, sample documents, and templates. I wrote this book to finally consolidate into one resource everything I know about the practice of UX strategy, which I learned from my work with start-ups, agencies, and enterprises.

I also hope that designers and product makers who are aspiring strategists will gain from my years of professional experience. I've had a lot of ups and downs in my professional and personal life, and they have informed my attitude toward trial and error. This is why even from the beginning I didn't want to write a dry business or technology book. I wanted to write a book that chronicles the vitality and fluidity of what we actually experience in the real world of product design. I wanted to depict the entrepreneurial spirit, which isn't just about success or techniques that always work. I wanted to share that journey with the hope that you won't get as scuffed up as I did along the way.

How This Book Is Organized

I organized this book based on how I have fine-tuned my teaching method over the years. Therefore, the first way to read this book is as it was originally intended—as a how-to guide to making an innovative digital product. If that's how you choose to read it, you'll want to begin with an idea or problem you hope to solve through a digital interface, because the only way to learn how to swim first is to get in the pool and become comfortable with freezing your butt off. As you and your team move through the chapters, you'll unlock techniques in a linear order. Then, when you're acquainted with all the techniques, you'll be able to practice them in the future in whatever order works best.

The book has 11 chapters. Chapter 1 establishes what UX strategy is and is not. Chapter 2 introduces the UX strategy framework that will shape all the tools and techniques in this book. Chapters 3 through 9 teach you how to perform those UX strategy techniques. Chapter 10 includes four interviews with top strategists around the globe to give you some insight to their different perspectives on the subject. And finally, Chapter 11 wraps everything up in a brief conclusion.

What Is the UX Strategy Toolkit?

This book comes with a complimentary toolkit so that you and your teams can begin using it immediately for nailing a stellar UX strategy for your product. I've been refining these tools for years with clients, using them both for collaboration and as an output deliverable. They might seem unwieldy at first, but they are a crucial starting place to learn how to conduct efficient UX strategy. As you read, you'll come across in-depth explanations of how each tool works and the benefits that each one provides.

To access the free UX Strategy Toolkit, go to the following URL:

http://userexperiencestrategy.com

After you download the toolkit—an Excel (*.xlsx*) file—simply import it into Google Drive as a spreadsheet. You will have full editing and sharing privileges; so, by all means, share it with your team. There are tabs at the bottom of the spreadsheet with which you can switch among the different tools.

UX strategy requires collaboration among team members and stakeholders. It doesn't matter whether you're a student in a classroom, a fledging startup, or a cross-functional team at an enterprise. The tactics don't work unless you all work together. The best way to collaborate in this digital age is through cloud-based tools, and the cloud-based toolkit for this book will help you to align your onsite and remote teams to a product vision. It's also great because you can work together in real time on the same document, virtually chat with teammates, or leave contextual notes for later.

Comments and Questions

Please address comments and questions concerning this book to the publisher:

O'Reilly Media, Inc.
1005 Gravenstein Highway North
Sebastopol, CA 95472
(800) 998-9938 (in the United States or Canada)
(707) 829-0515 (international or local)
(707) 829-0104 (fax)

We have a web page for this book, where we list errata, examples, and any additional information. You can access this page at:

http://bit.ly/ux_strategy

To comment or ask technical questions about this book, send email to:

bookquestions@oreilly.com

For more information about our books, courses, conferences, and news, see our website at *http://www.oreilly.com*.

Find us on Facebook: *http://facebook.com/oreilly*

Follow us on Twitter: *http://twitter.com/oreillymedia*

Watch us on YouTube: *http://www.youtube.com/oreillymedia*

Safari® Books Online

Safari Books Online (*www.safaribooksonline.com*) is an on-demand digital library that delivers expert content in both book and video form from the world's leading authors in technology and business.

Technology professionals, software developers, web designers, and business and creative professionals use Safari Books Online as their primary resource for research, problem solving, learning, and certification training.

Safari Books Online offers a range of product mixes and pricing programs for organizations, government agencies, and individuals. Subscribers have access to thousands of books, training videos, and prepublication manuscripts in one fully searchable database from publishers like O'Reilly Media, Prentice Hall Professional, Addison-Wesley Professional, Microsoft Press, Sams, Que, Peachpit Press, Focal Press, Cisco Press, John Wiley & Sons, Syngress, Morgan Kaufmann, IBM Redbooks, Packt, Adobe Press, FT Press, Apress, Manning, New Riders, McGraw-Hill, Jones & Bartlett, Course Technology, and dozens more. For more information about Safari Books Online, please visit us online.

Acknowledgements

This book would not be in front of your eyes without my constant collaboration with Sarah Dzida. I first met Sarah in my UX design class while she was pursuing a master's degree in writing. We eventually worked on a number of UX strategy and design projects together, which gave her firsthand insights into helping me tell the stories behind my business cases. In the end, she did everything from helping me write the book proposal to serving as my writing coach from sample chapter to final draft, acting as the lead editor and applying her genius talents to structurally weave all of the crazy narratives together across the chapters into a seamless epic. I'm forever grateful to her for sticking with me throughout my entire quest of becoming an author. I also want to extend my thanks and gratitude to the following people:

- Big thanks go to Lane Halley, my "Number 1" UX Guru and Lean Startup Queen, who has been my sounding board for this project since the first time it was presented as a lecture in Los Angeles.

- Thanks to the contributors including Chaim Diesto, Miles Frank (portraits of strategists), Ena De Guzman, Geoff Katz, Jared Krause, Zhan Li, Paul Lumsdaine, Peter Merholz, Holly North, Bita Sheibani, Michael Sigal, Milana Sobol, Michael Sueoka, Eric Swenson, and Laurel Wetzork.

- Thanks to O'Reilly Media and my editing team, Mary Treseler and Angela Rufino.

- Thanks to my awesome son Terry for giving me that special *raison d' être* to keep my eyes on the prize. I dedicate this book to him and the rest of my family.

- Thanks to all my ballet teachers for teaching me an art form and a practice that kept me sane throughout this project.

Thank you, Los Angeles, for being my home.

[1]

What Is UX Strategy?

I've seen the needle and the damage done,
a little part of it in everyone.
—NEIL YOUNG (1972)

A FEW YEARS AGO, A HIGHLY SUCCESSFUL SOFTWARE ENGINEER BECAME an entrepreneur because he had a problem—someone he loved needed treatment for a drug addiction. He embarked on a daunting journey that millions of Americans face each year—to find appropriate care at a reputable facility. However, the road was filled with uncertainty and pain points; there was no price transparency, no centralized place to research the facilities with unbiased reviews, and scads of liars running overpriced facilities while preying on desperate people just like him. But during the course of his research, he discovered that reputable treatment centers also struggled with certain things: they constantly had empty beds; they had difficulty sifting through referrals for appropriate patients; and it was a hassle to collect payments from insurance companies. At the end of his journey, the software engineer saw the opportunity to embark on a different kind of adventure. He could solve a market problem and at the same time help people with a personal problem about which he was very passionate. That's how his startup was born; his idea to connect the right patients with the right kind of treatment centers through an online interface.

Because his product had the potential to disrupt the marketplace,* he was able to gather a solid team and get investment capital. He developed relationships with reputable rehabilitation facilities. He developed a database for matching empty beds with the people who needed

---

* "Priceline Type Bed Auction Service Has Potential to Radically Transform Addictions Biz." *Treatment Magazine*, January 12, 2012. *http://tinyurl.com/8lj5wqa.*

them.[†] He developed a way to vet each facility to ensure that only the best were included in the database. And, of course, he and his team developed a consumer-facing website for customer acquisition.

They didn't leave anything to chance. They also conducted a couple of online surveys with people who had looked for treatment in the past. They hired public relations, marketing, and search-engine optimization (SEO) firms. They bought advertising in print and online publications; talked to industry experts; and found many business-side partners interested in their value proposition and who wanted to be a part of it.

When the site went live, they ran numerous online advertising campaigns using Facebook and Google to promote the financial savings and data-rich reviews that customers could get by using their service. From these campaigns, only a small amount of traffic trickled to their home page and then bounced away. Sometimes, a user registered with the service. Sometimes, they even came back. But over the course of 18 months, no one booked a treatment center through their website.

The software engineer's team knew that whatever they were doing, it wasn't working. They had the proof: millions of dollars spent building a product that hadn't gained them one customer. Their investors and business partners were getting anxious. Their publicist continued to find media that were interested in the concept, but the outlets wouldn't run the story without some activity on the site. Still, they had a lot of features and functionality built in to their interface to help users make the best decision possible.

"It must be the user experience," the team hypothesized, which is when and why they came to me.

Like many product makers before them, they asked my user experience (UX) team to just redesign the "look and feel" of the site, ASAP. After all, they needed to meet the growing concerns of their business partners, and because they had a lot of entrenched functionality, they

---

† "Making a Treatment Match." *Behavioral Healthcare*, February 25, 2013. *http://tinyurl.com/mv5gq8u.*

felt it would be easy for my team to just build off of it. But we refused, because they didn't just need a new UX design. They needed a new UX strategy.

Misinterpretations About UX Strategy

UX is an umbrella term that encompasses a lot of disciplines, and UX strategy lies somewhere at the intersection of UX design and business strategy. But the lines don't exist in a vacuum. Instead, they exist in an elaborate anatomical structure with a lot of dots to connect. This is why there are so many different interpretations floating around UX strategy.

I first came across the term "UX strategy" in 2008 in an advanced-level UX book called *Mental Models* by Indi Young.[‡] At the time of its writing, Young was attempting to help UX design ascend to the next level. As such, she offered her readers a mini-manifesto, which you can see in Figure 1-1.

Experience Strategy

The strategy that you develop for your product ought not evolve in isolation. Even though the value of user experience is clear, your over-arching reasons for providing something should be considered with equal weight. Jesse James Garrett describes the phrase Experience Strategy thusly:

Experience Strategy = Business Strategy + UX Strategy

A mental model helps you visualize how your business strategy looks compared to the existing user experience. Thus, it is a diagram that can support your experience strategy.

FIGURE 1-1

Sidebar from the book *Mental Models* © 2008 Rosenfeld Media, LLC

---

‡ Definition of Experience Strategy by Jesse James Garrett in Indi Young's book *Mental Models*, Rosenfeld Media, 2008; p 20.

I really wanted to understand what UX strategy meant, but aside from the fact that the difference between "experience" strategy and "user experience" strategy just seems to be one word, the book didn't delve any deeper into this abstract equation. Over the course of my career from working with big interactive agencies to enterprises, I've heard many other theoretical concepts about the intention of UX strategy. And that's something I want to sidestep in this book: the entirely semantic disputes about what "strategy" means or whether a theoretical framework has practical application. It's important that we avoid battles that boil down to these kinds of debates. They only confuse our clients and stakeholders, and this is ultimately what happened in the early 2000s when there was so much debate about the differences between the practices of "user experience design" versus "interaction design."

But misinterpretations, if they can do anything, can be useful in providing a grounding point for contrast. So, let's get the big ones out of the way.

MISINTERPRETATION 1: UX STRATEGY IS ABOUT IDENTIFYING A "NORTH STAR"

Reality: the North Star is not the brightest star in the galaxy, but it has been used for navigation throughout history because of its "fixed" location in the sky.[§] In the context of the digital age, a team identifies that fixed point as the goal of their game plan and then sets course for it. This traditional business-strategy approach can work to galvanize a team in a large slow-moving enterprise. But what if your solution is an innovative digital product about to be launched in a fast-moving consumer market full of uncertainties? This requires an agile process—one that is variable and iterative with continuous feedback loops at several points along the way. You don't want a North Star to guide your UX strategy; instead, you want a goal or point toward which to steer every time you pivot.

MISINTERPRETATION 2: UX STRATEGY IS A "STRATEGIC WAY" TO PERFORM UX DESIGN

Reality: I guess the opposite of this would be, what, doing nonstrategic UX design? UX design and UX strategy are two different things. When you are doing design, you are creating something. When you are doing

---

§   http://www.space.com/15567-north-star-polaris.html

strategy, you are coming up with a game plan before creating something. One way to explain it is to just substitute the word "product" for "user experience." A product strategist thinks about all the possibilities for the product and defines it after researching the potential customers and existing competitors. She thinks about how much the product will cost to make and be priced to sell at, and how it will be distributed to different customer segments. In contrast, a product designer actually fabricates the thing. They are two separate disciplines.

Too often, I have seen UX designers work on products without being informed of the overall business strategy. They are blind beyond what they've received in the business requirements document. This disconnect is why the Lean UX movement is so popular; it advocates that UX designers take on a bigger leadership role ("getting a seat at the strategy table") by becoming the glue that holds cross-functional teams together.

MISINTERPRETATION 3: UX STRATEGY IS JUST PRODUCT STRATEGY

Reality: Misinterpretation 2 points out the similarities between a product strategist and UX strategist. However, that doesn't mean that you can easily substitute one for the other (even if my parents think my little brother [a product director/manager type] and I do the same thing for a living). The people who design the real-world shopping experience of a brick-and-mortar Target as well as the products in that store are thinking about a very different set of issues than the people designing Target.com.

But UX strategy goes beyond just one digital product or online experience. It spans dozens of different digital products, services, and platforms; it interconnects all members of a digital interface family. Here are just a few examples to consider:

Apple
iMac, iPod, the physical Mac Store, iTunes, iCloud, and so on

LinkedIn
Desktop, mobile, and Premium

Adobe
Photoshop, Illustrator, and in the cloud

Amazon

Prime, AWS, Kindle, as a content creator, and so on

The UX strategy makes a case for all touch points and weaves them into a seamless ecosystem between buyer and seller through the UX design. It accounts for the user's entire journey down the funnel. (For more on this, see Chapter 9.)

MISINTERPRETATION 4: UX STRATEGY IS CLOSELY TIED TO BRAND STRATEGY

Reality: brand strategy is how, what, where, when, and to whom you plan on communicating and delivering your brand messages through your distribution channels. Aspects of brand strategy can help define aspects of your product's UX design, and vice versa. But it's easy to confuse these branding efforts and goals with a UX strategy. A poor UX can actually decrease the "brand value" of a product, but not so much the other way around. Even the brandiest of brands can't overcome the poor UX of a product.

In their book *Lean Entrepreneur*,¶ Brant Cooper and Patrick Vlaskovits say, "Marketing can increase awareness for the product, but if the product sucks, that's what the buzz will be." Apply this thinking to Google. It has a fantastic brand. Now, think about products like Google+, Buzz, and Wave. These products were consistent with the Google brand strategy, but they failed to stand up to public scrutiny on their own. When these products debuted, they baffled users and failed to acquire them. They bombed at the "Big Picture," which was to solve the user's dilemma over how to communicate to different networks of people through multiple products.

Another important thing to remember is that a solid UX design no longer differentiates brands. For companies such as Google, users assume the UX will be good. Google doesn't have to announce it anymore, and when it's bad, it's all the more jarring. That's why a UX strategy becomes even more potent. As the company grows and expands its digital properties, you need to constantly pivot and shift your game plan, baking your strategy into all online services effectively, reliably, and without friction. A product needs a good UX no matter what.

¶ Vlaskovits, Patrick and Brant Cooper. *Lean Entrepreneur*. Wiley, 2013.

So What the Hell Is UX Strategy?

UX strategy is the process that should be started first, before the design or development of a digital product begins. It's the vision of a solution that needs to be validated with real potential customers to prove that it's desired in the marketplace. Although UX design encompasses numerous details such as visual design, content messaging, and how easy it is for a user to accomplish a task, UX strategy is the "Big Picture." It is the high-level plan to achieve one or more business goals under conditions of uncertainty.

The purpose of any strategy is to create a game plan that looks at your current position and then helps you get to where you actually want to be. Your strategy should play to your strengths and be mindful of your weaknesses. It should rely on empirical, lightweight tactics that quickly move you and your team (because let's face it, you're probably not doing this alone) toward your desired destination. A solid strategy is the difference between success and failure. In the digital-product world, chaos—time delays, increased costs, and bad user experiences—get exacerbated when there is no shared product vision among team members.

Like any good general, you need to develop that strategy. That's why we convinced the beleaguered startup of our software engineer to step back and reformulate their game plan. Here's what our hands-on UX strategy achieved for them in about a month:

- We questioned all the current research and found a lot of it was based on business assumptions rather than factual user data. This is why the client allowed my team to put the redesign on pause.

- We conducted guerrilla user research using a *Minimum Viable Product* (MVP) prototype with the clients sitting at the table. By hearing firsthand from their presumed customer, the clients acknowledged that their customer segment actually wasn't "everybody" who was getting ripped off by bad treatment centers. Instead, they had built a business model that needed a direct marketing channel targeted at an affluent customer segment.

- We experimented on new value propositions by testing customer acquisition with landing pages. This helped open the clients' minds to other possible business models, such as a business-to-business (B2B) solution.

Sure, many of the findings were super depressing for the clients. They had spent a lot of time and money building a product that didn't work. Initially they blamed their site's "user experience." But by looking at the big picture, we showed them how a lot of their UX was actually getting hamstrung by other things that went beyond the digital interface.

Why a UX Strategy Is Crucial

A mental model is the conceptual model in a person's mind about how a thing works. For instance, when I was 10 years old, I believed the way my mom got cash was by going to a bank, signing a slip of paper, and then receiving the funds from the teller. When I was 20, I believed I needed to take a bank card and key code to access an ATM to get cash. But if you were to ask my 10-year-old son how to get cash, he would tell you to go to the supermarket and ask the cashier to give you some when you pay for your groceries. The 2015 mental model for getting cash is very different from the 1976 mental model. That's because new technologies and new business processes come together to offer a more efficient way for people to accomplish tasks. Stale mental models are overturned. Life is disrupted for the better!

This is why I love working with startups, because entrepreneurs are the biggest risk takers of them all. They quit their day jobs and go all in on one big idea that they are passionate about. Our software engineer was just that type of person—after a difficult personal experience, he wanted to solve a problem so that others would not have to experience his pain. He wanted to change a mental model.

Even though envisioning innovative products is fun, it's hard to get people to change their behavior. Customers have to see the value in the new way before they'll consider abandoning the old. Devising new products to solve serious dilemmas is not for the faint of heart. You must be passionate and at least a little crazy to run headlong into all the obstacles that inevitably will get in the way.

Yet, it's the passion to solve a problem, change the world, and make it an easier place to live in that makes for game-changing products. And this passion is not limited to entrepreneurs who quit their day jobs. It also emboldens people who have titles like product manager, UX designer, or developer. These are people who also are passionate about using technology to devise products that customers want. When you bring these types of people together, you have the necessary means to potentially make magic happen and destroy outdated mental models. Because time on earth is finite, why else would you want to build anything else?

My goal in this book is to demystify the practice of UX strategy so that you can do just that. You'll be able to immediately apply UX strategy techniques to your projects in a variety of work settings to keep you and your team from getting overwhelmed no matter what limitations you face.

I'll show you how it can happen through a variety of business cases. You'll meet some of my former clients—our aforementioned software engineer, a Hollywood producer, and an entrepreneur named Jared who wants to eliminate the need for currency with his transactional online platform. You'll meet two of my students—Bita and Ena—who participated in a UX apprenticeship in which they chased a made-up value proposition in order to document my UX strategy process. I'll even reach back into my family ancestry, because I know I was incentivized to be entrepreneurial from watching and learning from my parents. You'll see how the journey *is* a reward, no matter if you're the teacher, student, or maker. You'll also see that no matter the project or the circumstances, devising products is like being on a rollercoaster, and the only way to keep the product on the rails is to use empirical, cost-efficient strategy techniques.

As a UX strategist, I am paid to help my clients face dilemmas and chase dreams. This is why solid problem-solving skills are absolutely critical to mastering UX strategy. Strategy goes beyond the abstract nature of design and into the land of critical thinking. Critical thinking is disciplined thinking that is clear, rational, open-minded, and informed by evidence.** Product stakeholders and entrepreneurs use the critical thinking in a UX strategy to help them connect the dots among all the points—the customers, their needs, and the solution they all want to solve using technology.

It is in this way that UX strategists need to be equally passionate about technology, because the Internet continues to offer consumers an endless supply of digital options. Every click, swipe, and hover is a decision that users are able to make. They have choices—a gazillion of them—to

---

** *http://en.wikipedia.org/wiki/Critical_thinking*

buy or not buy, like or deride, share or forget, complete or cancel. You need to know what features to offer and how people actually use them. You need to understand all of the latest and upcoming devices, platforms, and apps so that you can consider their application for your solutions. You and your team need to do everything you can to ensure that Alice will fall down the rabbit hole and into Wonderland.

Are you ready to jump?

[2]

The Four Tenets of UX Strategy

"In war, let your great object be victory, not lengthy campaigns."
—SUN TZU, *ART OF WAR* *

A STELLAR UX STRATEGY IS A MEANS TO ACHIEVING DISRUPTION IN the marketplace through mental-model innovation. And to keep me from forgetting this, I have the sticker shown in Figure 2-1 on my laptop lid.

FIGURE 2-1
The sticker on my laptop lid

---

* Sun Tzu, *Art of War*. first published by Lionel Giles in 1910.

Because what's the point in spending time and energy crafting a digital product that isn't unique? Or, at the very least, is a much better alternative to current solutions found in the online marketplace?

To achieve that disruption, we need a framework in which to connect all the dots that will build a cohesive UX strategy. In this chapter, I'm going to break down the most important tenets that you need to understand in order to successfully implement the tools and techniques in this book. Think of it as a primer to get you and your team thinking like a UX strategist.

How I Discovered My UX Strategy Framework

In the digital world, strategy usually begins in the *discovery phase*. This is when teams dig deep into research to reveal key information about the product they want to build. I've always liked to think of the discovery phase as similar to the pretrial discovery process used by attorneys in the United States. To avoid a "trial by ambush," lawyers can request to see the evidence of the opposing counsel in order to prepare sufficient counter-evidence. In this way, the attorneys try to avoid surprises, and you, as a product maker, should also want to *strategically* do just that.

My first chance to practice UX strategy occurred in 2007. At the time, I was the UX lead at Schematic (now Possible) for the website redesign of Oprah.com. Along with the other team leads, I flew into Chicago to kick off our discovery phase.

Before that moment, my 15 years of professional experience focused on interface design and integrating new technologies (such as Flash) into interfaces to create "cutting-edge" products. Often, I was handed a massive requirements document that listed hundreds of "essential" features. Or, I was given a flimsy project brief with pretty comps that stated what the final product should accomplish. From there, I made a site or application map that catered to a specific set of user scenarios that enabled those interactions. Based on these documents, I could only infer whether my creation solved the problem or not because it was typically too late at that point to challenge the rationale behind the product vision. I was just supposed to design it on time and on budget.

But in 2007, it was so fascinating to watch our UX director, Mark Sloan, get a dozen contentious stakeholders—no, Oprah wasn't there—on the same page. Mark used consensus-building techniques such as affinity maps, dot voting, and forced ranking[†] to help us understand all the different parts—content and critical functionality—that would make up the system we had to digitize. This discovery opportunity helped us (the stakeholders and product team) in examining our goals to make a better platform for the millions of devoted Oprah fans in the world.

One week later, after all the workshops, the product team and I presented the discovery brief defining the product vision. The brief contained typical deliverables such as user personas, concept map analyses, and a recommended feature list. Because the stakeholders were anxious to get started, they immediately approved it. Our digital team was off and running on the implementation phase, which took over six months of emotionally fueled hand-offs. There were hundreds of pages of wireframes and functional specifications traded between stakeholders, designers, and developers.

But the discovery brief was never referenced again. The personas and proposed solution were never validated by existing customers. The stakeholders went back to fighting for whatever prime real estate they could grab for their particular business units. Yet, there was something good that came out of that discovery phase for me: I was a UX designer who finally got a taste of what a UX strategy could potentially be. I was ruined. I couldn't imagine just being a wireframe monkey anymore.

A full year later, the redesigned site launched. I never looked at it because I had moved onto to another interactive agency (HUGE) with other high-profile clients. In my new position, I was able to focus my energy more directly on the discovery phase of projects in which user research and business strategy were given more weight. I also had a seat at the table to help shape the UX strategy and decide how a product vision should be implemented. I no longer had to feel fraudulent for spending so many waking hours building products for which I lacked a deep understanding of the customer segment and the business model.

---

† Gray, David, Sunni Brown, Jamews Macanufo. *Gamestorming: A Playbook for Innovators, Rulebreakers, and Changemakers.* O'Reilly, 2010.

Today, I run my own practice that specializes in UX strategy, and since my first discovery phase, I've learned a lot about how to make it an iterative, lightweight, and empirical process of intense collaboration among stakeholders, designers, developers, and so on. Because when everyone shares a product vision, you and your team really have a chance at changing the rules of the game for your product, company, and future customers.

However, I do want to acknowledge that my methodology is my version of UX strategy and might be different from other strategists'. That's precisely why I included Chapter 10, which contains profiles of people I respect who have been practicing UX strategy and design as well. However, you'll also see that we align on a lot of things. That's what happens when a new discipline or methodology arises: people will find their own approach, but even within those differences, there are connective tissues that bind them together to make UX strategy identifiable and unique.

So, with all that said, cue the drum roll to introduce my UX strategy framework, as presented in Figure 2-2.

FIGURE 2-2
The four tenets of UX strategy represented as plates at the dinner table

My formula is this: UX Strategy = Business Strategy + Value Innovation + Validated User Research + Killer UX Design.

These are the four tenets that make up my framework. I have seen them in play every day since my first discovery phase. It's not enough to understand your marketplace if you don't talk directly to your customers. It's not enough to validate that your product works if you're not creating something unique. Good enough just isn't good enough, and just identifying these tenets won't be enough to get your team flying. You'll need to understand how they interact and affect one another. Then, the real trick will be to keep all four of these tenet "plates" spinning in the air while you move through the techniques and tools in the subsequent chapters.

Lessons Learned

- The discovery phase is where UX strategy begins. UX strategy is based on four tenets: business strategy, value innovation, validated user research, and killer UX design.

- The output of the discovery phase should be based on empirical data, such as getting direct input from target users before going straight from an idea to wireframes and development.

- How a team executes a discovery phase can be the deciding factor between how a product will ultimately deliver real value through a killer UX *and* create real value for the stakeholders.

Tenet 1: Business Strategy

Business strategy is the top-line vision of the company. It is why the company exists. It ensures the long-term growth and sustainability of the organization. It is the basis for the core competencies and offerings, which are the products. In this book, I will use the term "products" to refer to both digital products and digital services.

The business strategy is what gives product makers the direction to grow in the marketplace while beating the competition. The business strategy identifies the company's guiding principles for how it will position itself and still achieve its objectives. For this to happen, the business *must* continually identify and utilize a competitive advantage. A competitive advantage is essential to the company's long-term existence.

In his classic book, *Competitive Advantage*,[‡] Michael E. Porter lays out the two most common ways to achieve a competitive advantage: cost leadership and differentiation.

The advantage behind cost leadership comes from offering the lowest price for products in a particular industry. Whether it is the cheapest car, television, or hamburger, this was the traditional way that companies achieved dominance in the marketplace. After all, allowing the private sector to compete without government regulation is what free market economy is all about! I mean, look at the rampant success of stores such as Walmart and Target. They can offer consumers the best prices and widest selection of merchandise. But what happens when prices hit rock bottom? Then, the battle needs to be about what makes the product better.

This brings us to Porter's second type of competitive advantage: differentiation. Because we are product inventors planning to build disruptive technologies, this is where our actual power lies. With differentiation, the advantage is based on a new or unique product or a unique aspect of the product for which customers will pay a premium because of its perceived value. As consumers, we choose one product over another based on the things we personally value, ranging from the product's usefulness to how much pleasure we derive from it. That perceived value is what transforms a simple little café and cup o' joe into the crazy success story of Seattle-based Starbucks. There's a reason why people pay $5 for a cafe latté—it's the *experience* that's also wrapped into the product. It starts the moment a customer steps into the store and ends when that person tosses his cup and sleeve into the trash.

Today, a UX differentiation is the digital-product game changer. Differentiated user experiences have completely revolutionized the way we communicate with the world. Consider what the world was like before microblogging. When it was released in 2006, Twitter confounded users with its 140-character limit. But the limit turned out to be a valuable perk, especially with respect to updates. Today, users

---

‡   Porter, Michael. *Competitive Advantage*. New York: The Free Press, 1985.

don't check traditional news outlets for instant updates; they instead check Twitter. When Hurricane Sandy pounded the East Coast in 2012, the power went out, but more than 20 million Tweets occurred among users, residents in the storm, and media and government outlets.[§] I know I spent some time on Twitter, tweeting to friends in New York about the hurricane updates I saw on TV from my home on the West Coast.

Another tool that has distinguished itself from the competition with a UX differentiation is the map app Waze. It combines social traffic with GPS navigation, thereby allowing users to find the quickest route of the moment to their destination. By merely driving around with Waze open, users passively contribute traffic and other road data to the network. Users also can take a more active role by sharing road reports on accidents, police traps, or any other hazards along the way, helping to give other users in the area a heads-up about what surprises might ahead of them. In June of 2013, Waze (an Israeli startup) was acquired by Google for $1.1 billion. Now, Waze still offers its distinct UX to its users, but its data is also channeled into Google Maps.[¶] Clearly, Google recognized the competitive advantage of UX collaboration and chose to adopt Waze for what it could add to its product rather than compete against it.

A UX competitive advantage is important to understand in this brave new world of technology. Traditionally, the purpose of a competitive advantage was to make a product that was self-sufficient through a revenue stream. A revenue stream is how the company gets paid. And when a customer pays more for the product than what it costs to make, value is created for the stakeholders. To many people, this is the heart of a product's business model. Today, though, a UX differentiation doesn't necessarily mean big bucks when your product hits the market. Instead, the goal of many entrepreneurs is mass adoption. Products such as Facebook didn't kick the collective asses of competitors like MySpace or Friendster's because it was a cheaper alternative. Facebook won the field because, a) it offered a differentiated UX that was perceived by users as more valuable, and b) *everyone* adopted it. From that

§   *http://www.journalism.org/2012/11/06/hurricane-sandy-and-twitter/*

¶   "New features ahead: Google Maps and Waze apps better than ever." *Google Maps Blog*, August 20, 2013, *http://tinyurl.com/lx9sq8c.*

point, Facebook innovated a new kind of business model that relied on monetizing its user data for selling targeted advertising.[**] In 2013, Waze did a similar thing when Google bought it. Waze made a lot of money by selling access to its devoted users, and Google will make a lot of money because so many users continue to use both the Waze and Google Maps apps. The two companies essentially turned their users into customers because they were able to monetize them, and because of this, from here on out, I am going to use the terms "user" and "customer" interchangeably.

Still, a good business model doesn't just define the revenue stream of a product. Nor does it just rely on a ridiculous number of users adopting it. This is something often lost on young tech entrepreneurs. Because they grew up in a world in which products like Facebook became solvent and conquered the world without an obvious business model, they don't realize what an uphill battle they have ahead of them to acquire users. They also forget that the megasuccessful digital products that continue to define our everyday lives didn't just stumble onto their business models. These game-changing companies experimented, tested, and failed before they hit on and innovated the right one. And if, like me, you worked on the Web when the dot-com bubble burst in the 1990s, you have firsthand experience of all of the risks involved in creating products without proven business models. When the investment money runs out, and there isn't any more coming in, life *is* bleak.

The process of business-model construction is foundational to a business strategy. As Steve Blank writes, a business model describes the "flow between key components of the company."[††] This quote comes from Blank's Customer Development manifesto, in which he challenges product founders to stop writing static business plans. Instead, he encourages them to adopt a flexible business model that requires all of the key components to be validated using empirical, customer-facing discovery methods. To get a sense of these key components, let's take a look at a tool called the Business Model Canvas.

[**] Kirkpatrick, David. *The Facebook Effect: The Inside Story of the Company That Is Connecting the World.* Simon & Schuster, 2011.

[††] Blank, Steve and Bob Dorf. *The Startup Owner's Manual.* Wiley, 2012.

In their seminal book *Business Model Generation*,[‡‡] authors Alexander Osterwalder and Yves Pigneur deconstruct each of the nine essential building blocks of a business model so that visionaries can systematically think through the logic of how the company will eventually make money. Blank also refers to this tool in his own work on business-model creation. What's relevant to us in this book is how many of these components align with the UX strategy for a digital product. They are as follows (see also Figure 2-3):

Customer segments
> Who are the customers? What are their behaviors? What are their needs and goals?

Value propositions
> What value (either qualitative or quantitative) do we promise to deliver?

Channels
> How will we reach our customer segment? Is it online or offline?

Customer relationships
> How are we going to acquire and retain our customers?

Revenue streams
> How does the business earn revenue from the value proposition? Are the customers going to pay for it? Or are there other options?

Key resources
> What unique strategic assets must the business have to make the product work? Is it content, capital, or patents? Is this something we must develop?

Key activities
> What uniquely strategic things does the business do to deliver its proposition? Are we optimizing an outdated business process? Are we creating a platform to bring customers together to transact?

Key partnerships
> What partnerships and suppliers do we need in order to deliver our value proposition?

[‡‡] Oswerwalder, Alexander and Yves Pigneur. *Business Model Generation*. Wiley, 2010.

Cost structure

What are the major costs that will be incurred to make our business model work? Are we trying to cut costs by throwing out the thrills? Are there fixed costs that won't go away?

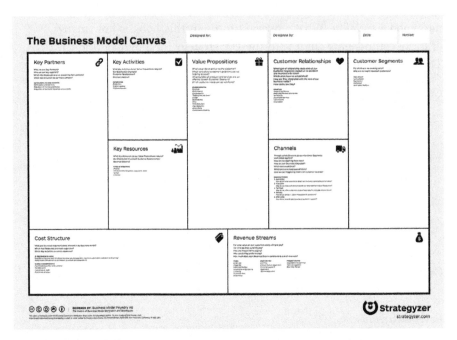

FIGURE 2-3

Business Model Canvas showing the nine essential building blocks of a business model

By using the canvas, product makers collect all their hypotheses about their product into one place. They then revise it as they move through the discovery phase, and it's something you'll see as we develop all the techniques in this book. For this tenet, however, it is another place in which we can see how business strategy and UX strategy really intersect. So many of the concerns of the Business Model Canvas—customer segments, value propositions, revenue streams, and customer acquisition and retention—are elements that are essential to creating a product's user experience, which as you've learned, is key to our competitive advantage.

When you don't see these connections, you can potentially end up in the same position as our software engineer in Chapter 1. His business model relied on an affluent customer segment to provide the company's revenue stream, but he had not correctly identified that segment before he built his product. If he had not come in contact with that user during my team's customer discovery, he might have pushed ahead with a lengthy and expensive campaign to blitz media and online advertising outlets. This, as my team's UX strategy proved, would have been very problematic because the campaigns wouldn't have reached out to the user segment actually interested in the value proposition.

This leads us to how the Business Model Canvas also calls out the importance of collaboration among stakeholders and team members in the discovery phase. Categories such as key resources and partnerships aren't something that a digital product manager or UX designer should think up in a vacuum. Rather, these categories are where the stakeholders can offer a wealth of information and leads. Other categories, such as key activities, customer segments, and value propositions, will more likely rely on the guidance of the digital team to lead the stakeholders to the best product. But the digital product team must also recognize that these same categories need input from actual users before a hypothesis can be changed to a fact, which is what our UX strategy research demonstrated to the software engineer.

We need to recognize that building a business strategy isn't about formulating and executing a perfect plan. Instead, it's about being able to research what's out there, analyze the opportunities, run structured experiments, fail, learn, and iterate until we devise something of value that people truly want. Also, as the product scales and the market evolves, the business strategy must be nimble. For a new product, a strategy probably revolves around just getting enough product/market fit to raise financing, or grabbing enough market share so that its customer base is the competitive advantage. But, for a more mature company, the strategy is about building out the company's core value proposition while trying to keep the company's infrastructure and internal processes in place. It is in this way that what might have been the business model or competitive advantage in the early life cycle of the product might not be the same in later phases. Nevertheless, in chasing this moving target, companies must continue to experiment with varied offerings so that they can scale, remain competitive, and continue to offer value to users in an ever-changing marketplace.

Tenet 2: Value Innovation

As digital product inventors, we must be hyperaware of all the changing digital market dynamics. We must understand how and why people use their digital devices and what defines a successful and a failed UX. This is because a user's first contact with the interface generally determines success or failure. It provides the user with their first impression of your value innovation, and it is value innovation that disrupts or creates new mental models for people. We definitely want to do that.

Before we dig into value innovation, let's discuss the word "value." The word is used *everywhere*. It's found in almost all traditional and contemporary business books since the 1970s. In *Management: Tasks, Responsibilities, Practices,*§§ Peter Drucker discusses how customer values shift over time. He gives an example of how a teenage girl will buy a shoe for its fashion, but when she becomes a working mother, she will probably buy a shoe for its comfort and price. In 1984, Michael Lanning first coined the term "value proposition" to explain how a firm proposes to deliver a valuable customer experience. For a business to generate wealth, it needs to offer a superior product to that of its competitors but at a manufacturing cost below what customers pay for it. That same year, Michael Porter defined the term "value chain" as the chain of activities that a firm operating in a specific industry performs in order to deliver a valuable product. Figure 2-4 illustrates a traditional value chain for a physical product manufacturer.

FIGURE 2-4
The value chain

That is the business process that Toyota uses to make vehicles and that Apple uses to make computers and devices. During each of the activities in this value chain of events, opportunities exist for firms to outperform their competitors. But, all those terms apply to physical products. By contrast, virtual products allow for a value chain to have faster repeat loops and in some cases for the activities to happen in parallel.

---

§§ Drucker, Peter. *Management: Tasks, Responsibilities, Practices.* HarperBusiness, 1973.

This is part of why traditional business-strategy principles do not perfectly map to digital product strategy. When producing digital products, we must continuously research, redesign, and remarket to keep up with the rapidly evolving online marketplace, customer values, and value chains that are required to keep our products in production.

This brings us to another challenge of designing digital products: the software, apps, and other things that users find on the Internet and use every day. As mentioned, a product needs to be valuable to customers to entice them use it. It also needs to be valuable to the business so that the business can sustain itself. However, the Internet is full of digital products for which the users don't have to pay for the privilege of using them. If a business model is supposed to help a company achieve sustainability, how can you do that when the online marketplace is overrun with free products?

Value innovation is the key. In the book *Blue Ocean Strategy*,¶¶ authors W. Chan Kim and Renée Mauborgne describe value innovation as "the simultaneous pursuit of differentiation and low cost, creating a leap in value for both buyers and the company." What this means is that value innovation occurs when companies align newness with utility and price (see Figure 2-5). Companies pursue both differentiation and cost leadership to create high-value and low-cost products for the customers *and* stakeholders. Consider how Waze found a sustainable business model—sharing its crowd-sourced data made it lucrative to other companies such as Google. Yet, to get the data, it had to provide a new kind of value to customers for mass adoption, and that value was based entirely on taking advantage of a disruptive innovation through the UX and business model.

¶¶ Kim, W. Chan and Renée Mauborgne. *Blue Ocean Strategy*. Harvard Business School Press, 2005.

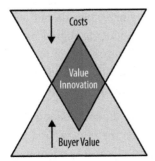

FIGURE 2-5

Value Innovation = The
simultaneous pursuit
of differentiation and
low cost

Disruptive innovation is a term that was coined by Clayton M. Christensen in the mid-1990s. In his book *The Innovator's Dilemma*, he analyzed the value chain of high-tech companies and drew a distinction between those just doing *sustaining innovation* versus *disruptive* innovation. A sustaining innovation he described as any innovation that enables industry leaders to do something better for their existing customers.[***] A disruptive innovation is a product that a company's best customer potentially can't use and therefore has substantially lower profit margins than the business might be willing to support. However, this is where disruptive innovation can blindside established competitors. Christensen says that disruptive innovation usually is "a process by which a product or service takes root initially in simple applications at the bottom of a market and then relentlessly moves up market, eventually displacing established competitors."[†††]

Innovative means doing something that is new, original, and important enough to shake up a market, and this leads us right back to the book *Blue Ocean Strategy*. In the book, the authors discuss their studies of 150 strategic moves spanning more than a 100 years and 30 industries. They explain how the companies behind the Ford Model T, Cirque du Soleil, and the iPod won because of how they entered *blue-ocean* markets instead of *red-ocean* markets. The sea of other competitors with similar products is known as a red ocean. Red oceans are full of sharks that compete for the same customer by offering lower prices and eventually turning a product into a commodity. In contrast, a blue ocean is uncontested territory; it is free for the taking.

[***] *http://www.strategy-business.com/article/14501?pg=all*

[†††] *http://www.claytonchristensen.com/key-concepts/#sthash.47B9F4IW.dpuf*

In the corporate world, the impulse to compete by destroying your rivals is rooted in military strategy. In war, the fight typically plays out over a specific terrain. The battle gets bloody when one side wants what the other side has—whether it be oil, land, shelf space, or eyeballs. In a blue ocean, the opportunity is not constrained by traditional boundaries. It's about breaking a few rules that aren't quite rules *yet* or even inventing your own game that creates an uncontested new marketplace and space for users to roam.

When we transpose *Blue Ocean Strategy* to the world of digital products, we must admit that there are bigger opportunities in unknown market spaces. A perfect example of a company that took advantage of a blue-ocean market is Airbnb. Airbnb is a "community marketplace" for people to list, discover, and book sublets of practically anything from a tree house in Los Angeles to a castle in France. What's amazing about this is that its value proposition has completely disrupted the travel and housing industry (see Figure 2-6).‡‡‡ Its value proposition is so addictive that as soon as customers try it, it's hard to go back to the old way of booking a place to stay or subletting a property.

CNET › Internet › NY official: Airbnb stay illegal; host fined $2,400

NY official: Airbnb stay illegal; host fined $2,400

An administrative law judge decides that a man leasing a condo broke New York's laws after he rented out part of his home on Airbnb.

by Donna Tam 🐦 @DonnaYTam / May 20, 2013 5:00 PM PDT

FIGURE 2-6

Airbnb in the news

Airbnb achieves this value innovation by coupling a killer UX design with a tantalizing value proposition. And, as I mentioned earlier, true value innovation occurs when the UX and business model intersect. In this case, they intersected in a blue ocean because of how Airbnb broke and reinvented some rules.

---

‡‡‡ "NY official: Airbnb stay illegal; host fined $2,400." *C/Net*, May 20, 2013. *http://tinyurl. com/k7oyx3j*.

For example, Craig's List was a primary means for users to sublet before Airbnb, but it was a generally creepy endeavor. There were no user profiles. There was no way to verify anything about the host or guest in the transaction. Yet, that was the norm! Airbnb enabled a free-market subeconomy in which quality and trust were given high value in the UX, much like in Amazon, Yelp, and eBay. Airbnb's entire UX was built around the idea of ensuring that each guest and host was a good customer. It required its users to change their mental models. Formerly unwritten social etiquette now had to come into play if users were to host strangers or stay in a stranger's home and for both parties *to feel good about it.*

For instance, I just came back from a weekend in San Francisco with my family. Instead of booking a hotel that would have cost us upward of $1,200 (two rooms for two nights at a 3.5 star hotel), we used Airbnb and spent half of that. For us, though, it wasn't just about saving money. It was about being in a gorgeous and spacious two-bedroom home closer to the locals and their foodie restaurants. The six percent§§§ commission fee we paid to Airbnb was negligible. Interestingly, the corporate lawyer who owned this San Francisco home was off in Paris with her family. She was also staying at an Airbnb, which could have been paid for using some of the revenue ($550-plus) from her transaction with us. Everybody won! Except, of course, the hotels that lost our business.

Airbnb's business strategy is that they cater to both sides of their two-sided market—the people who list their homes and those who book places to stay. They offer incredible value through feature sets like easy calendaring tools, map integration for browsing, and, most crucially, a seamless transactional system that had not been previously offered by other competitiors like VRBO, Homeaway, or Craig's List. Ultimately Airbnb offered a more usable platform that minimized the risk of dealing with scary people coupled with fair-market value pricing. All of this added up to serious disruption through value innovation for all customers and stakeholders in the online *and* offline experience. That's why it is winning so decisively.

---

§§§ The service fee that guests pay on AirBnb varies from 6 to 18 percent, based on the subtotal.

There are many other products causing widespread disruption to the status quo through their combined value innovation of cost leadership and differentiation in blue-ocean marketplaces. And through their UX strategies, they are ultimately making people's lives easier, bringing together customers in new ways and smashing mental models. Companies such as Airbnb, Kickstarter, and Eventbrite have completely upended how people rent homes, fund business ventures, and organize events, respectively. In fact, Eventbrite is how I tested my hypothesis that there were people out there with a thirst for knowledge about UX strategy. Using its interface, I quickly set up a 60-seat lecture at the price of $40 per person, and sold it out. If I didn't have Eventbrite to experiment with as a promotional platform, there might have been no book for Jaime Levy. Thank you Eventbrite for enabling the one value innovation that other platforms like Meetup failed to offer: the ability to host paid ticketed events.

Tenet 3: Validated User Research

Not realizing a product's value is one of the primary reasons why that product will fail. Stakeholders are dreamers in that they assume what is valuable to their customers instead of verifying it. Much like Kevin Costner in the movie *Field of Dreams*, these entrepreneurs believe that if they build it, they [the users] will come. But the truth is that any product is a risk. Remember our software engineer at the beginning of this book? His assumptions about what his customers wanted turned out to be wrong. His heart was in the right place. His idea was timely, different, very innovative, and even had a unique and sustainable business model. Nonetheless, the users didn't come. And when my team eventually went out and asked his target users, we discovered that they wouldn't pay for the product as it was being positioned.

User research is how you verify that you're on the right track with your value proposition. There are lots of ways to do it—ethnographic field studies, contextual inquiries, focus groups, diaries and journals, card sorting, eye-tracking, personas, and more. I don't want to talk about any of these traditional methods. Instead, I want to talk about *Lean Startup*.

It's weird to admit, but before 2011 when Eric Ries' *Lean Startup*[¶¶¶] (which you must read) went critical mass, founders didn't make it their mission to confront customers "early and often." The empirical, fast-moving, and transparent nature of Lean Startup riffed on ideas from Steve Blank's customer development methodology[****] and the highly theoretical *Design Thinking* approach. Sure, organizations had UX designers around to do "user-centric" design (as opposed to engineer-centric), but Lean Startup made conducting validated user research a make-or-break aspect of moving forward on a product. Lean Startup forced user research to become measurable.

This leads us to our third tenet—validated user research. "Validation" is the secret sauce of the Lean Startup business approach. Validation is the process of confirming that a specific customer segment finds value in your product. Without validation, you are simply *assuming* that customers will find use for your product. Validated user research goes beyond just observing and establishing empathy for potential users. It is a process based on a reality-check that focuses on direct feedback from interaction with users. It helps your team to determine if the vision of your product is a dream or a potential nightmare.

Eric Ries popularized the term Minimum Viable Product (MVP). It simply means learning if potential customers want your product by building just the core features of your value proposition. This is far different from traditional product development in which building a prototype was often a simulation to show potential investors the future product. By getting customer buy-in on your value proposition early, you are de-risking your product. And if users don't like what they see, we need to either "pivot" to a different customer segment or pivot to a different problem that our value proposition can address.

Iterations like the MVP require your team to conduct research and gain validation before developing a solution. It helps verify that your team is targeting the *right* customer (something our startup in Chapter 1 failed to do) and not just a general persona. When you've validated a specific pain point that needs addressing, you can continue to add features and then test those features using the same research methods. This is

¶¶¶ Ries, Eric. *Lean Startup*. HarperBusiness, 2011.
**** Blank, Steve. *The Four Steps to the Epiphany*. K&S Ranch Press, 2005.

known as the Lean Startup feedback loop of *build-measure-learn*. Use your research to validate your decisions and ensure that the product vision is aligned with the end user's needs.

Validated user research is a collaborative process that should involve as many members of the product team as possible. Collaboration will actually help organically build consensus on the value proposition and any pivots that follow. Now, this might sound naïve, given that we are all working in different environments with a range of folks with dynamic personalities who are in various positions of power. In an enterprise environment, there are typically many stakeholders who each have a say on the product requirements based on their personal agenda or preference. When I work for agencies, the product requirements are typically locked in stone during a requirements-gathering phase that I'm not involved in. For me to suggest doing validated user research or creating an MVP to test during the design phase is blasphemy because it's counterintuitive to the agency model. The last thing an account executive wants to hear from his UX resources are ways to cut the project fee down for his client.

If you happen to find yourself in this familiar position, that's the exact moment that you need to become *intrapreneurial.* Intrapreneurship is the act of behaving like an entrepreneur while working within a large organization. You need to decide to take the fate of the product into your own hands through assertive risk-taking and innovation. Stand up and ask for the extra week or two to conduct validated user research. If you get a "no" or are too afraid to ask, it's time to start working off-hours. The worst thing that can happen is that you will discover something about yourself and/or start looking for ways to improve your own work process.

The bottom line is that confronting your target customers is nonnegotiable. We must learn as quickly as possible if the idea we are working on is stupid and worthless. We need to have an open mind to experiment and to fail. That's right, we are betting. And the odds are against us. In the end, though, this approach is more cost-effective and efficient.

Tenet 4: Killer UX Design

In *Lean Entrepreneur*[††††] Patrick Vlaskovits and Brant Cooper advocate, "If you are doing best practices, you are not innovating." This is a provocative statement, because established interaction design patterns help make consistent user experiences. Then again, there is no harm in breaking a rule or two through experimentation to make a killer user experience.

The "user experience" (UX) is how a human feels when using the interface of a digital product while attempting to accomplish a task or goal. Yes, we can say a door handle is an interface and go off the nondigital highway into the world of 100 percent physical products. But in practice, the term "user experience" refers to whether a person has a good or bad time trying to utilize a digital product.

Traditionally (if I dare use that word for a discipline barely two decades old), UX design is associated with deliverables for development and design execution—site maps, wireframes, process/task flows, and functional specifications. Recruiters for enterprises and agencies identify UX design with the job titles that create these deliverables, including interaction designer, information architect, and UX designers. These definitions are used by large enterprises and agencies and are pretty much how UX design is currently practiced. Yet, what ultimately happens in this "traditional" system is that the UX designer and therefore the UX design are often more focused on the issues of user engagement and design rather than customer development and business-model generation.

The common problem that many product makers don't realize is how much their UX decisions are tied to customer acquisition. Just think about any transactional website or even a simple sign-up process. The UX design should be very concerned with barriers to entry, which can prevent validated leads who have previously engaged with the product from converting to customers. We'll talk more about this in Chapter 9. Interfaces and user flows should be geared toward the desired response of the user. It's all about engagement.

[††††] Vlaskovits, Patrick and Brant Cooper. *Lean Entrepreneur.* Wiley, 2013.

This is what distinguishes a novice UX designer from a killer UX designer. Killer UX designers know now to guide the value innovation of a product in the following ways:

- They work collaboratively with stakeholders and teammates at the idea's inception. Then, the UX designer can be involved in designing structured experiments for validation. These experiments need to be focused on how successful the value proposition can be communicated to the customer from the moment the customer opens the landing page. Using measurable results, design decisions can be made based on real evidence rather than hunches.

- They help determine the key moments and features that are absolutely critical to your product. Chapter 6 focuses on tactics for helping you discover value innovations, concentrating on the primary utility of the product. We explore techniques such as storyboarding that will weave key experiences together in simple and elegant ways. We look at ways to poach and cherry-pick features from both competitors and noncompetitors so that we can put them together in new ways.

- They learn everything about the existing market space to identify UX opportunities that can be exploited. This allows your team to find ways to create a leap in value by offering something that makes peoples lives more efficient.

- They talk directly to potential users or existing power users of the product to discover and validate its primary utility with respect to the problem that must be solved.

- They weave the UX through all touch points—online and offline— enabling an experience that is *frictionless*. This is especially relevant in products such as Airbnb and Uber in which the transaction begins on the Internet, is fulfilled in the real world, but then loops the user back to the interface to write reviews.

You can't merely "design think" your way to a killer UX design. It's only when the UX is informed by and affects the other three tenets that mental models are broken. Disruption erupts!

Over the course of the book, I will discuss several case studies of products that have killer user experiences. These are UX designs that didn't just "happen" through good luck or "genius design." They're killer through the manifestation of the tenets. It's only with practice and mindfulness that we will come to understand the product as a sum of both its tangible and intangible parts. The examples include the following companies.

Airbnb

The listing service that is disrupting the travel industry (Figure 2-7).

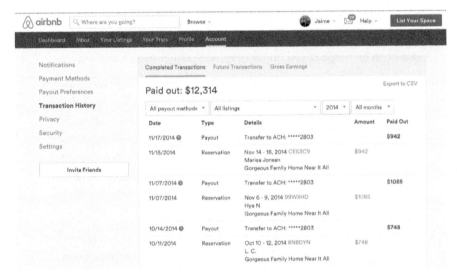

FIGURE 2-7

Airbnb's killer UX

Uber

The ridesharing application that is disrupting the taxi-service industry (Figure 2-8).

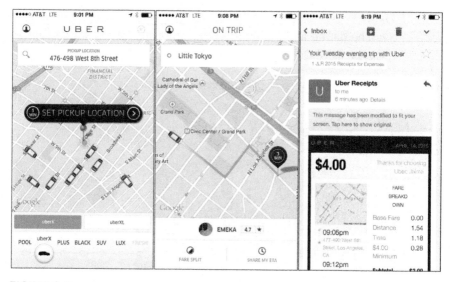

FIGURE 2-8

Uber's killer UX

Waze

The map application that is disrupting how people get from Point
A to Point B in their cars (Figure 2-9).

FIGURE 2-9

Waze's killer UX

Tinder

The dating app that is threatening former dating-site disruptors such as OkCupid and Eharmony (Figure 2-10).

FIGURE 2-10
Tinder's killer UX

These products all got to where they are not by execution of a static business plan or a two-week UX discovery phase, but through experiments, failure, and iterations over months and sometimes years. It was the insights born out of structured strategic meanderings that blossomed into awe-inspiring product interfaces. It's how the founders and teams behind-the-scenes took risks while assembling the building blocks of their products' business models. They fine-tuned their value innovation and acquired fervent customers, which led to a competitive advantage such that they now swim in a blue ocean.

Top 10 Not-UX Strategies!

1. A killer idea for a new product!

2. A laundry list of features!

3. A thoroughly researched game plan for which all possible scenarios have been considered and is ready for implementation. No need for customer feedback because you are 100 percent certain you have nailed it!

4. A creative permutation of trending buzzwords that were just used by another startup that raised financing (for instance, peer-to-peer sharing economies).

5. A generic set of motivational statements (such as Go Team Challenge Conquer).

6. An arrogant statement from some expert—"Our product sprung from the genius of Professor I.M. Awesome, the visionary of Social Lean Disruption."

7. A hypothesis that has nonvalidated risky assumptions—"Well, all women do like pink."

8. A grandiose vision that doesn't align with its core values that your company has no capability of delivering (for instance, a patent-pending, new-method-of-discovery dream).

9. A vague affirmation that sounds like a good Hallmark card—"You, too, can achieve Social Lean Disruption."

10. The North Star.

Recap

UX strategy is a way of thinking. It's not a means of formulating and executing a perfect plan; rather, it's about being able to research what's out there, analyze the opportunities, run structured experiments, fail, learn, and iterate until you devise something of value that people truly want. While devising a UX strategy, you will need to take risks and accept failure. You'll learn how to fail smartly by doing small-structured experiments to validate that your strategy is moving your team in the right direction.

[3]

Validating the Value Proposition

"To know what a business is we must start with its purpose. Its purpose must lie outside of the business itself. In fact, it must lie in society since business enterprise is the organ of the society. There is only one valid definition of business purpose: to create a customer."[*]
—PETER DRUCKER, 1973

At the beginning, you don't just define your product vision. Rather, you first need to figure out what problem you're going to solve and what kind of customer needs it solved the most. That's a lot to figure out, and getting one part wrong could turn your vision into a delusion. So, to stay grounded, you're going to really dig into Tenet 1, Business Strategy, and Tenet 3, Validated User Research (see Figure 3-1 and refer to Chapter 2 if you need a refresher on the four tenets of UX strategy). In this chapter, you will learn how to create a value proposition, which is the magical thing that you must make tangible for customers. Then, you will go over how to validate it through experiments to prove whether that hypothesis is correct.

FIGURE 3-1
Tenet 1 and Tenet 3: Business Strategy and Validated User Research

---

[*]   Drucker, Peter. *Management: Tasks, Responsibilities, Practices.* HarperBusiness, 1973.

The Blockbuster Value Proposition

When I was in the eighth grade, I used to pretend I had a stomachache so my mom would take me to work with her. She was a legal secretary at Burbank Studios, and I loved wandering the back lots, hiding on sets and watching crews shoot television shows and movies. Once, I even had a chance to meet Ricardo Montalbán on the set of *Fantasy Island!* The younger me of 1978 just couldn't imagine a cooler job. And that's why the older me of 2012 was particularly excited when a blockbuster movie producer arranged a meeting with me at a bungalow on the same lot. He wanted to consult with me on an idea for a product to see if it "had legs."

```
FADE IN:

EXT. BUNGALOW - MORNING

The shot starts long and then pans up through the
window of the bungalow.

                                          CUT TO:

INT. BUNGALOW - MORNING

A production assistant leads our UX strategist
JAIME into the room. The movie producer PAUL is
seated behind his desk. He stands up to greet her.
They shake hands and then settle into their seats.
The assistant leaves the room.

                    PAUL
     So I have an idea for an ecommerce site, and
     I'm hoping you can help me with it.

                    JAIME
     Let's hear it.

                    PAUL
     It's like an Amazon.com Wish List for the
     Busy Man who needs help shopping for his
     wardrobe.

                    JAIME
     Can you tell me more about this "Busy Man"?
```

Paul gets really excited. He leans forward and gesticulates a lot while describing the Busy Man to Jaime.

                    PAUL
        He's the guy whose life is his work. He makes
        good money but doesn't have time to spend it.
        He loves high-end products but hates shop-
        ping for them. He's sick of repeating himself
        to salespeople but still wants to get the VIP
        treatment.

Jaime leans forward, hands resting on her knees. She takes a beat before speaking.

                    JAIME
        That's very specific. But do you think this
        is a problem for most busy men? Do you think
        they need it solved?

                    PAUL
        Absolutely! I certainly do!

In Los Angeles, it's easy to run into both Hollywood types who pitch movie ideas and tech entrepreneurs who pitch Internet product ideas. What's funny is how similar they are. Both want to create something original and compelling that makes lots of money. Both need to raise a ton of cash to make their ideas into reality. But, this requires "spinning" a good story in order to convince potential stakeholders and investors that there is an audience out there who will want the idea.

Most investors know that the odds are not in their favor because the market is constantly being inundated with schlock—crappy movies and crappy apps. Then again, when something is truly great, the payoff can be major. And not just in terms of the money. Having a "hit" is also what gives us fulfillment as content and product creators. We want to create something that people find useful and meaningful—something maybe even our mom will like!

However, there is one major difference between making movies and making digital products. With films, regardless of the strategy—casting big-name actors, sequels to board games, well-worn plots and tropes—there are hardly any opportunities in the process of making the film to "de-risk" it through empirical feedback. Sure, filmmakers can test early cuts on their target market, but typically at that point, reshooting is an unaffordable option. With digital products, you can "test market" your concepts on your target audiences much earlier and with much less fidelity to the intended idea. You can reality check your team and ensure that everyone is on the right path. There is no reason to live on *Fantasy Island* unless you enjoy the risks of big gambling.

Lessons Learned

- Just because your stakeholders (or you) really want your product, doesn't mean anybody else will. Most startups fail because the market doesn't necessarily need the product.

- You need to ground your stakeholders and team in reality with empirical evidence. You must turn assumptions into facts.

- Don't take what your stakeholders or team says at face value. To learn what potential customers want, hunt them down in person.

What Is a Value Proposition?

Generally, a value proposition takes the form of a statement and is usually the first sentence out of the mouth, as it was for my movie producer client. Think of it as an elevator pitch—when you distill something into a discrete, easy-to-remember, compelling, and repeatable phrase. Its primary purpose is to communicate the benefits that the customer can expect from your offering. Here are examples of value proposition statements for a few well-known products:

- Airbnb is a community marketplace for people to list, discover, and book unique spaces around the world through the Internet.

- Snapchat is the fastest way to share messages, photos, videos, texts, and drawings with friends for a limited amount of time.

- Waze is a social traffic and navigation app based on the world's largest community of drivers sharing real-time road information and contributing to the "common good" while driving.

No matter what environment you work in as a product maker, you are constantly getting pitched or pitching value propositions. Before their products became household names, just imagine how many times the teams at Airbnb, Snapchat, and Waze had to repeat their value proposition statements with investors until they finally "clicked."

All this is to say that the little sentence, "It's like *Avatar* meets *Die Hard!*" is really important. But, you might be thinking, how hard could it be to come up with one? It's not, actually. In fact, there's even a website called *itsthisforthat.com*, which generates random value propositions as fast as you can click the refresh button. I generated the one shown in Figure 3-2.

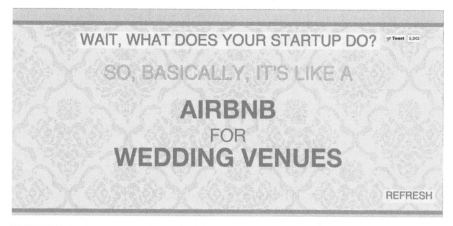

FIGURE 3-2
A machine-generated value proposition that says "Airbnb for Wedding Venues"

Let's deconstruct the website's value proposition formula:

It's *<famous platform or app goes here>* for *<type of customers or customer need goes here>*!

The "this" essentially describes the magical powers of the product. The "this" for the dating app Tinder is how you can immediately let someone know you find them attractive with a swipe interaction. The "this" for Waze is how you can find a driving shortcut because other people around you have their Waze app open and are providing you with real-time data to maneuver around traffic jams. The "this" is the mental model; it's how people understand the interactive dynamics of a product and how it affects the outcome of how they use it.

The "that" describes either or both the specific customer segment and its need or goal. The "that" for Tinder is people looking for an easier way to "hook up" instead of having to fill out a time-consuming dating profile. The "that" for Waze is drivers who want to avoid getting stuck in traffic even if it means taking routes off the beaten path. The "that" clues us in on who might want or need the "this" and why. What this formula does is give us a fast way to articulate the solution.

But value propositions are not valuable if they do not solve a real problem. I'm not talking minor problems like a scraped knee; I'm talking about painful broken-leg problems. I'm talking about those problems that hinder a certain set of people from doing what they need to do in a timely manner. By solving this kind of problem, a solution would give relief or joy to this large set of people. You need to know everything you can about those problems and people *before* you build out those solutions, because building software takes time and money. Thus, it's a risky endeavor to just begin building a new innovative product based on a hunch.

Because what if you are wrong?

Or your boss is wrong?

Or the client is wrong?

Or even the successful movie producer guy is wrong?

Or this digital value proposition that we generated in .05 seconds is wrong?

The answer is simple. If the person with the big hunch is wrong and your team doesn't find out until after the money is gone, everyone has failed in making something with a *true* value proposition. Everyone involved has only succeeded in wasting their resources. And because this is the infancy stage of your product vision, you don't want to get too attached to any ideas—especially without proper validation that *real* customers will *really* want the solution.

IF YOU DON'T WANT TO LIVE ON FANTASY ISLAND...

Just follow these five steps, which I will walk you through in detail:

Step 1: Define your primary customer segment.

Step 2: Identify your customer segment's (biggest) problem.

Step 3: Create provisional personas based on your assumptions.

Step 4: Conduct customer discovery to validate or invalidate your solution's initial value proposition.

Step 5: Reassess your value proposition based on what you learned!

(Rinse and repeat until you have product/solution fit.)

It's that easy! We just need to be empirical in our process.

Step 1: Define your primary customer segment

Because you and your team are launching an innovative product, you are starting with zero customers. Therefore, if you think your customer is everybody, think harder. Otherwise, you're facing an uphill battle in customer acquisition. Which is easier: getting everybody to use your app, or getting people who really need it to sign up? Many hit digital products have done just that. When Facebook launched, it was exclusive to students at Harvard University, not the entire world. Airbnb tested out its product on the 2008 Democratic National Convention, and even Tinder did its initial pilot project by focusing on college students at the University of Southern California.[†]

The customer is a group or segment of people with a common need or pain. Your primary customer's pain point must be severe, because there is a lot of risk involved in trying to change how people do something in a familiar way to an unfamiliar one in an uncontested market space. Examples of customer segments are international college students in Los Angeles who have a hard time making friends with native students, aspiring musicians in big cities who want practice gigs, or busy suburban moms who can't manage their kids' schedules. These segments can be identified by a combination of demographic and psychographic attributes, but what is most essential is that they describe in 10 words or fewer a set of people on whom you can zero-in.

So, let's go back to the computer-generated value proposition and imagine the most obvious primary customer. Who the hell needs to plan a wedding on a budget? Hmmm... As Figure 3-3 demonstrates, maybe a bride-to-be? Yes, let's go with it!

---

† *http://en.wikipedia.org/wiki/Tinder_%28application%29*

FIGURE 3-3
Mock-up of typical first page of a pitch deck

Step 2: Identify your customer segment's (biggest) problem

The problem should be a specific one that a specific customer segment is having. Nonetheless, you need to acknowledge that you and your team are working solely on assumptions, and that's just the reality of where you begin when making a product. You make assumptions about your users, their needs, and how to solve them. You just need to be very honest about the assumptions you're making and to take them for what they are: facts people take for granted. Or, as the great Coach Buttermaker (Walter Matthau) in the movie *Bad News Bears* said to his baseball team, "When you 'ASSUME,' you make an ASS out of U and ME."

At the beginning of the chapter, Paul the movie producer stated that he understood his customer's problem because it was his own: he was a busy man with money who didn't have time to shop. Therefore, all busy men needed an online shopping experience to build a high-end custom wardrobe. If that logic worked for every value proposition, I could easily look at the digital value proposition and say, "When I planned my own wedding, I was a bride-to-be on a limited budget, and my biggest pain point was finding a wedding venue in Los Angeles that I could afford." Which was true for me, but is it true for every frugal bride-to-be?

This is where you want to write out the customer and problem hypothesis in a statement. Here's what it could look like:

> Brides-to-be in Los Angeles have a hard time finding wedding venues that are affordable.

Which, if proven true, would validate an important need for the value proposition:

> Airbnb for Finding Wedding Venues.

It would seem, then, that the next logical step would be to start dreaming up the entire feature set for this much-needed solution, right? No. Not yet.

Remember the software engineer from Chapter 1? He jumped straight into building out the solution for his startup. He assumed that customers like him (addicts' loved ones) would be interested in a digital platform with which they could negotiate prices with treatment centers. He also assumed that there would be a lot of customers like this or at least enough to help keep the business model afloat. Yet, these assumptions were just that: assumptions. He could not pinpoint the reason why his product was unsuccessful until my team ran validated user-research experiments. The experiments exposed the fallacy to him, which was that customers, including those with a decent budget, were highly unlikely to book a treatment center over the Internet the same way they would book a hotel room. He heard directly from the potential customers what he initially didn't want to believe: booking a treatment center was just too much of a highly emotional decision to be done entirely online.

Here's a pro tip:

> Don't build your product's UX around a value proposition unless you have tangible evidence that people will want the product!

If you are a problem solver (which is instinctual for UX designers, product makers, and entrepreneurs), this process at first feels backward. That's because it is. We are reverse-engineering the solution to validate the assumptions about the customers and their problem. This approach is particularly important for those of you who have produced dozens of products, including ones that have been very successful. Don't believe your own hype. Instead, approach every new product or project like an experiment.

As I mentioned in the Preface, I've been a part-time college professor for more than 20 years. I have always run my courses the same way. The first week, the students have to think of problems they would like to try to solve using technology. Each week, they build toward the final course project, which is to pitch a real product that they've tested using the methods I'm teaching you in this book. In the spring of 2014, I offered UX apprenticeships to my students Bita and Ena to take on the "Airbnb for Weddings" product vision. I'm going to present their methods and results to show how you can give any value proposition a real shot to see if it is viable. This was their first assignment: the provisional persona.

Step 3: Create provisional personas based on your assumptions

Personas can be a helpful tool in giving stakeholders and the product team an empathetic sense of what the end user's needs, goals, and motivations are. In this way, they can make a product more "user-friendly." However, the concept of provisional personas has had a tumultuous history with advocates on both sides of the table, so I'm going to give you a little lesson on it to explain why I'm using them here and now.

In the early days of software design, the engineers who developed and programmed the products were also typically the designers of the product interfaces. These product interfaces were rarely "user-friendly," because they were not tested on the end user of the product. Too often, interfaces were pasted together in a hurried fashion to meet a shipping date.

Alan Cooper, a widely recognized Bay Area software designer and programmer, knew this problem all too well. In 1988, Cooper created the visual programming language that would become Visual Basic, an innovation that ultimately enabled an open marketplace for software companies that wanted to build applications for Microsoft Windows.[‡] In 1995, he invented personas and wrote books to help software teams to embrace his goal-directed design methodology. Personas were also a

---

‡ http://en.wikipedia.org/wiki/Alan_Cooper

critical tool to inspire product stakeholders to make more user-friendly interfaces.[§] But to achieve this kind of persona, it meant that months of qualitative "ethnographic" research had to be conducted to create an authentic model of each end user.

By 2002, personas were a popular tool in the designer toolbox, but they weren't often used to achieve their original purpose. Instead, big interactive agencies such as Razorfish or Sapient used personas to upsell the research/discovery phase to clients. When used in this way, personas were often laughable caricatures packed full of stereotypical details based on nothing more than marketing data. In fact, this is what happened with the three personas conducted for the Oprah.com redesign I talk about in Chapter 2. The personas that made it to the discovery brief were depicted as three people from different minority backgrounds but only because Oprah had a massive multiracial following. In reality, ethnicity had little to do with the UX of the product. Did African-American Oprah fans need a different interface or feature set than Caucasian Oprah fans? In this way, the personas failed in informing the UX strategy process in a basic way, such as when Cooper writes, "Don't confuse persona archetypes with stereotypes. Because personas provide a precise design target and also serve as a communication tool to the development team, the designers must choose a particular demographic characteristics with care."

By the third edition of Cooper's book *About Face* in 2007, he added a new section called "When Rigorous Personas Aren't Possible: Provisional Personas."[¶] The concept was geared for product makers who did not have the time, budgets, or corporate buy-in to perform the fieldwork necessary to gather detailed qualitative data. They were a simple collaborative group exercise for designers and nondesigners to create quickly. In fact, the product designer and author Jeff Gothelf also reintroduced them as a *Lean UX*[**] technique to help align teams on how they think about the customer before doing customer discovery. This is where personas become useful to you in this book, because a provisional persona will be a helpful communication tool to depict your hypothesized customer and align your team. It also gives everyone a starting point for

---

§   Cooper, Alan. *About Face*. Wiley, 1995.

¶   Cooper, Alan. *About Face 3*. Wiley, 2007.

** Gothelf, Jeff with Josh Seiden. *Lean UX*. O'Reilly, 2013.

the validation process. Thus, you can think of a provisional persona as a "back-up" or "low budget" persona, which is better than having no persona at all. (Also see what the long-time UX executive Peter Merholz has to say about profiles in Chapter 10.)

Provisional persona layout and breakdown

The provisional personas will collect and present the assumptions you are making about your primary customer segment. Therefore, all information will be contextual to the hypothesized customer and relevant to the value proposition. Specifics such as demographic details or user goals aren't necessary unless they are essential to the product. Instead, you want to focus your personas on what you assume is important to customers and how they are currently dealing with the problem.

The provisional persona is made up of these four parts:

Name and snapshot/sketch

What is the customer's name? What does she look like? If you're going with a certain gender or demographic—in this example, perhaps a woman in her late 20s or early 30s—search for popular baby names of the early 1980s. If you can sketch, draw her. If you have a photo of someone who fits the part, just paste it. If not, find a good reference photo using Google Images or Flickr.

Description

What factors personally motivate the customer? The description should be a composite archetype of the customer that is relevant to the product idea rather than a stereotype of psychographic or demographic details. For example, your team only cares about the customer's taste in cars if you are solving a problem related to cars.

Behaviors

This category can be answered in several ways. The first is how the customer is trying to solve the problem now. Is it via a workaround on the Internet? In the real world or a hybrid of both? Is the customer tech-savvy enough to use the Internet to solve his problem? Is he using social networks to do it? Or are there general behaviors for customers who are using similar types of digital products that are relevant to your solution? The second is how the person's personality affects his behavior. For example, if the person is professionally successful, does that make him a good problem solver? Is the customer trusting or skeptical?

Needs and goals

This category explains what motivates the customer and causes her to act a certain way. For example, what is she missing from the current solution? What specific needs or goals aren't being satisfied by the customer's current behaviors? What are the deal-breaker issues she faces? What are compromising points?

Because you are using the provisional persona purely as a thinking tool to get a sense of your primary customer segments, you and your team want to keep the layout and content simple. In the provisional personas that follow, Bita and Ena use a two-by-two grid with a section for each part. They've pasted the image of their primary customer in the upper-left section, and they've created five to six bullets in each of the other three. Observe how the assumptions about their customers seem relatively easy to prove. You only want statements in your provisional personas that can be externally verified.

Figure 3-4 shows the provisional persona that Bita did for her first homework assignment, for "Airbnb for Weddings."

Jennifer, a value conscious bride-to-be (by Bita)

Description
• Late 20s/early 30s
• Lives in Los Angeles
• Educated
• Employed full-time
• Makes a decent salary

Behavior
• Very busy and on-the-go
• Savvy and resourceful: leverages large social and business networks online and offline
• Values opinions from friends on large purchases
• Values high efficiency—will try tools that will simplify her life. Has heard of or used Airbnb for travel
• Looks for high rated reviews online to make final purchase decisions

Needs & Goals
• Dreams of a romantic, elegant, mid-sized wedding
• Can't afford to have time wasted—needs to get information efficiently
• Wants to plan wedding via a reliable wedding service
• Wants everything to be perfect, i.e. ceremony, location, amenities
• Cautious and fiscally conservative, wants best value for hard-earned money

FIGURE 3-4
Bita's provisional persona for a bride-to-be

Figure 3-5 shows what Ena developed.

Stephanie, a budget-conscious bride-to-be (by Ena)

Description
- Mid 20s
- Lives in Los Angeles with her roommate
- Some college
- Freelancer, creative field
- Lives on a tight budget

Behavior
- Has time to seriously research her options
- Uses a spreadsheet to keep track of venues/vendors
- Internet savvy with strong social media presence
- Asks friends for advice
- Reads blogs for the latest trends, new ways to save, cool spaces, purchases, and reviews

Needs & Goals
- Dreams of a small outdoor wedding
- Wants the wedding to be affordable and manageable
- Wants the food to be good, but not fancy
- Needs relevant information to do comparison shopping
- Wants her friends and family to have a good time

FIGURE 3-5
Ena's provisional persona for a bride-to-be

What's most telling about the personas is how different the customers are even though each student worked on the same value proposition. They each assumed the primary customer was a very different kind of bride. Bita assumed that her customer was a professional woman named Jennifer in her late 20s or early 30s. She earns a decent income and is value conscious. Ena, however, assumed that her customer was a younger 20-something bride named Stephanie. This younger bride is in a very different place in her life than the more established and professional Jennifer. This creates more distinctions between the two brides. For instance, price is an issue for the younger Stephanie, but she wants people to have fun. She's willing to compromise and not have fancy food or that big of a wedding. However, Jennifer is efficient and a problem solver. She has high expectations that everything will be perfect. She needs a solution that will help her save time and get good value.

Which persona is the right one? It doesn't matter right now, because Bita and Ena are just working with assumptions anyway, and what they've built in the provisional personas are just more assumptions. Perhaps in the final product they might be able to suit the needs of both personas, but until then, everything in the personas remains an assumption until proven true or false. Regardless of who ends up being more "correct," though, the provisional personas helped Bita and Ena paint a clearer picture of their hypothesized customers. Now they just need to find those customers in real life and see what the brides really think!

Step 4: Conduct customer discovery to validate or invalidate your solution's initial value proposition

Customer discovery

In 2005, Steve Blank, a long-time Silicon Valley entrepreneur, published *The Four Steps to the Epiphany: Successful Strategies for Products that Win.*[††] Although his methodology revolves around four phases, I'm going to ruminate on the first one, customer discovery, as part of your UX strategy.

Customer discovery is a process used to discover, test, and validate whether a specific product solves a known problem for an identifiable group of users; it is essentially conducting user research. However, you don't want to just watch people, empathize with them, and then make judgments. Instead, you want to "get out of the building" and get customer validation, which is foundational to the Lean Startup business approach (and Tenet 3). You want to actively listen to people and engage them because your goal is to uncover the specific problem that they need solved.

This might sound like an obvious thing to do, but shockingly, the majority of stakeholders whom I work with in startups and enterprises don't talk to customers. In fact, before Lean Startup, the norm was that companies would just build the product without talking them. Much like Paul the movie producer, the stakeholders or product team assume that if they have the problem or associate with it, this means that they understand it. I think the real reason stakeholders don't talk to customers is fear. Product visionaries are like screenwriters sweating away at a script that they never show anyone. They're frightened of what their *real* customers might think—nobody wants to hear that their baby is ugly.

---

†† Blank, Steve. *The Four Steps to the Epiphany.* K&S Ranch Press, 2005.

In an ideal world, customer discovery is a collaborative process involving as many members of the product team going out into the field as possible. Collaboration will also help organically build consensus on what exactly the vision is for the product. If the people you work with don't want to do customer research, do it for yourself. Do it on the sly without waiting for permission from your boss, the client, or any naysayers. What is crucial is that it *is attempted*. You can come back from your research and share your discoveries anecdotally with your team. If nobody wants to listen, you can decide at that point if you want to continue working on that project or with your current team, or with your current employer. But at least get *out there* and discover evidence that might make your product better in the time that you have to work on it. Own your destiny.

We've already touched on some reasons why product makers become very protective of their ideas. They put a lot of energy and love into them. If you're a UX designer, you know exactly what I'm talking about. Clients such as Paul typically come to you with an idea for the product that they want to build. They've assumed that customers want their product. But as I've already stated, the UX strategist wants to know whether those assumptions are correct. As you're learning in this book, you don't want to get too attached to any ideas, especially without proper validation that real customers want the solution.

Fortunately, Bita and Ena aren't emotionally attached to the value proposition I generated off the Internet. They just need to validate their initial assumptions. And that's exactly what they're going to do. They're going to get out of the building (office or classroom) to conduct problem interviews.

The problem interview

During customer discovery, the goal of the interview is to talk to real people. My students have personas, and they need to talk to the people who match those personas.

Let's remember Tenet 3: Validated User Research. You want to use the approach of the Lean Startup, which means research should be meaningful, effective, and swift. You want to get into the Build-Measure-Learn loop as quickly as possible (see Figure 3-6). That loop begins with the smallest build of an idea. This build leads to some form of data that can measure what the customers say. Based on that, you then learn from that feedback about how to make the build better. And at this infancy stage of a value proposition, this means getting out of the building to validate provisional personas.

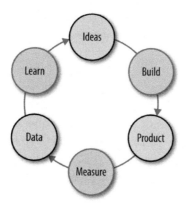

FIGURE 3-6

The Build-Measure-Learn feedback loop from the book *Lean Startup* by Eric Ries

You need to identify two or three nearby locations where you can make direct contact with your proposed customers. You can't hide behind your desk. Think creatively about where your customers lurk by focusing on the types of activities they might be doing. If you can't find them in the real world, you need to find them on the Internet (more on that in Chapter 8).

In the case of Bita, her provisional persona was of an upper-middle-class yet value-conscious bride-to-be. Bita decided to hit the malls of Los Angeles where she thought she could find people who matched her persona. Her first stop was the Westside Pavilion in West Los Angeles. This mall had plenty of kids' clothing stores such as Gymboree and Baby Gap where mothers with babies shopped. This was certainly different than what I was thinking, which was that Bita would find women in the midst of shopping for wedding gowns.

Bita's assumption was that these new mothers might give her insight about planning a wedding because they probably had a wedding before starting their family. And because they had very young children, their wedding was most likely recent. Bita dressed professionally and appropriately. She carried a notebook on which her questions were written and always approached her targeted customer with a smile and only if the timing was right (typically, their baby was asleep in a stroller). This was her script:

> Hi, I'm Bita. I'm conducting research on a product idea for an Internet startup. Can you spare a few moments to answer questions related to wedding planning?

The problem interview is actually made up of two parts: the *screener* and the *interview*. A screener is a list of questions used to qualify potential participants for a study. You need these questions because you cannot assume that every person you approach is in fact the customer you need and want to validate your persona assumptions. The screener questions will identify the "control group," on whom we will ultimately validate our hypotheses.

Therefore, good screener questions must help you quickly weed out the wrong people. They should seem nonintrusive to the participant, but you know they are deal-breaker questions. It might be helpful to work backward. What are the exact answers you must hear from someone to qualify them for this mini-experiment? Sometimes, it takes a few iterations of your screener questions to truly ensure that you are talking to the right people. Be okay with fine-tuning your questions on the fly to either make them more general or more specific, based on what happens "in the wild" as you begin talking to people.

Let's get back to Bita. If the woman she confronted seemed open to chatting, Bita immediately launched into her screener questions.

Phase 1: The screener questions

1. Were you married within the last few years?

   - Yes (continue to question 2)

   - No (kindly end the interview)

2. Did you happen to get married here in Los Angeles?

   - Yes (interview the person)

   - No (kindly end the interview)

Based on Bita's persona, the goal of her screener questions is to identify if the woman she's interviewing recently planned a wedding in Los Angeles. She needed participants with fresh memories about what happened at their weddings. Also, she needed them to be married in sunny Southern California, in which they probably had an outdoor venue like a park, beach, or fancy backyard. This detail was crucial to validating the Airbnb for Weddings value proposition, because she assumed that these outside locations (such as someone's fancy backyard overlooking the beach) would have solved this potential participant's wedding venue woes.

Phase 2: The interview

If a woman passed the screener test, Bita was able to move on to her actual interview questions.

Typically, this is when product makers and tech entrepreneurs like to extol the virtues of their awesome value proposition. But, if you just start pitching ideas at strangers, they tend to just nod their heads in agreement to quickly get the hell away from you. That's not the validation you need or want. Remember customer discovery is about listening and not selling. Let's take a look at how Bita handled it in her interview questions:

1. How did you go about planning your wedding?

   • Prompt for both ceremony and reception locations

   • Prompt for tools/means, such as Internet, word-of-mouth

2. Did you have a budget for venues and were you able to stay within that budget? (If not, by how much more?)

3. How many people were you planning to have at the reception (for example, 50 to 200)?

4. What were some of the challenges you faced in finding the venues (Prompt: e.g., finding the ideal location, such as by the beach)?

5. How did you overcome these challenges? Did you end up having to compromise on your ideal wedding?

These questions actually set up the context for our solution. Now that the participant has that context, it's time for Bita to ask her money-shot question. Bita:

Excellent, thank you so much for all this great feedback. I have two last questions for you.

6. Have you ever heard of or tried a website called "Airbnb"?

   - Yes (continue to question 7)

   - No (quickly explain what value prop is of Airbnb with respect to the part about short-term subletting and continue to question 7)

7. If there were a website, like Airbnb, that gave you a numerous choices of gorgeous homes with big backyards in LA that you could rent specifically for a wedding event, what do you think?

You end with your money-shot questions, which are when you actually pitch your hypothetical value proposition. Again, you want to listen and not sell. See how open-ended Bita's questions are? She's just pulling the trigger on the solution to see what response she gets without trying to bias the participant in favor or against it. When you ask the money-shot question, just capture the essence of the person's response and, if they apply, ask any relevant follow-up questions. Then that's it! Thank the person profusely and let him go on with his day. Ideally, you will try to collect 10 complete interviews from screener to money-shot.

Two-sided markets

Now, it's time to do a serious reality check about your primary customer, because this book is talking about digital products for twenty-first-century consumers. Therefore, you need to think about *all* of your potential customers. Sometimes they are paying customers, and sometimes they are customers who use the product for free. As you probably already noticed, I use the terms "user" and "customer" interchangeably, because users who don't pay for a product such as Facebook or YouTube are still customers. Facebook and YouTube need buy-in from these nonpaying customers so that paying customers—advertisers—will want to engage with the product. All this is to say that sometimes you only have one primary customer segment for which you need to validate a UX. Here are some examples:

- A video-streaming website such as Netflix needs movie viewers.

- An online publication such as the *New York Times* needs news readers.

- A financial website such as Citibank needs customers with bank accounts.

But, what if you need *two* distinct user types for your product to have value? Two-sided markets are what make the Internet go around. They drastically affect the UX strategy because they require two distinct user experiences—one for each customer segment—to be validated and created. eBay has buyers and sellers. Airbnb has hosts and guests. Eventbrite has event producers and event attendees. These digital products are insanely good at providing value to both of these customer segments through their feature sets, and that's something that you might also need to do.

The real Airbnb is a digital platform that facilitates one set of customers (hosts) subletting their properties to another set of customers (guests). Airbnb then collects a small percentage of the transaction from both "sides." Bita and Ena's value proposition is based on Airbnb's innovative business model, which is based on the peer-to-peer sharing economy. For them to solve the problem of helping brides find an affordable venue for weddings, they must match them up with the other side of the market: people who are willing to rent their homes out for a wedding event.

Ena realized this during her customer discovery. Consequently, she took a step back and created a provisional persona of her other primary customer, which you can see in Figure 3-7.

John and Susan, homeowners open to hosting weddings (by Ena)

Description
- Late 40s/early 50s married couple
- Live in a good part of Los Angeles
- Educated
- 100–200k household salary
- Have kids in college

Behavior
- Know how to use the Internet
- Use Airbnb for world travel
- Have listed their home on Airbnb and Home Away
- Enjoy sharing their beautiful home and making it nice
- Flexible and open to trying new things

Needs & Goals
- Need to find more ways to supplement their income
- Need a reliable service for subletting their home
- Want to put their spacious house to good use
- Need to know the guests are trustworthy
- Need the entire experience of subletting to be easy

FIGURE 3-7

Ena's provisional persona for a wedding venue host

This is the customer segment that also must exist to make her value proposition work. Ena needs people like John and Susan: people who own nice homes in Malibu and are open to innovative solutions for taking advantage of their home's value. They are probably older than our brides-to-be and quite concerned that their homes don't get trashed, or so Ena's persona assumes.

I asked Ena how she planned to validate this provisional persona. Where would she find people of this type? Would she knock on big fancy doors of homes by the beach? Good luck. Maybe she could ask people who were shopping at the high-end grocery store in Malibu if they would rent their home? I was concerned that she was chasing a persona that wouldn't be easy to verify. So I sent her out to do more customer discovery.

The following week Ena came back with some pretty cool validation, which is shown in Figure 3-8. She had put on her bride-to-be hat and contacted some real hosts on the real Airbnb. She asked them if they would consider renting their homes out for a wedding event. She even asked how much they might charge. As it turns out, people are already doing this.

Hi Ena,

Thank you for your inquiry! We would love to host you, and your guests :) The base price is $1500/night (up to six overnight guests), and $40 per person for the wedding attendees. For example, with 50 people it would be an additional $2000. Plus a cleaning fee of $500.

It looks like you are from California, so you probably know Malibu well, but just in case wanted to let you know that our house is on La Costa beach which is a private beach - no public access. It's perfect for hosting weddings.

I look forward to hearing from you.

Best,

Kate

FIGURE 3-8

Example of a positive response from hosts on Airbnb for Ena's inquiry about renting their home for a wedding

Hosts on Airbnb were already bending the system. They were creating pricing packages totally separate from the Airbnb business model and UX, and the responses showed Ena how familiar hosts were with wedding inquiries. So, how did this information affect Ena's value proposition? Let's find out!

Step 5: Reassess your value proposition based on what you learned! (And continue to iterate until you have product/market fit.)

As you can see, conducting validated user researcher does not need to be costly or time-consuming. For Bita, it cost her one Saturday to validate whether her assumptions were right, which she then compiled into the results shown in Figure 3-9.

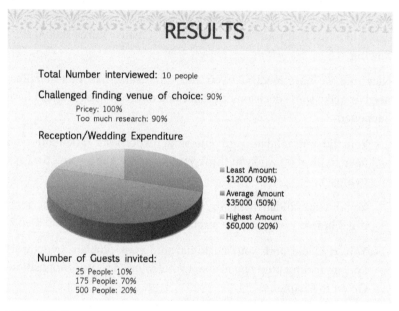

RESULTS

Total Number interviewed: 10 people

Challenged finding venue of choice: 90%
    Pricey: 100%
    Too much research: 90%

Reception/Wedding Expenditure

- Least Amount: $12000 (30%)
- Average Amount $35000 (50%)
- Highest Amount $60,000 (20%)

Number of Guests invited:
    25 People: 10%
    175 People: 70%
    500 People: 20%

FIGURE 3-9
Bita's customer discovery results

Yes, she only talked to 10 people who passed her screener questions, but she found that 9 of them had a huge problem finding an affordable venue. Obviously, the value proposition's hypothetical problem was real. However, she also learned about how much those people spent on their weddings and how many people they invited. This knowledge affected how she thought about her value proposition because it meant the detail of venue size was actually more important than she originally assumed. It made her question whether there were homes large enough in Los Angeles to accommodate the needs of her personas. It was a reality check.

In contrast, Ena's customer discovery revealed that there is already an existing solution for Airbnb for Weddings, and it was...Airbnb! Moreover, she also learned that Airbnb is not designed to address the purpose, problems, or perspectives faced by the host or bride-to-be. For example, you currently can't search for homes that will allow private parties. You have to look at each house, one listing at a time, and then contact the owners individually just as Ena did. Yet people (both hosts and brides-to-be) are currently using Airbnb as a Band-Aid solution because there is no better alternative! It's when you stumble on evidence like this that your "value innovation" creative juices should start flowing.

Now that we have feedback, you and your team, like Bita and Ena, need to make some decisions, because one of three things should have happened:

- You did not validate your customer hypothesis. Therefore, you need to pivot on who you think your customers really are. Go back to Step 1.

- You did not validate the pain point your customers were experiencing. Therefore, you need to pivot on the problem. Go back to Step 2.

- You validated both your customer and your problem hypothesis and are feeling pretty good about your solution's value proposition. Go on to Chapter 4.

Recap

At the beginning of this chapter, I talked about great value propositions from amazing companies like Waze, Airbnb, and Snapchat. Some of these value props are very different from what their founders started with before their products had substantial traction. Value propositions of products evolve with a great understanding of customers' needs. Not to quote Peter Drucker *ad nauseum*, but he did say, "Strategy requires knowing what our business is and what it should be."‡‡

By mashing up customer-discovery techniques with traditional user-research tools such as provisional personas, you now have a cost-efficient way to determine if you are on the right track with your

---

‡‡ Drucker, Peter. *Management: Tasks, Responsibilities, Practices.* HarperBusiness, 1973.

product. Even if you are intimidated by users, new to research, locked in by a requirements document, fighting a looming deadline, or staring at a two-line vision statement, you want to reach out to users when you are at the starting point for a product development cycle. Because doing so is always far better than making an "ASS out of U and Me."

[4]

Conducting Competitive Research

You were right. I was on the wrong track.
We're deep in the valley, how deep in the gulley.
And now in the canyon. Out in the yonder.
—SONIC YOUTH (1984)

NOW THAT YOU HAVE A STRONG POSITIVE SIGNAL THAT YOU'RE ONTO something, you need to ask, "Why hasn't this solution been built yet?" I hesitate to say that everything has been done, but pretty much everything has been *attempted*. It's because individuals and companies have been designing products for distribution and consumption on the Internet for more than 20 years! Knowing what has actually worked or failed is crucial to identifying a competitive advantage. So, in this chapter and the next, we will look more deeply into Tenet 1, Business Strategy (Figure 4-1).

FIGURE 4-1
Tenet 1: Business Strategy

Learning Lessons, the Hard Way

Doing solid investigative market research is like peeling an onion. The more layers you peel, the more you reveal. And it also might bring tears to your eyes if you discover that your product vision is not actually unique. But don't you want to know what it will take to beat the competition sooner rather than later? If you don't know what you don't know, you are at risk of learning the hard way.

Take, for instance, my dear father. In 1976, at the age of 38, he got up the courage to quit his full-time job as the area management supervisor for a popular California restaurant chain. He'd been working for others since he graduated from UCLA with an accounting degree and was eager to be an entrepreneur. His good friend did well for himself by opening several hot dog stands in the Los Angeles area. So, my father was confident that his own management experience would bring him success.

He soon found a hot dog stand for sale next to a carwash in North Hollywood. He watched the operation briefly and saw how very few customers came to the stand even while their cars were being washed. The place was run down, and the owner appeared indifferent to his customers. My father saw an opportunity for turning the stand into a profitable business and bought it immediately.

Figure 4-2 shows how he gave everything a fresh coat of paint, updated the menu, and put up a big sign that said the stand was under "new management."

FIGURE 4-2
Polaroid of Alan Levy in front of his hot dog stand in 1978

On opening day, though, he sold fewer than 10 hot dogs. Worse, cockroaches crept across the serving counter, and my dad kept trying to squash them before customers walked up. At the time, my brother and I (then 10 and 12) would hang out at the stand on the weekends, and we could see that my dad didn't know what to make of his new business. Eventually, he realized that in spite of all his efforts, he couldn't turn it around. His management expertise did not translate into the emotional stamina and physical strength required to perform the daily operations of the business. So he put it up for sale.

One morning someone responded to his "Hot Dog Stand For Sale" ad. The man showed up to the stand at noon and introduced himself. He bought a hot dog and then sat down at a table to observe the entire lunch shift. In the first hour, an elderly woman who lived at the nearby senior-citizen home walked up and bought a hot dog. After one bite, she asked for her money back. She said, "It didn't taste right."

The man came back the next day and watched another lunch shift. Before he left, my father asked him what he thought of the business.

"To be honest, Alan," the man replied with a heavy Armenian accent, "You are married to a corpse."

That comment depressed my father for days. He decided to accept his fate and sold the stand at a significant loss, which was truly tough for my family. But the whole experience taught my father (and us kids) lessons that were huge.

Lessons Learned

- Before you start a new business, learn everything you can about how it works. Don't let your enthusiasm dull your logic.

- Investigate your competition. What are they doing right? What are they doing wrong? Why should customers come to you?

- And when you can't figure out how to make it work, admit defeat. It's totally okay to fail! But move on. Or pivot!

Using the Competitive Analysis Matrix Tool

You and your team might think you are creating a new marketplace with your product, but how can you be sure? Chances are you actually are entering an existing market. Therefore, you want to study how all the current digital solutions address the needs of your target customers.

To be competitive, you need to know what's out there, what has worked, and what has not worked. That's why conducting market research on the competition is a crucial component of business strategy. You want firsthand knowledge of the good and bad user experiences provided by your competitors. If done thoroughly, the research can provide a treasure trove of insight into current trends and outdated manifestations of mental models. It will also help your team learn about the competitors, their best practices for design, and what types of customer segments use their products. To connect the dots, though, you first need to collect them.

I have found the most efficient way to do a comprehensive competitive analysis is to collect all of the data in a matrix. It's the most obvious way to do a cross-comparison, and by using a spreadsheet, I can methodically collect data and not miss anything while I'm surfing around to research. The matrix helps keep track of everything that needs to be compared. When it's complete, I can rationalize my position with a cogent understanding of numerous qualitative and quantitative data points.

I use Google spreadsheets instead of Excel because I prefer a free cloud-based tool that is easily accessible to as many people—teammates and stakeholders—as possible. It's important that everyone has access to the most up-to-date research, and this way I avoid blank stares during important discussions.

Figure 4-3 depicts an example of a spreadsheet that I created using Google documents specifically for conducting competitive research. I am going to use the research that I conducted on the Busy Man's Shopping Site for explanation and sample data. (As I first mentioned in the Preface, I've included a toolkit with this book. It's for you to use with your teams. Refer to it for details on accessing the Competitive Analysis Matrix.)

Competitors	URL of Website or App Store Location	Usernames and Password Access	Purpose of Site	Year Founded
DIRECT COMPETITORS				
Trunkclub	http://www.trunkclub.com/	usn: jim@castersblues.com pwd: Learning000	Your own virtual personal stylist will shop and send you men's apparel. Trunkclub helps guys discover awesome designer clothes without any of the shopping. Hand-selected outfits from exclusive designers, free shipping both ways.	2009
Bombfell	http://www.bombfell.com/	usn: jim@castersblues.com pwd: Learning000	Bombfell was a monthly subscription for clothes. Join now to get clothes picked just for you by a stylist, so you can spend your time doing awesome guy stuff.	2012
JackThreads	https://www.jackthreads.com/	usn: jim@castersblues.com pwd: Learning000	JackThreads is an online Flash sales shopping community selling apparel, shoes, and accessories from top-tier streetwear and contemporary fashion brands.	2008
INDIRECT COMPETITORS				
Fab	http://fab.com/	usn: jim@castersblues.com pwd: Learning000	Daily curated design flash sales featuring the world's leading designers and manufacturers.	2011
Gilt	http://www.gilt.com	usn: jim@castersblues.com pwd: Learning000	Flash sales-Gilt Groupe hand selects both established and up and coming brands relevant to its membership base. Each Gilt Groupe Shopping Event is designer-specific and held over a one day period.	2007

FIGURE 4-3

Competitive market research spreadsheet example

Your ultimate goal is to devise a solution that creates a competitive advantage. The market research your team does in the tool will force everyone to look across the competitive landscape with an eye for gaps or inconsistencies in how the competitors deliver their user experiences. The devil *is* in the details, and it's in those details that Tenet 2, Value Innovation, can happen. (See Chapter 6 for more on this.)

When solid research is the input, solid analysis can be the output. This sounds obvious, but it's amazing how many quick decisions are made after only a cursory examination of the marketplace. As strategists, we need to help our clients filter the market research into bite-size, actionable takeaways in which everyone can make smart, analytical decisions. Let me break it down slowly. At the end of this adventure, you will see that *knowledge truly is power.*

Understanding the Meaning of Competition

Let's begin with some basics about conducting market research to analyze the competition. First let's agree on the boundaries of the market. Take an index finger and draw a big circle in the air in front of you. Now, imagine that inside the circle is anybody on this planet who has regular (or consistent) access to the Internet. Anybody outside of the circle is everyone else. Let's get rid of them and focus on the people inside the circle.

As digital product makers, the marketplace you all serve and dominate is the Internet. It's not only your marketplace; it's your distribution medium. You and your team create for, deliver products to, interact with, and acquire more users than any other medium through this digital highway. This is why the Internet is *far* more powerful than traditional mediums like television and radio.

Another special thing about your marketplace is that it contains all of your existing and future customers. They can be either paying or nonpaying customers. They can be of almost any age range, so long as they can interact or engage with the product digitally. If a company in this space offers a product that is similar or even similar-ish to yours, they are your competitors. They have the ability to cut into your share of the potential two-plus billion people in the market.

However, not all of these two-plus billion people are necessarily your customers. (If you think they are, please reread Chapter 3, right now.) If you realize this from the start, it will be easier to pinpoint your competition.

TYPES OF COMPETITORS

A competitor is a person, team, or company that shares your goals and is fighting for the same thing that your product team wants. If you are entering a new market, there might be no true "direct competitors." Still, the chances are that the market for your product already exists, and you just might not know about it yet.

Direct competitors are companies that offer the same, or very similar, value proposition to your current or future customers. This means that the customers you want are alive right now and spending their time and money on the Internet using a direct competitor's product instead of yours to solve their problem—whether it is the best interface or not!

In my research for Paul the movie producer from Chapter 3, I found that the biggest direct competitor was a site called Trunk Club, shown in Figure 4-4.

FIGURE 4-4

Direct competitor's website: Trunk Club

Trunk Club is a great solution for Paul the movie producer's intended customer segment because Trunk Club addresses his hypothesized users' problems. For example, the Busy Man doesn't want to deal with annoying sales people. If the Busy Man joins the VIP-ish sounding "Club," he also gets high-end clothing sent to him to try on in the privacy of his own home. That seems to hit all the points Paul brought up in Chapter 3, doesn't it? That's why Trunk Club is a direct competitor.

Indirect competitors offer a similar value proposition to a different customer segment; or, they target your exact customer base without offering the exact same value proposition. For instance, an indirect competitor's primary service might not be your value proposition, but their secondary service definitely is. Or, your customer base is using an aspect of an indirect competitor's interface to solve the problem that our soon-to-be-amazing product will!

In my research for the Busy Man's Shopping Site, I discovered that the online shopping site Gilt (see Figure 4-5) is an indirect competitor.

FIGURE 4-5
Indirect competitor's website: Gilt

Gilt is an indirect competitor because it offers a partial solution to the Busy Man customer segment. With Gilt, the Busy Man could avoid annoying salespeople and get access to top brands. However, Gilt has a flash sales business model. That means that single products are only on sale for a brief period of time (perhaps just 24 hours). This makes it possible for Gilt to offer its targeted customer base deep discounts, but Paul's intended customer base doesn't want that at the expense of flexibility and time. Time limits and curated selections would actually prevent Paul's intended customers from putting together the personalized wardrobe of their dreams. So, although customers of the Busy Man could solve some of their big fashion needs with Gilt, it wouldn't be the their ideal solution.

But no matter, whether the competition is direct or indirect, the Internet is an intense marketplace. Make sure that you consider *all* of your competitors because they will affect the overall success of your product. The reality is that people often use products or combinations of products in ways that the product makers do not expect. (Remember what Ena discovered about hosts for wedding venues on Airbnb!) Research everything because that is how you and your team will ensure that you have an edge over others in your industry.

HOW TO FIND YOUR COMPETITORS AND COMPILE YOUR COMPETITION LIST

There are many ways to learn who your direct and indirect competitors are. In fact, you will most likely begin to learn about competitors before you sit down to do the competitive analysis. During customer discovery or other research, users might share names of products they're using. During stakeholder interviews, the client, investors, and other product owners will probably drop the names of products they admire and want to emulate. Or, they might mention a product that they've heard is similar to what your team is proposing. That's why it's crucial to keep track of competitor names somewhere so that you don't forget them. Make a list somewhere in an email, word processing program, or a writing pad. Otherwise, you can jot the names down in your spreadsheet tool. Just track that list somewhere because you are going to need it very soon.

Of course, you could also stumble on a few products by surfing the current marketplace on the Internet. There are hundreds of web research tools for doing effective market research. Google, obviously, is the most popular search engine for doing generalized research. The advanced search filters are very powerful. However, it doesn't hurt to use Yahoo!, which is powered by Microsoft's Bing, to compare result sets. I will dig into this method more deeply now by demonstrating how to build a competitor list for the Busy Man's Shopping Site.

Searching for competitors

First, you look for direct competitors—products that compete head-to-head with your value proposition. Paul the movie producer's vision was of a platform for the busy, wealthy, and particular guy who wants to buy high-end products. Therefore, you need to figure out keywords the Busy Man might use to search for similar products. In this scenario, it might be a good idea to reverse engineer—how would Paul's customers search for a product? Here are some possible examples:

- Men's ecommerce site
- Men's shopping site
- Top brands
- Wardrobe online
- Personal stylist

Ideally, you want to be as quick and precise as possible when scanning your results. What sets a professional web researcher apart from an amateur is how fast he is able to determine if the product matches your criteria. A good search result will often yield more than potential competitor websites on the search page, too. It will lead you to niche media platforms like blogs in which you can find "Top 10" or "Best of" articles from experts. These pieces of media are another great jumping-off point to find competitors. Other tactics include using Crunchbase, which collates the largest dataset of startup activity. You can also use advanced search tools such as the "more like this" button within Google AdWords, as illustrated in Figure 4-6. Clicking the button opens the window shown in Figure 4-7. It's also a good idea to click through to the landing page of potential competitors. Read their About pages. Scan their products. Does it match your value proposition in any way? If it does, add the competitor to the list. If it doesn't, quickly click the Back button. Then, just rinse and repeat!

FIGURE 4-6

This is the "more like this" keyword feature in Google AdWords. When you click the button, it displays the results shown in Figure 4-7.

Keywords	Add around 15-20 keywords. These are the search terms that may trigger your ad to appear next to search results.	
	Keyword	Search popularity ?
	men's shopping	170 ✕
	men shop	1000 ✕
	mens shops	880 ✕
	mens shopping	4400 ✕

FIGURE 4-7

The "More like this" feature results in the most popular and relevant keywords

You won't get much information about your industry if you only examine two or three competitors. Unless you really have hit a blue ocean and there are only a handful of competitors in your market, shoot for identifying the top five direct competitors and obtaining at least three indirect competitors. Otherwise, keep your list diverse with established competitors versus newer players who have recently entered the market. You want to get a panoramic view of how the new products might be more innovative to what best practices define their established competition.

Quick Tips

- Try different permutations of keyword searches by using quotations.

- Don't be lazy. Be systematic and review all the links to ensure that you don't miss anything.

- Don't limit yourself to the first page of results. Look through at least 5 pages (the top 50 results) and see what treasures might be buried.

FILLING OUT THE MATRIX WITH DATA

Now we have a list of direct and indirect competitors, and that means we can start gathering the rest of our data. Go ahead and open the Competitive Analysis Matrix from the UX Strategy Toolkit if your computer is handy.* As Figure 4-8 illustrates, I've provided a blank template for you to use. Plunk your competitor list into the leftmost column of the Y-axis.

COMPETITIVE RESEARCH & ANALYSIS: <Value Proposition or Product Name Goes Here>				
Competitors	URL of Website or App Store Location	User Names and Password Access	Purpose of Site	Year Founded
DIRECT COMPETITORS				
Competitor Name 1				
Competitor Name 2				
Competitor Name 3				
Competitor Name 4				
INDIRECT COMPETITORS				
Indirect Competitor Name 1				
Indirect Competitor Name 2				
Indirect Competitor Name 3				
Indirect Competitor Name 4				

FIGURE 4-8

Competitive Analysis Matrix template

Separate the direct competitors from the indirect competitors. Include the website address or app store, too, as demonstrated in Figure 4-9 (for example, Google Play versus Apple Store). This is reference for your team and you. It will make it easier for you to double-check data and verify facts. The list will eventually need to be reorganized; I go over how to do that in Chapter 5, after you gather your research and are ready for the analysis. For the time being, I want to just focus on correctly capturing your research.

Competitors	URL of Website or App Store Location
DIRECT COMPETITORS	
Trunkclub	http://www.trunkclub.com/
Bombfell	http://www.bombfell.com/
JackThreads	https://www.jackthreads.com/
INDIRECT COMPETITORS	
Fab	http://fab.com/
Gilt	http://www.gilt.com

FIGURE 4-9

Lists of competitors going down Y-axis

---

* You can access the UX Strategy Toolkit at *userexperiencestrategy.com*.

Okay, now take a deep breath, because we are about to jump into the labor-intensive process of conducting research and capturing results. Pace yourself so that you can capture data as quickly and thoroughly as possible. Try to also keep an open mind because the only bias you should have is whether or not the product is actually a competitor.

However, research can be time-consuming, so when you go down the rabbit hole, be sure to come up for air. For your first pass, spend up to an hour filling out as many cells as possible in each row. Set a timer for 30 minutes to give yourself a reality check at the halfway point. Less is more! Keep your documented research brief and to the point. This way, if you or anybody needs to refer back to the spreadsheet, it won't require scanning excess or unrelated information.

If you look at our cloud example, you'll see how rows represent competitors, whereas columns represent competitor attributes (see Figure 4-10). The rightmost column is the analysis column, which you can ignore for now until Chapter 5, after you collect all your research.

Competitors	URL of Website or App Store Location	Usernames and Password Access	Purpose of Site	Year Founded	Funding Rounds
Revenue Streams	Monthly Traffic	# of SKUs / Listings (estimate)	Primary Categories	Social Networks	Content Types
Personalization	Community/ UGC Features	Competitive Advantage	Heuristic Evaulation	General Notes	Questions/Notes to Team

FIGURE 4-10
Horizontal (X-axis) attributes go across the columns

We're going to attack each row, evaluating each competitor based on a range of market and UX attributes. I will explain the attributes that need to be captured in each column. Not all of the attributes are applicable or relevant to all digital products. Just skip or delete the ones that don't apply to your product. There also might be attributes that need to be considered that are not in this spreadsheet; feel free to add anything relevant by adding a new column or replacing one that you don't need to use. What is crucial is that the pros and cons of the UX are clearly evaluated.

URL of website or app store location

This is where you put the primary online location that customers use to access the product. For desktop-only products, it will be the website address (URL), as depicted in Figure 4-11. For multiplatform products, you can list website URLs, links to app store preview pages, and so on. You want to make the information easy for your team to reference regardless of what device everyone has. They shouldn't all need to download an app to see how it looks. Here are sample links to the Waze app listing for Apple and Android:

Apple

   https://itunes.apple.com/us/app/waze-social-gps-maps-traffic/ id323229106?mt=8

Android

   https://play.google.com/store/apps/details?id=com.waze&hl=en

If a product is a mobile app with a nonessential desktop counterpart used only for marketing or support (such as Tinder's website, *http:// www.gotinder.com*), it's not crucial to list both platforms.

URL of Website or App Store Location
http://www.trunkclub.com/

FIGURE 4-11

URL/App location result sample

If you find that the competitor's website and mobile app are both crucial to the customer experience of the product, I recommend that you break the competitors into two separate rows, especially if they offer distinct user experiences or feature sets (for instance, the Airbnb desktop versus the leaner mobile version). This way you can evaluate each platform separately.

Usernames and password access

To beat your competitors, you need to know exactly what they are doing. You want to know the unknowns. In many cases, the only way to learn this is through your competitor's experience and/or sales funnel by becoming a user yourself. That's right, you want to create an account or download the app. The column shown in Figure 4-12 is where you keep track of that information.

FIGURE 4-12

Usernames and Password Access

usn: jim@castersblues.com
pwd: Learning000

The benefit of tracking the access information is that it saves time for you and the rest of the team. They won't have to create and pseudo-personalize a profile, too. This is especially useful if you're researching a two-sided market in which you need two types of accounts (for example, buyer and seller). Don't be dumb when creating all of these new accounts, however. Be very cautious about the usernames, passwords, and the personal information you choose to share.

Here are a few pro tips:

- Create one global username and password for use on all the products in your audit. It makes it a lot easier to remember and distribute to your team. Include a capital letter and number in your password because that criterion will be required by some of the products.

- Don't ever use personal information such as your kid's birthday, your own passwords, or profanity. You will potentially share this information with clients or colleagues.

- Do not log on (single sign-on) using your personal or professional Facebook (or any social network) account ever.

- If you are creating profiles on social networks, *do not* use your personal or work email address! Instead, create secondary accounts on Gmail or Yahoo first. Then, use these fake email accounts to create fake profiles.

- If it is a transactional website you are researching, purchase something. If it is an app that you must purchase (versus a free one), pay for it. Don't be cheap! It's usually only a few dollars here or there. Having one user account for your entire team to learn from is worth the financial investment.

Why Are We Being So Covert?

Here are two reasons why you probably don't want to use accounts that personally identify you:

Reason 1: When I worked on the treatment center startup, I needed to find competitors for the value proposition. One way to do this was through social media accounts such as Twitter, in which I could tweet that I was looking for advice about drug rehab and treatment centers. I didn't want to use my personal account because it might risk the professional reputation I had with colleagues. Also, I didn't want my friends and family to become concerned that I was personally looking for treatment.

Reason 2: The startup world is fierce. If your competitor is in beta, it might know that you're the competition, too. If it recognizes your account or becomes aware that you're gathering competitive intelligence, it could cut off your access.

Purpose of site

The purpose of the site is why it exists; it's basically the high-level description of the product or the value proposition. Think about how the competitor might explain it to a user or investor. As Figure 4-13 demonstrates, your description should be one to two sentences that describe the primary customer and the solution provided by the product.

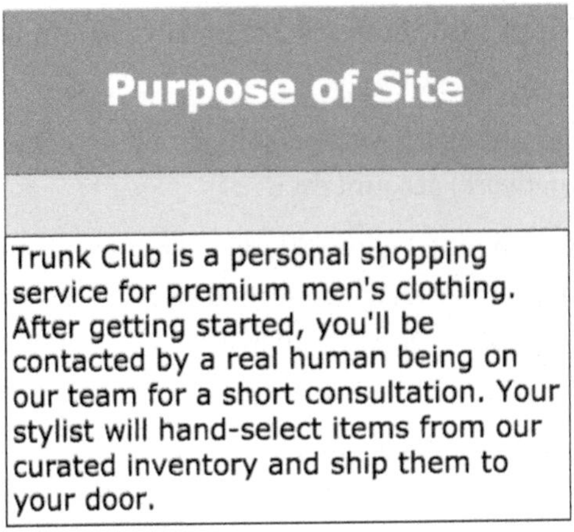

FIGURE 4-13
Purpose of Site result sample

Purpose of Site

Trunk Club is a personal shopping service for premium men's clothing. After getting started, you'll be contacted by a real human being on our team for a short consultation. Your stylist will hand-select items from our curated inventory and ship them to your door.

You can often find this information by looking in the following places:

"About" or "About Us" section

The value proposition is often written here by the competitor.

Crunchbase

Both the "Company Overview" and "Detailed Description" section have company descriptions.

iTunes or Google Play app stores

The first two lines of the "description" are generally what you're looking for.

Social networks such as Facebook, Pinterest, Twitter, and YouTube

These sometimes provide information about the value proposition.

Online annual report

All publicly traded companies must release an annual report that often has a description of the company near the beginning of the report. Simply Google the competitor's name and "Annual Report" to find it!

Year founded

What year was this company founded or the product launched (Figure 4-14)? You should be able to find this in the same place you found the value proposition; for example, the About Us section, Crunchbase, and so on. It's useful information to have when you do the analysis, because you can see what players (products and/or services) are new to the market and who's been around for a while.

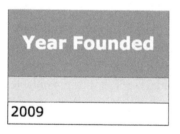

FIGURE 4-14

Year Founded result sample

Funding rounds

A funding round is a discrete round of investment by which a business or other enterprise raises money to fund operations, expansion, capital projects, acquisitions, or some other business purpose.[†] (See Figure 4-15.) Again, the obvious places to find this information are Crunchbase and/or the competitor's website. This information is important because competitors with funding have a competitive advantage.

---

† *http://en.wikipedia.org/wiki/Securities_offering*

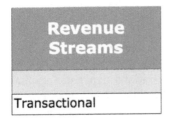

FIGURE 4-15
Funding Rounds result sample

Funding Rounds
$12.4 Million in 4 Rounds from 5 Investors

Revenue streams

A revenue stream is how the product brings in money. As Figure 4-16 depicts, it could be via a transaction fee, advertising, monthly fees, or Software as a Service (SaaS), or by selling user data and trends to other companies. OkCupid is a dating site that's free for users. The company makes money through premium features and advertising. Facebook uses data mining as its first revenue model, selling competitive intelligence to third parties from unsuspecting users. eBay's success hinges completely on users being able to easily buy from and sell to one another. Adobe charges a monthly SaaS fee for its cloud-based service.

How a product is potentially monetized should be directly tied to the UX strategy because that's what will make the product valuable to the user and the stakeholder. A successful competitor's revenue model will probably reflect that. If you're not sure how a certain competitor is monetizing its product, spend more time using its website. If the competitor wants to survive in the long run, it needs to eventually charge someone for something. Is there advertising on the website? Click the "Advertise with Us" link to see how it position itself. How do your competitors charge for membership? Look at their annual report if they're available.

Revenue Streams
Transactional

FIGURE 4-16
Revenue Streams result sample

Monthly traffic

This is actually a measurable, quantifiable attribute. If you have access to Comscore, you can get super-accurate data—traffic (see Figure 4-17), minutes-on-site, and so on. about other websites. But there are also dozens of free websites that monitor monthly traffic. Usually all you need to do to get the data is type in the domain name of the site you're researching. Check out Compete.com, Quantcast, and Alexa. You can pilfer free data from these sites and many others. By looking at multiple data points, you can triangulate an average of the traffic data, which is a lot better than not having any traffic data at all. For iPhone downloads and stats, there are great sites such as App Annie, AppFigures, Mopapp, and Distimo.

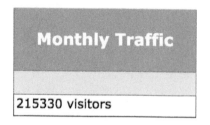

FIGURE 4-17

Monthly Traffic result sample

of SKUs/listings

This cell is optional because this information is often difficult to ascertain. Here, you will track how many items or listings are available for the product. In the case of an ecommerce site like Zappos, you'll track SKUs (stock keeping units, see Figure 4-18). Each SKU represents one item for sale on the site. For example, on Zappos I can currently see that there are more than 13,828 men's shoes (SKUs) for sale by simply clicking the link for the top level of the men's shoes category. You could use this as a point of comparison to other sites selling in that category. In the case of a video-sharing or content-producing site, you'll want track how many videos/articles are actually on the site. In the case of a transactional product/platform, you'll want to know how much stuff is in there, even if it's a rough estimate based on a few search queries.

The problem with this attribute is that there's no magic button that you can click to give you this information. In many cases, there are design conventions such as "infinite scroll" that prevent you from easily knowing how many more results could be displayed. Try searching for a common word that would apply to a lot of listings. For a clothing site, you could try a word like "shoe" or "shirt." The goal is for you to have data to compare. For example, what is the total result of one product—watches, for example—across multiple competitor products? You want to establish how empty or full the competitor's site is. Is it actually offering what it's promising to the user?

If it's a social networking platform, try to determine how often and how many users are interacting with one another. You might get different results with a variety of word combinations. We are looking for something to estimate against, and you can change the title of the column so it more accurately reflects the substance of your data.

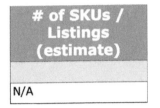

FIGURE 4-18

SKUs/Listings result sample

Primary categories

If the site is selling products (like Honda.com) or offering content (like Oprah.com), you need to understand how everything is categorized. The site probably (hopefully) already does this, so check out the site's global navigation menu. If the category list is small (women's, men's, kids', and so on), you can just copy that into your spreadsheet, as illustrated in Figure 4-19. If the list is long or complex, as on Amazon or eBay, the site is probably a *horizontal marketplace*. A horizontal market tries to meet the needs of a wide range of customers by offering products or services across many sectors. If you're studying a horizontal marketplace, try to ascertain what the most active categories are. Look at what's featured on the home page. What does the site promote as "most popular" or "best selling"? In either case, just include the categories that correlate to the products on the site. Don't include noncontent/product categories such as "About us" or the Help section.

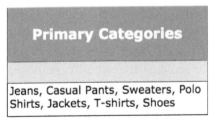

FIGURE 4-19

Primary Categories result sample

Social networks

Is the competitor's brand also on Twitter, Facebook, or others? Which social platforms is it truly using? Most products these days integrate with these platforms, but they don't fully leverage anything with all of them. Figure 4-20 shows that you need to determine what social media strategy each competitor is trying to harness well. You can find most of this information by simply searching the product's name on Twitter, Facebook, Instagram, Pinterest, and any other popular relevant social platform, or by just checking out the competitors' sites.

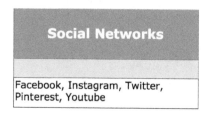

FIGURE 4-20

Social Networks result sample

Content types

Use this to capture what type of content is on the competitor's site, as depicted in Figure 4-21. Is the bulk of the content text, photos, or video? How much content dominates the site and how is it presented? Is the content well organized? Is it easy to scan and/or read? How detailed and informative is the information displayed on the product detail pages?

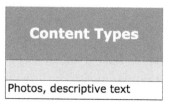

FIGURE 4-21

Content Types result sample

Personalization features

Personalization, shown in Figure 4-22, is one of the most crucial features to get customers engaged with an application or website. It should provide a value-added experience. On Airbnb, Amazon, or eBay, you don't need to be logged on to perform a basic search. However, you will need to log on as soon as you want to take an action (for example, save to favorites or make a purchase). The more time people spend personalizing their experience, the more engaged they will get with the product. (Think: Facebook!) Personalization features include favoriting, watch lists, user profiles, wish lists, custom content experiences, custom interface experiences, messaging, saved shopping carts, and so on. Sign up for the competitor's newsletters, too.

Another way to check out the personalization features is to go to the "My Account" section of each competitor. See what the site or app allows you to do that's particularly useful and helps achieve the value proposition. How can customers customize their experience? Is the experience *sticky*—meaning so engaging that the user will really want to "stick" to this product? Does it display the user's name? Does it remember and display the last item the user looked at? Does it let the user make a list of favorite items? As you look at all of the competitors, it will soon become obvious which personalization features are crucial and which are not.

Personalization Features
Your own virtual personal stylist will shop and send you men's apparel. Trunkclub helps guys discover awesome designer clothes without any of the shopping. Hand-selected outfits from exclusive designers, free shipping both ways.

FIGURE 4-22

Personalization
Features result sample

Community/UGC features

User-generated content (UGC) or crowd-sourced content is content that is created by the users. Some products such as Yelp, Waze, eBay, and Airbnb would be useless without user-generated content. In contrast, brands like Levis and ABC have mostly editorial content. Editorial content is created by people who work for or associate professionally with the site. In this column, you want to estimate the amount of user-generated content versus the amount of editorial content, as illustrated in Figure 4-23. You want to get a sense of where most of the content is coming from.

Look for features like message boards, the ability to post content (reviews, stories, and so on), and user comments. Be specific about which features are crucial and try to cite concrete examples of how they bring value to the product's other customers.

Community/UGC Features
Invite a friend feature, No user-generated content

FIGURE 4-23

Community/UGC
Features result sample

Competitive advantage

Think different! Differentiators are distinct features that a product provides that are not found in its competitors. They give a product a competitive advantage, such as those depicted in Figure 4-24. They can be a combination of attributes that make the product better. Some attributes might be specific to the online experience and others to the offline experience.

For instance, Zappos made a name for itself by providing an amazing customer experience. It is known for having a great browsing experience as well as simplifying product returns. Vine's initial differentiator was how easy it was to record a video by touching anywhere on the screen. What makes it different now is that it's a massive social network owned by Twitter. Kayak had the ability to filter live search results long before Priceline did. Kayak made the experience even better by providing the simplest of interactive patterns—a slider—to make this live filtering fun.

Figure out the top three differentiators of each product and list them in this cell. Ask yourself questions such as which features were successful because the product was first-to-market? Can those features be easily replicated? Which is better, the filtering or the large database of options? Which attributes are specific to the online experience?

FIGURE 4-24
Competitive Advantage result sample

Heuristic evaluation

Heuristic is a fancy word that means experimentation and trial-by-error. In other words, get firsthand experience using the product to see how it works for you, personally. What do you think?

You basically want to quickly evaluate whether the site is usable. You probably don't have time for anything exhaustive, so just do a quick evaluation, such as that shown in Figure 4-25, and give the product an overall grade of "A" to "F." You can use the following questions as a guide:

- Does the experience allow the user to easily accomplish her primary goal? Is it intuitive?

- Are the navigation, page/screen layouts, and visual design consistent?

- Is it easy to find, search, and browse the content or services being offered?

- Is the user feedback (for instance, error messaging) satisfactory? Is there a live help or a support system in place?

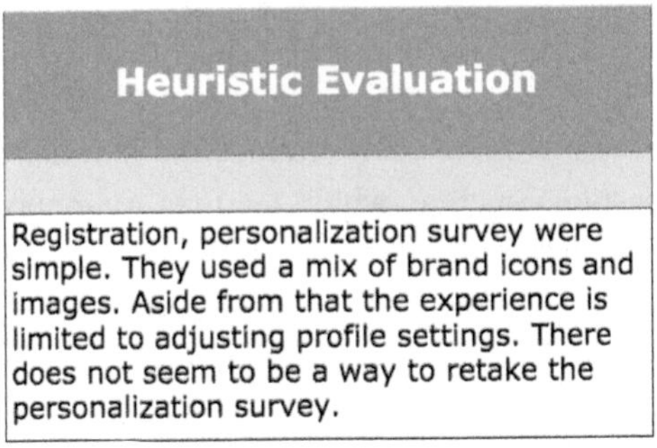

Heuristic Evaluation

Registration, personalization survey were simple. They used a mix of brand icons and images. Aside from that the experience is limited to adjusting profile settings. There does not seem to be a way to retake the personalization survey.

FIGURE 4-25

Heuristic Evaluation result sample

Customer reviews

This is a summary of the amount (that is, hundreds or thousands) of customer reviews that you can find on a product outside of its website. For mobile apps, you can find these in the app stores where you download the product. For websites, you can sometimes find these on Quora or other similar message-board platforms where users reach out to the general public for troubleshooting advice. You are looking for the latest recurring customer complaints about a product because those potential pain points are something your team might be able improve upon.

General/miscellaneous notes

This is miscellaneous information that doesn't fit into the other columns. You can use this for any research relevant to your product that you want to track. Feel free to change the name of this column if needed.

Questions/notes to team or self

Remember this is a collaborative document. Other people will be reading your research as you fill it out and could provide valuable information. Thus, you might put things in here such as, "This site doesn't work on Chrome not sure if it's me." "Hey Steve, do you think you can expense a pair of shoes on this site so we can see how the entire transaction works?"

Sometimes, you will have a miscellaneous note that you want to remember. You can also use this column as a parking lot for attributes that need to be examined across all sites.

Analysis

You get to skip this for now until you finish up all the other competitors. Chapter 5 covers how to do the analysis section.

One last note: often product teams and stakeholders don't keep an eye on the market after they've moved on from the research process. However, this is a mistake because the Internet is a fast-moving target. Things change really fast. The competitive landscape is always shifting; consequently, competitive research will never be final. One competitor might tank but two others will pop up. It's like playing whack-a-mole. For instance, I did the competitive research for the Busy Man Shopping Site in 2012. I'm sure if you look at the landscape now, it's very different. That's why you and your team always need to be on your toes, agile, and ready to grab your competitor's newest ideas and immediately see how they might affect your product vision.

Conducting UX-Focused Market Research

There are many benefits to having your market research conducted by the UX lead or a UX team member:

Design enhancement Oftentimes, what separates a killer UX design (more on this later) from an average one is nuance. A better visual design might just have a slightly different shade of color. A better music composition might contain a tone played at the perfect beat. When studying UX, you'll find nuance in the articulation of an unexpected capability (or power for the user) through a subtle enhancement in either the interface or flow of screens. It might be a prompt that appears only once but at the precise time of need. Content messaging ("Saving...saved") is one of my favorite forms of nuance.

Simplicity   UX designers think about the number of clicks and how easy it is for someone to accomplish a task. They often spot an opportunity for improvement by changing an interaction design pattern. Think back to our Tinder example, and how a simple swipe left versus right became a major binary decision.

Cost   It's faster to have the same UX designer research and build the product. He'll see which interaction-design best practices (like "Advanced Search") actually work the best by examining the competition. He'll become expert in the subject matter by researching each site's taxonomy and content.

Tag team   It's an opportunity to let a UX lead or strategist mentor a junior-level researcher. The lead will be more efficient when the junior team member does the research and the lead provides analysis. The entire UX team will become familiar with the design of all of the competitors.

UX innovation   Improving UX design is almost always possible. People are becoming more familiar with more sophisticated tasks as we offer them solutions worth the time to explore. The Internet is only going to become more powerful, fast, complicated, and pervasive as it becomes entrenched in the daily lives of people of all ages.

Recap

To build something unique, you cannot ignore your competition. In this chapter, I discussed how to conduct competitive research to learn about the marketplace. You learned how to identify direct and indirect competitors. You relentlessly searched the Web, capturing a range of qualitative and quantitative data points to help understand what kind of marketplace your product might be entering. Now, it's time to analyze that grid and extract meaningful intelligence that will inform the UX. That might sound complicated, but don't panic. Just move on to Chapter 5.

[5]

Conducting Competitive Analysis

*"[Analysis is] the skilled application of scientific and non-scientific methods and processes by which individuals interpret data or information to produce insightful intelligence findings and actionable recommendations for decision makers."** *

—BABETTE BENSOUSSAN AND CRAIG FLEISHER, *BUSINESS AND COMPETITIVE ANALYSIS*

THE DEVIL IS IN THE DETAILS THAT YOU HAVE JUST COLLECTED BY doing a thorough investigation of the marketplace. In this chapter, I'm going to cover the basics for tackling the analysis section of the Competitive Analysis Matrix. By the end of the chapter, you'll know several useful techniques that will help you to easily convert the mounds of raw data in your grid into actionable learnings. My goal is to prepare you to take a stance on the viability of your product and to make recommendations about how to move forward—in other words, Tenet 1, Business Strategy (Figure 5-1).

FIGURE 5-1
Tenet 1: Business Strategy

---

* Bensoussan, Babette E. and Craig S. Fleisher. *Business and Competitive Analysis.* Pearson Education, 2007.

The Blockbuster Value Proposition, Part 2

Let's return to the unfolding drama we left in Chapter 3, in which our UX strategist, Jaime, talks to Paul, a big-time movie producer, on a Hollywood backlot about his idea for a shopping site for the wealthy Busy Man. He's just revealed how his value proposition also solves his personal problem.

INT. BUNGALOW – MORNING

The shot frames JAIME and PAUL. Paul is cocksure. JAIME is inquisitive.

>   JAIME
> Do you know if there are any competitors
> already in the space? Is anyone already
> doing this?

PAUL throws up his hands. He's super amped about his idea.

>   PAUL
> My wife and I have looked around, but we
> haven't found anything that really nails it.

>   DISSOLVE TO:

INT. BUNGALOW — MORNING

It's two weeks later, and Jaime is back in the bungalow. Paul is staring at hard copies of the Competitive Analysis Finding's brief. He seems baffled and annoyed.

>   JAIME
> As you can see from my research and analy-
> sis, there are actually several competitors
> with significant funding already delivering
> your product idea in the marketplace.

>   PAUL
> I have never heard of these companies. So
> you think it's risky to try to directly com-
> pete against them?

                              JAIME
Well actually, I think we should consider
doing more research about the customer you
want to target. And explore how they currently solve their problem.

                              PAUL
I already know there are lots of guys like
me who hate shopping.

                              JAIME
How about we interview them and run some
experiments to test variations on your value
proposition?

                              PAUL
I feel like we can just start building out a
website and see how things go.

                              JAIME
Why don't you take a closer look at all the
sites from the market research and see how
they work. Or have your wife look at them?
I also made some other recommendations on
other ways to attack the problem with an
ecommerce business model.

                              PAUL
I still think my original idea has legs.

                                        END SCENE.

Paul obviously wasn't happy with the market analysis, but guess who
was? His wife! She sensed that this idea could be a money pit and was
glad to have a strong second opinion to back up her instincts. In the
end, Paul the movie producer dumped this idea and went back to making movies. I never heard from him again.

Lessons Learned

- You must question your stakeholders and clients about their understanding of the competition and ensure that whatever statements they make are thoroughly backed by empirical research.

- The analysis should also recommend alternatives, especially if the initial product vision and business model have risks. After all, you do want to help clients convert their dreams into an executable strategy.

- Sometimes, people have fixed ideas, and no amount of research will change their minds. That's when the strategist has to ask a personal and ethical question of herself: will I help this person make the product regardless of the research, or do I walk away?

What Is an Analysis?

When analyzing things, you are essentially trying to convert a lot of information into smaller actionable bites. You are trying to find relationships among different inputs to make inferences about why certain things are happening. By breaking larger problems into smaller problems, you and your team can more easily tackle big-picture outcomes.

Converting information into meaningful intelligence is actually one step in a larger process called *competitive intelligence* (see Figure 5-2). Business author Jim Underwood writes, "Competitive intelligence is the process of legally and ethically gathering, analyzing, and acting on information about an organization's market environment, competition, and other forces that may impact its future success."[†] What Underwood is saying is that the impartial research should lead to impartial decisions. And that's one reason why clients hire consultants—to help them to avoid emotionally fueled judgments.

---

† Underwood, Jim. *Competitive Intelligence for Dummies.* John Wiley & Sons, 2013.

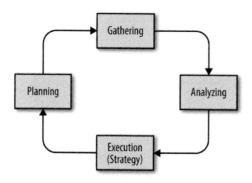

FIGURE 5-2

Gaining competitive
intelligence is a four-
step process

This analytical approach also ties into the Build-Measure-Learn loop
from Lean Startup. It should continuously inform the strategic and
tactical business decisions of your product. What's true today might
not be true tomorrow. If your team plans to build an innovative product, you must always keep gathering data, analyzing it, and acting on
it to be successful. Your gathered intelligence should strive to remain
competitive.

Because you've already looked closely at your digital competitors, you're
now ready to develop the intelligence about what's working, why it is
working, and what opportunities are available for your product in the
evolving marketplace. After all, you don't want to just launch a product that copies all your competitors' features as is. You also don't want
your ultimate analysis to just be a side-by-side feature comparison of
them. (For example, "This is how all the competitors use a Subscribe
button." Or, "All of our competitors have these features, so we should,
too!") My hero Steve Blank wrote a "Death by Competitive Analysis"
rant[‡] in which he argues that making a "my features versus their features" document will ultimately sink the ship. Simply offering as many
features as you can overlooks the holistic UX and business model, and
it doesn't address what features the customers actually want or need to
accomplish their primary goal. It's your job to analyze everything and
ultimately cherry-pick and recommend to the team the crucial features
and opportunities that will create value innovation (Tenet 2). To make
the competition irrelevant, you will have to offer something unique
that radically improves on their current options, and you'll figure this
out by diving into the spreadsheet and analyzing the raw data.

---

‡   *http://steveblank.com/2010/03/01/death-by-analysis/*

THE FOUR STEPS TO A COMPETITIVE ANALYSIS
AND MARKET OPPORTUNITIES

Just follow these four steps, which I will walk you through in detail:

1. Scan, skim, and color-code each column for highs and lows.

2. Creating logical groupings for comparison.

3. Analyze each competitor by benchmarking product attributes and best practices (this goes in the last column of the spreadsheet).

4. Writing the Competitive Analysis Findings Brief.

It's that easy! We just need to be methodical in our process.

You're going to use these steps to turn your market research into meaningful competitive intelligence. When you're done with the entire labor-intensive process, you'll use the major takeaways to create a Competitive Analysis Findings Brief with recommended action plans.

Step 1: Scan, skim, and color-code each column for highs and lows

The end goal of the spreadsheet analysis is to distill your learnings into a form, brief, or presentation that explains the rationale behind your recommendations. To do that, you need to do what is called *systems thinking* to organize information and processes. (See the interview with Milana Sobol in Chapter 10 for more on systems thinking.) So, let's begin doing that by looking at the heap of raw data in your spreadsheet.

Scanning and skimming the data

After inputting all the data into the spreadsheet, it's probably a good idea to reacquaint yourself with all rows (competitors) and columns (attributes) before analyzing them. To do that, I use two speed-reading techniques: skimming and scanning. Skimming means moving your eyes rapidly over text to get the basic meaning of it. Scanning is rapidly covering a lot of material while searching for a specific thing. I skim and scan a lot during a data analysis but not to be sloppy or to cut corners. Instead, I want to quickly discern how simple or complicated the task at hand is. Is my spreadsheet 5 rows by 5 columns or 12 rows by 24 columns with lots of missing data? Estimate the density and completeness of the content you are about to analyze so that you'll know how long it will take. This matters because you probably have a fixed amount of time to do this task, and you don't want to waste precious project hours going down a rabbit hole on just one row of analysis. For instance, if you have 20 competitors to analyze and 20 hours in which to complete this task, you have 1 hour to analyze each competitor. Time blocking for both research and analysis is essential because you want to have a balanced perspective—no blind spots.

Also notice if something looks incomplete or missing. Did you or whoever it was who did the research overlook an obvious competitor that really needs to be considered? Is the column with the monthly traffic or apps downloaded blank? That attribute could be quite important to know, and it's a colossal distraction to have to stop an analysis to switch gears back into research mode.

Measuring raw data points

A *data point* is a discrete unit of information. Any single fact or observation is a data point. In our analysis, data points can help us illuminate whether something is a failure or success. There are two kinds of data points to keep an eye out for in our columns: quantitative data and qualitative data.

Quantitative data is numbers and statistics. How much traffic did a site get? How many transactions happened on the site? How many SKUs are on the site? Numbers can be metrics, transactions, and/or a finite set of options. Unlike qualitative data, these numbers have logic or order applied to them. For example, the quantitative data points of a Starbuck's latte might be the size of the cup, the temperature of the coffee, the price, or the time it took the barista to make it.

Qualitative data is descriptive and subjective. It's the stuff that makes up interesting content such as opinions, reactions, emotions, aesthetics, physical traits, and so on, but in most cases it's not quantifiable. These data points can't be easily measured or ordered. The qualitative aspects of a Starbucks latte are its taste, the aroma, how frothy the cream is, the aesthetics of the environment in which it is made, or the service.

QUANTITATIVE DATA	QUALITATIVE DATA
Numbers (metrics, data sets)	Descriptive
Can be measured	Can be observed, but not measured
Length, area, volume, speed, time, and so on	Opinions, reactions, tastes, appearance
Objective	Subjective
Structured	Unstructured

Sometimes, the difference between quantitative and qualitative data isn't obvious at first glance. So make sure that you're careful. For example, on a dating site, you might think "men with brown eyes" is a qualitative attribute. It's a color after all and could imply how people perceive the man's attractiveness. However, what if the site makes male users choose an eye color when they sign up, and they only have five options to choose from—brown, blue, hazel, gray, and green. This is actually information that could be measured. The data point is objective; you have a number to quantify it.

Fun with color-coding

You can color-code the spreadsheet to keep track of meaningful data points, trends, and other patterns, as shown in Figure 5-3. For example, use yellow to highlight the most telling information (for instance, all competitors struggle with a feature). Use green to highlight positive attributes (highest monthly traffic). Just remember to keep it simple and use colors effectively. Creating a complex code in this initial pass won't help your analysis, and it can confuse other team members who are also popping into check out or add to the raw data. The color code should be used sparingly to highlight things that are crucial to remember.

521816 visitors	Mens' Shoes, Shirts, Pants, Jackets, Sweaters, Sweatshirts, Denim	Facebook, Twitter, Instagram	Magazine-like images, Zoom, Item descriptors and sizes/dimensions, Sizing charts
381536 visitors	Sales categories ranging from home products to clothing to jewelry to art work.	Facebook, Instagram, Twitter, Pinterest	Photos, Zoom, Item descriptors and sizes/dimensions, Sizing charts
1810842 visitors	Coveted fashion and luxury lifestyle brands at sample sale prices. Gilt Groupe includes sales for men, women, and home as well as Gilt City (geo-specific), Gilt Taste (food), and Jetsetter (travel).	Facebook, Instagram, Twitter, Pinterest	Photos, Zoom, Item descriptors and sizes/dimensions, Sizing charts

FIGURE 5-3

Highlighted cells showing color-coding of meaningful attributes

Step 2: Creating logical groupings for comparison

Now that you have an overall sense of your data, you need to do a little housekeeping to make the process of analysis very efficient. You want to compare the sites and apps in your analysis that have things in common. You want to compare apples to apples, oranges to oranges, and mobile apps for fresh produce delivery against mobile apps for fresh produce delivery. Thus, you need to manually sort and filter the competitors in the list into subgroups that you can compare practically.

Using logical groupings, you can place competitors that have common traits into "buckets." You already have two of them: direct and indirect competitors. If you don't have any groupings to make beyond those two, you might want to reorganize the rows at the very least. It doesn't need to be very complicated. For example, you could do something as simple as rank your direct competitors from most threatening to least threatening to the value proposition.

Here are examples of potential subgroups:

LOGICAL SUBGROUP EXAMPLES
Desktop versus mobile platform
Content type (for example, ecommerce, publishers, or aggregators)
Horizontal markets (Craig's List to Amazon to eBay or Target to Walmart)
Vertical markets (clothing, health, banking, and so on)
Business models

Here are examples of different ways in which you can order the list of competitive products:

- Highest traffic or most downloads (I always put the most popular competitors at the top)

- Alphabetically

- Newest to oldest in the market

- Numerous features to minimal features

- Largest to smallest in terms of SKUs, articles, or listings (this should be tied to traffic)

Remember your goal is to make it easier to identify which factors give other products their competitive advantage. You are looking for commonalities and differences so that you and your team can truly understand why certain products are more successful than others.

Step 3: Analyze each competitor by benchmarking product attributes and best practices

The term *benchmark* originates from the chiseled horizontal marks that surveyors made in stone structures to ensure that a leveling rod could be accurately repositioned in the same place in the future. These marks were usually indicated with a chiseled arrow below the horizontal line, as demonstrated in Figure 5-4.[§]

FIGURE 5-4
An Ordinance Survey cut mark in the United Kingdom. "BmEd" licensed under Creative Commons.

Benchmarking in the business world helps organizations identify and examine key facets of another identity so that comparisons can be made. This analysis leads to reducing costs, optimizing the sales funnel, and improving the product so that it delivers more value to the target customer. In this similar vein, when you analyze your data, you're going to benchmark by comparing the entire collection of products (sites or apps) in the matrix to one another, and you're going to do this on an attribute-by-attribute basis.

Each column on the spreadsheet represents a different attribute, and you've collected data points about each one, whether it's downloads of an app or a specialized content category. These quantitative and qualitative data points give you the ability to measure, score, and identify best practices versus lame practices.

[§] *http://en.wikipedia.org/wiki/Benchmark_(surveying)*

When you benchmark direct competitors, you want to find a competitive parity among their products. You're looking for a baseline that defines the bottom-line criteria that future customers will expect when your team delivers on the value proposition. Do customers expect that a product detail page will have photos, videos, and reviews? Does the most popular site have the most merchandise and/or the widest selection? Does the company behind the most innovative and downloaded app have lots of funding?

When you benchmark the indirect competitors, you're analyzing how these digital products offer alternative ways to solve a problem. For example, in the Busy Man's Shopping Site competitive analysis, I benchmarked the monthly traffic of the indirect competitors. The website Gilt had monthly traffic of 1.8 million users, but Fab—a direct competitor of Gilt—only had 380,000 users. This data point really seemed important to me because it made me wonder: why was the disparity between their monthly traffic so huge? What was Gilt doing better?

You are looking for trends, patterns, gaps, and an overall sense of the look of the landscape. Often, you will notice common patterns being repeated across many sites within a vertical market. You might wonder why they're all broken in the same way. You might realize that they are all overlooking an especially useful capability that could be the secret sauce you use in your value innovation. (See Chapter 6 for more.) Are most of the losers missing on content, traffic, stickiness, personalization, a bad browse or search experience? Determine the causes. By benchmarking the competition, you'll find opportunities to create value by either innovating or optimizing on the best UX and business model practices of other competing products. You'll also want to extract these golden nuggets as recommendations to put in your brief.

The analysis column of each competitor

The reason you waited until now to do the analysis column in the Competitive Analysis Matrix template is that you needed to collect as much data as possible about the entire competitive landscape of your value proposition. But now, you're finally ready to fill it out.

At this point, you should see nuances among competitors. You've benchmarked attributes. You can gauge which competitors are a success or failure. You can say which competitor is number one, number two, and who's doing something impressive even if they're farther behind in the marketplace race than others. You have a sense of the diversity of business models in play.

Use your analysis to answer the following questions about each competitor in a brief paragraph:

- How is it competing against your value proposition?
- If it's a direct competitor, what is it doing great or particularly badly?
- If it's an indirect competitor, is it competing with a similar solution or is it going after a similar customer segment?
- What are the big takeaways the stakeholder should know if she only reads this cell?

You can see how I answered those questions in the Busy Man's Shopping Site Competitive Analysis Matrix in Figures 5-5 and 5-6. There's an example for a direct and an indirect competitor.

Analysis

TrunkClub is a direct competitor. Their business model is with inventory management, buying wholesale and selling at retail prices. Centralized stylists out of Chicago allows them to manage the skill/quality of their stylist offerings effectively. The Chicago fitting/showroom should also be noted as customers can travel there to get face-to-face time with a stylist. The model has proven so popular they've begun planning for and considering opening up offices in Atlanta, Boston, Dallas and San Francisco. Atlanta and Dallas being Southern and transit hubs of significant size comparable to Chicago, Boston and San Francisco being growing sectors of affluent tech savvy busy workers. Copying the personal consult model phone/email/IM/VideoChat/centralized physical space should be considered.

FIGURE 5-5
Direct competitor analysis sample

Analysis
Gilt is an indirect competitor. It is a flash sales site that targets users hungry for top-of-the-line brands, but making them acquirable by giving them deep discounts. However, our proposed target customers are not looking for deep 60% discounts. There is a recent feature ""Pin it to Unlock," that is something to be considered. The feature works like this- If a product's image from Gilt's site on Pinterest has been pinned 50 times, the pin will link to a hidden sale on Gilt.com where shoppers will have the opportunity to purchase the special item. Another feature worth considering is their concept of early-bird access for customers who share a certain number of items or who invite a certain number of friends.

FIGURE 5-6
Indirect competitor analysis sample

Notice how the analysis cell imparts a picture of the competitor. This is really important because if your team and stakeholders have access to your raw data, you should assume that they might not necessarily look at all the other cells; they might only read this column. But that's your job anyway. The analysis cell is where you're going to sum up everything they should understand even if they never read the entire spreadsheet.

Step 4: Writing the Competitive Analysis Findings Brief

Abductive reasoning is a form of logical inference that goes from observation to a hypothesis. It accounts for the reliable data (observation) and seeks to explain relevant evidence.[1] It shapes your rationale for making recommendations, and making recommendations is the purpose of the Competitive Analysis Findings Brief. The findings brief is an easy-to-read summary of your competitive analysis along with your recommendations about how to move forward. This is your final judgment after doing your deep dive into the competitive landscape. It's

---

[1] *http://en.wikipedia.org/wiki/Abductive_reasoning*

about articulating your final, unbiased view of the marketplace in as user-friendly a way as a face-to-face conversation. This document will be what your client takes away from your research.

Before you begin writing the findings brief, however, take a moment to step away from your spreadsheet. Zoom out from the details and think hard about the big picture. First, you should be able to answer the following questions about the marketplace:

- Which competitors are closest to delivering a similar value proposition (that is, an online shopping site featuring high-end brands)? Are their products failing? Why? Or are their products succeeding so well that there's no room for your product?

- Which competitors directly appeal to your customer segment (wealthy men)?

- Of those competitors, how do you think customers discover them (perhaps paid advertising)?

- What products offer the best user experiences and business models? Who is doing something unique? What is working well for them? What do they have that your users like?

Second, you need to address in the brief if there's room in the market for your product. What opportunities exist for it? What gaps could it fill? Perhaps your market research and analysis have shown you that your team has hit the entrepreneurial jackpot. Perhaps your product is one or all of the following:

- First-to-market with something unique (such as Pinterest)

- Offers users a better method to use or save time or finances (Amazon Prime saves customers from having to waste time running errands.)

- Creates value simultaneously for two different customer segments (Airbnb does so for hosts and guests; Eventbrite for event planners and attendees.)

This is a blue ocean, which was discussed in Chapter 2. The thesis of the book *Blue Ocean Strategy* by W. Chan Kim and Renée Mauborgne[**] is of the uncontested marketplace in which the competition becomes

---

** Kim, W. Chan and Renée Mauborgne. *Blue Ocean Strategy*. Harvard Business School Press, 2005.

irrelevant because there is none. A blue ocean is full of customers with unmet needs. A red ocean is a market full of sharks fighting for the fish. In writing your brief, you must be able to say with certainty whether your product is in a blue, red, or somewhere-in-between purple ocean (such as the lovely vista in Figure 5-7).

FIGURE 5-7
A purple ocean

If you have found a blue or at least purple ocean, you can suggest specific ways that a killer UX and/or business model could help knock a product idea out of the park. That's when we, as UX strategists, can provide real value that could determine success or failure.

In short, your goal is to determine if there's room to win, and that's when you need to address the opportunities based on the research. Now, I'm not aware of any specific guideline for how to create a Findings Brief. But based on what I've seen and delivered over the years, I've noticed some primary components. I'm going to walk you through a sample Findings Brief so you can get a sense of what they are. (You can also learn what Geoff Katz puts in his Creative Briefs in Chapter 10.)

FINDINGS BRIEF, SECTION 1: INTRODUCTION/GOALS

The introduction presents the goals of the brief and tries to hook the stakeholder into, a) reading it, and b) reviewing it with an open mind. You might find that you need to rewrite this page several times to get it right. Don't be too afraid to draft a quick summary of what you think this page should be, and then return to edit it after you've pulled the rest of your data together.

Here are some elements to include on this page (see also Figure 5-8):

State your purpose.

[Your team] conducted a competitive analysis on [market or markets] to see what other products do [client's value prop]. Be sure to state the client's value proposition clearly so that there is no confusion as to what you were focusing on. Include the month and year in which the study was conducted, because the analysis is truly a snapshot in time that will become outdated as the competitive landscape evolves.

Make a general statement about the current marketplace.

You could say something like, "There are tons of sites that allow trading." Or, "The market is splintered into these core groups...." You might also include an introduction to the distinct competitor subgroups from your deep dive into the spreadsheet or overview of the business models at play. At the very least, list all the competitors you looked at, broken out by direct competitor and indirect competitor.

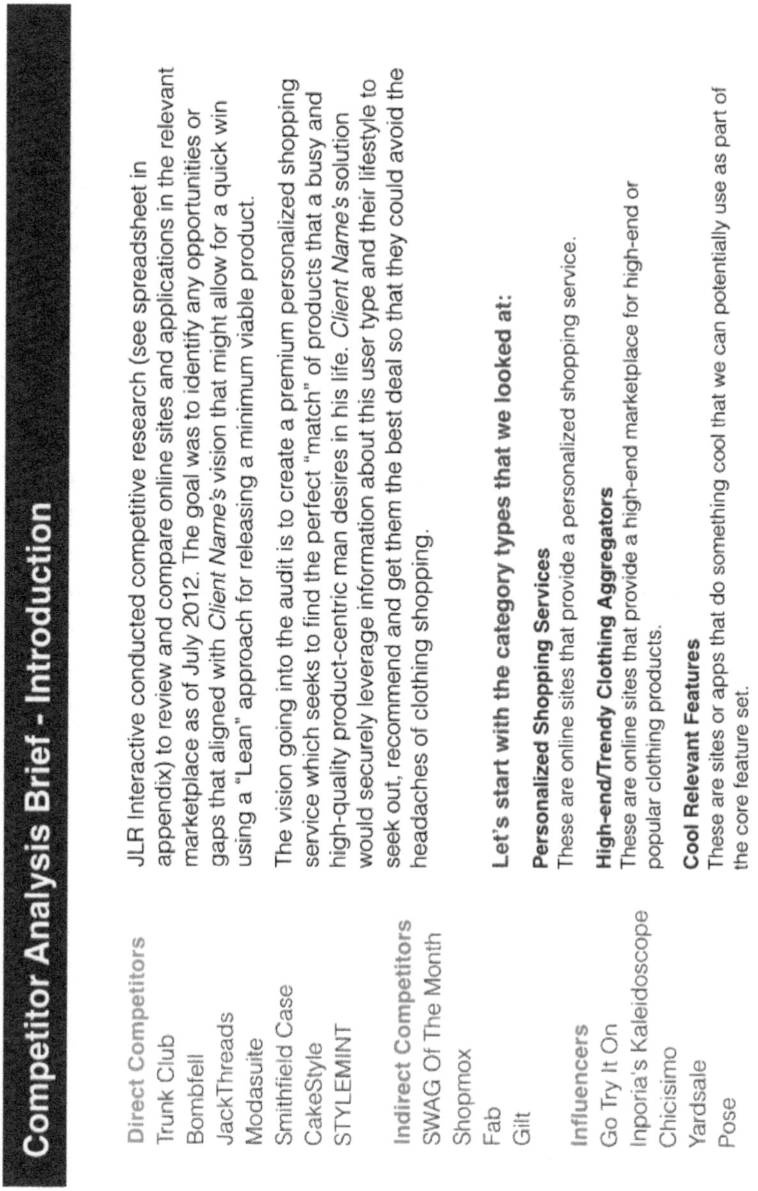

Competitor Analysis Brief - Introduction

Direct Competitors
Trunk Club
Bombfell
JackThreads
Modasuite
Smithfield Case
CakeStyle
STYLEMINT

Indirect Competitors
SWAG Of The Month
Shopmox
Fab
Gilt

Influencers
Go Try It On
Inporia's Kaleidoscope
Chicisimo
Yardsale
Pose

JLR Interactive conducted competitive research (see spreadsheet in appendix) to review and compare online sites and applications in the relevant marketplace as of July 2012. The goal was to identify any opportunities or gaps that aligned with *Client Name's* vision that might allow for a quick win using a "Lean" approach for releasing a minimum viable product.

The vision going into the audit is to create a premium personalized shopping service which seeks to find the perfect "match" of products that a busy and high-quality product-centric man desires in his life. *Client Name's* solution would securely leverage information about this user type and their lifestyle to seek out, recommend and get them the best deal so that they could avoid the headaches of clothing shopping.

Let's start with the category types that we looked at:

Personalized Shopping Services
These are online sites that provide a personalized shopping service.

High-end/Trendy Clothing Aggregators
These are online sites that provide a high-end marketplace for high-end or popular clothing products.

Cool Relevant Features
These are sites or apps that do something cool that we can potentially use as part of the core feature set.

FIGURE 5-8

Introduction to Competitive Analysis Findings Brief slide

FINDINGS BRIEF, SECTION 2: DIRECT COMPETITORS

In this section, you should highlight at least two or three of the top direct competitors and why their value propositions are relevant to yours. How you choose to showcase them depends on what showcase will best support your recommendations at the end of the brief (see Figure 5-9). Be sure to include screenshots of home pages or features that you want to point out, especially if they offer a visually appealing design, a solid UX, or insight into the viability of the business model. For example, there are many astrology sites. They all have a "Here's your horoscope" feature, but some of them have better personalization or superior content, and therefore they deliver a more powerful experience.

You can also discuss each direct competitor, mentioning specific things that give them a competitive advantage (see Figures 5-10 and 5-11). You can use arrows to point to aspects of the UX that you want to call out to your team and stakeholders. Call out a competitor if it's a serious threat—if it has a large market share, if it caters to your intended customers, if its product is solid, if it has copious financing to scale quickly. Point out features or layouts that you believe should be replicated. Also discuss any of the competitors' weaknesses. What features should be avoided? Which competitor did something particularly badly? Or can this negative aspect of its UX be an opportunity for your product?

Direct Competitors

Trunk Club
www.trunkclub.com

Description
Trunk Club is a personal shopping service for premium men's clothing. A stylist handpicks clothing for you and then it is shipped in a trunk so you can try it on in the privacy of your own home.

Pros
Centralized stylists out of Chicago allow them to manage the skill/quality of their stylist offerings effectively. The Chicago fitting/showroom offers users who can travel there to get face-to-face time with a stylist.

Cons
The clothing options are quite expensive. Their mobile experience has limited functionality.

JackThreads
www.jackthreads.com

Description
JackThreads automates the style recommendations based on user's preferences and showcases the newest and best clothing options.

Pros
JackThread collects personalized data by allowing shoppers to star favorite categories and track their favorite brands and products.

Cons
They offer too many choices with a heavy focus on price instead of style recommendations. Their mobile app does not yet offer search capabilities.

Bombfell
www.bombfell.com

Description
Bombfell is a monthly subscription for men's clothing where members get clothes picked for them by a stylist.

Pros
Since Bombfell operates on a pretty forecastable monthly subscription model, it doesn't have to carry a ton of inventory month-to-month to support its growth. They used a mix of brand icons and images to make registration and the personal survey simple.

Cons
It creates too niche a user base, given the test bed for this service offering is primarily tech-savvy well-to-do Bay Area males.

FIGURE 5-9

Direct competitors high-level view slide

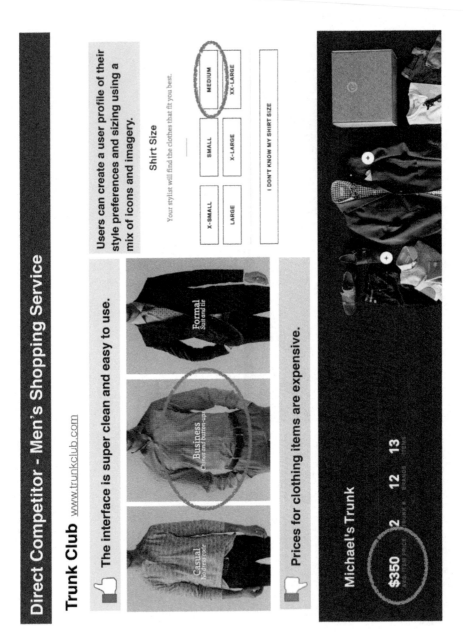

Direct Competitor - Men's Shopping Service

Trunk Club www.trunkclub.com

👉 The interface is super clean and easy to use.

Casual
No dress code

Business
Chinos and button-ups

Formal
Suit and tie

Users can create a user profile of their style preferences and sizing using a mix of icons and imagery.

Shirt Size

Your stylist will find the clothes that fit you best.

| X-SMALL | SMALL | MEDIUM |
| LARGE | X-LARGE | XX-LARGE |

I DON'T KNOW MY SHIRT SIZE

👉 Prices for clothing items are expensive.

Michael's Trunk

$350 PER ITEM PRICE — 2 TRUNKS — 12 BRANDS — 13 ITEMS

FIGURE 5-10

Calling out relevant aspects of the direct competitor's product

Direct Competitor - High-end Trendy Clothing Aggregator

Jack Threads www.jackthreads.com

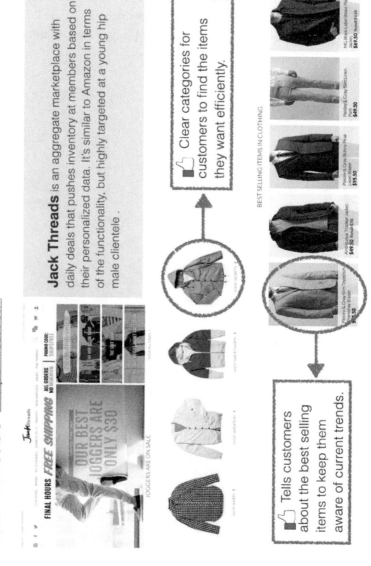

Jack Threads is an aggregate marketplace with daily deals that pushes inventory at members based on their personalized data. It's similar to Amazon in terms of the functionality, but highly targeted at a young hip male clientele.

Clear categories for customers to find the items they want efficiently.

Tells customers about the best selling items to keep them aware of current trends.

FIGURE 5-11

Calling out relevant aspects of the direct competitor's product

FINDINGS BRIEF, SECTION 3: INDIRECT COMPETITORS

With indirect competitors, you want to demonstrate what they're doing right with respect to your value proposition (see Figure 5-12). The negative aspects are less consequential because they are not direct competitors.

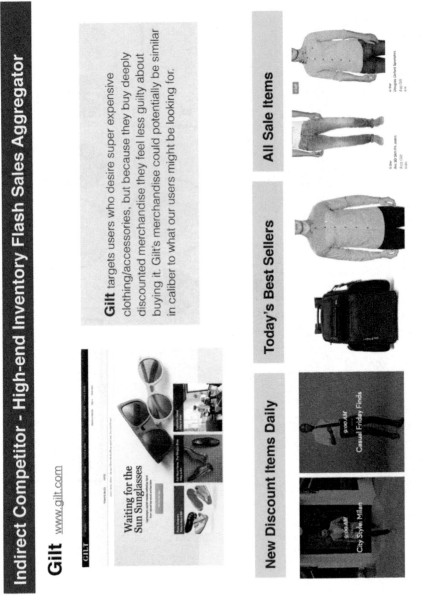

FIGURE 5-12
Indirect competitor slide

Look for clues in these areas:

- Revenue streams for monetization

- Mental model for the navigation system or transaction flow

- Features that simplify the experience

- New and interesting visual treatments and animations

- Improved messaging and content strategy

Use arrows to point out aspects of the UX that are relevant to the solution that your team is pursuing. Explain why you're pointing them out and what insight they offer into market opportunities. You will organize these points based on what you want the stakeholder or team to understand by the end of the brief.

FINDINGS BRIEF, SECTION 4: COOL FEATURES FROM INFLUENCERS

In this section, write about any cool or relevant UX features or findings about the marketplace that might not come from competitors (see Figures 5-13 and 5-14). I call these types of products "influencers" because they are not in your product's competitive landscape but could offer insight into your product's value innovation. An influencer doesn't even have to be an online product. As long as it has an interaction, transaction, or capability you're trying to accomplish, it's an influencer.

Often, an influencer might have a very cool feature that could be the differentiator your product is looking for. A good example of this is how Airbnb utilized the Yelp map functionality. Yelp is not a direct or indirect competitor for Airbnb, but Airbnb saw how refining a user's results set by zooming in and out of a map might be a useful differentiator for its subletting service. It allowed the influence, and that map feature is now a very distinctive feature of Airbnb!

In the course of your research and analysis, it's probable that you've already identified or noted influencers. Maybe you sighed to yourself and thought, "If only this product was more like [insert product name]." That product is most likely a good influencer. It's also possible that an influencer inspired your original value proposition. For example, Paul the movie producer was originally inspired by Amazon's Wish List feature. Even though Amazon.com itself would have been neither a direct nor indirect competitor to his product, the UX of Amazon could definitely influence the product in a positive direction and distinguish it from the competition. Therefore, it should be presented here in the brief in a way that is similar to the direct and indirect competition.

Cool Features from Mobile App Influencers

Inporia's Kaleidoscope

Kaleidoscope helps users figure out what kind of "look they are going for" by allowing them to browse and break down fashion styles in magazine-type spreads by item.

Pose

Pose rips off the Pinterest UI for viewing and collecting images wherein a user discovers trends and clothing from a user-generated image database.

Go Try It On

The user can submit a photo of themselves wearing an item and get feedback from a stylist. Other users can vote on the outfit with "love it" or "change it" votes.

FIGURE 5-13
UX influencers from the mobile space slide

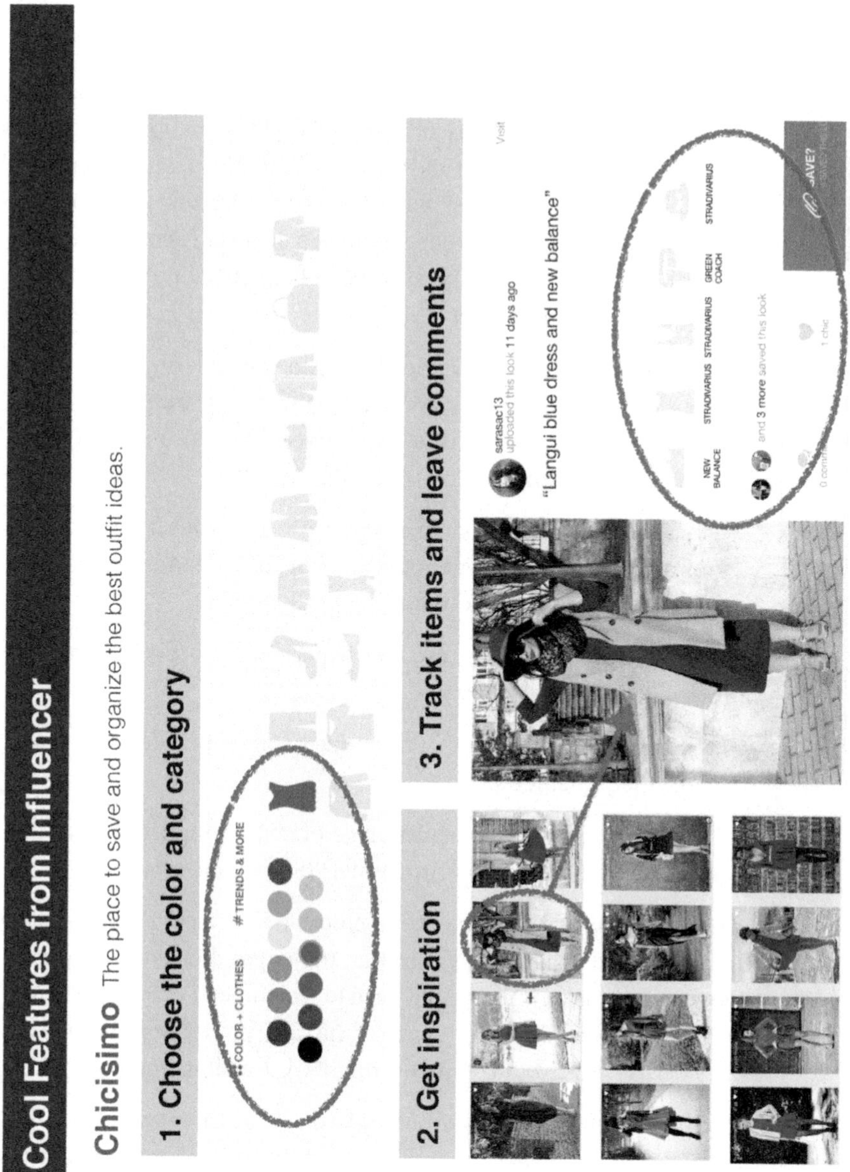

FIGURE 5-14
UX Influencer slide

FINDINGS BRIEF, SECTION 5: TAKING A STAND/YOUR RECOMMENDATIONS

This is the most important section. You need to voice your opinion in a strong, authoritative way. This summary should be an honest and balanced assessment about what the current competitive landscape looks like (see Figure 5-15). However, you don't want to leave your client with nowhere to go. Think about what the client's original vision was for the product and what aspect of that vision can be realized no matter if the market is blue, red, or purple.

If your analysis supports the value proposition, your recommendations will probably suggest specific ways to capitalize on market opportunities and gaps through the user experience. Your recommendations might answer these questions:

- Can a specific function such as the Browse or Search capability be improved to help customers discover or find something that currently takes a lot of work to find? (See Chapter 6.)

- How can you make the product experience more personalized? (See Chapters 6, 8, and 9.)

- How can your team create or optimize a funnel to increase engagement? (See Chapter 9.)

- How can your team take advantage of something like social networks to drive people to your funnel? (See Chapter 9.)

If your analysis reveals that the value proposition is facing certain risks, your recommendations need to pivot on the targeted customer segment or the specific problem. You would need to recommend that your team or stakeholder pursue a different version of the value proposition and/or business model. As such, your comments might try to address these scenarios:

- Is this an expensive endeavor to take on or are there ways to de-risk the vision by experimenting with Minimum Viable Products (MVPs)? (See Chapters 7 and 8.)

- Do you see another possible angle that addresses aspects of the stakeholder's vision, or do you recommend that the team pivot on the customer or its problem? (See Chapters 3 and 8.)

- Does more research need to be conducted to really know if the value proposition is viable, such as with Guerrilla User Research (see Chapter 8) or using landing page A/B tests? (See Chapter 9.)

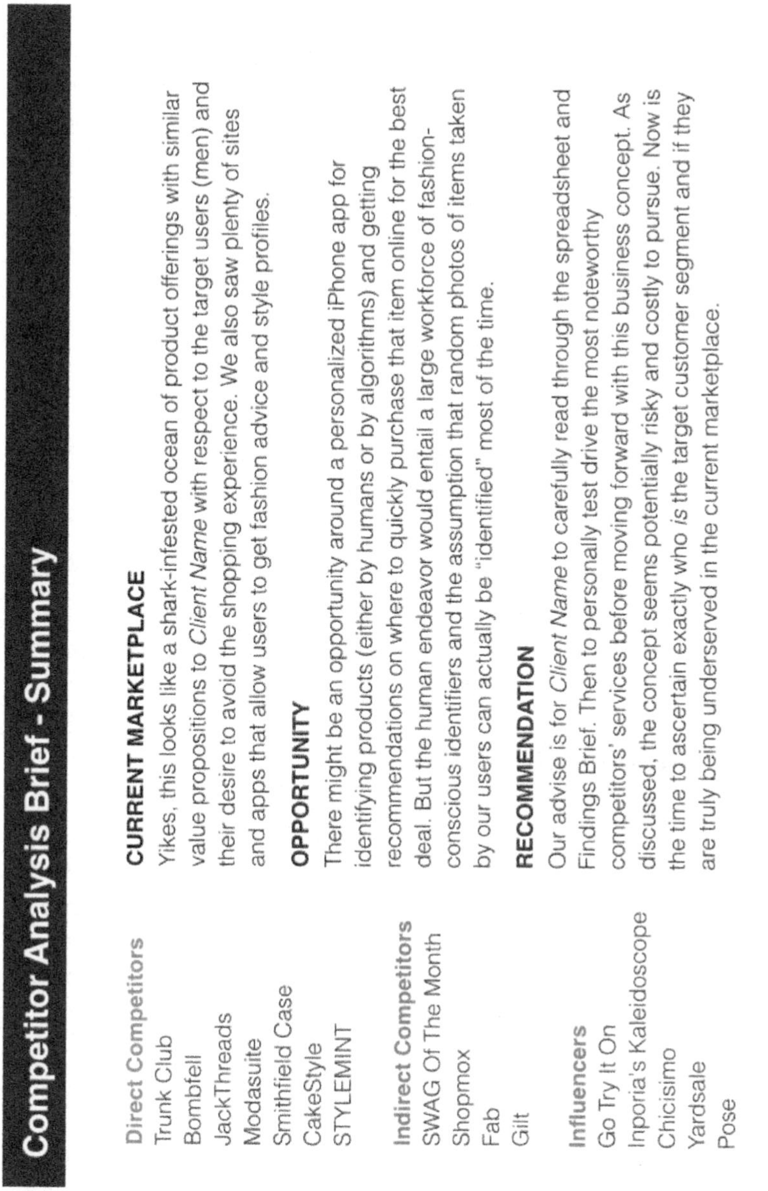

Competitor Analysis Brief - Summary

Direct Competitors
Trunk Club
Bombfell
JackThreads
Modasuite
Smithfield Case
CakeStyle
STYLEMINT

Indirect Competitors
SWAG Of The Month
Shopmox
Fab
Gilt

Influencers
Go Try It On
Inporia's Kaleidoscope
Chicisimo
Yardsale
Pose

CURRENT MARKETPLACE

Yikes, this looks like a shark-infested ocean of product offerings with similar value propositions to *Client Name* with respect to the target users (men) and their desire to avoid the shopping experience. We also saw plenty of sites and apps that allow users to get fashion advice and style profiles.

OPPORTUNITY

There might be an opportunity around a personalized iPhone app for identifying products (either by humans or by algorithms) and getting recommendations on where to quickly purchase that item online for the best deal. But the human endeavor would entail a large workforce of fashion-conscious identifiers and the assumption that random photos of items taken by our users can actually be "identified" most of the time.

RECOMMENDATION

Our advise is for *Client Name* to carefully read through the spreadsheet and Findings Brief. Then to personally test drive the most noteworthy competitors' services before moving forward with this business concept. As discussed, the concept seems potentially risky and costly to pursue. Now is the time to ascertain exactly who *is* the target customer segment and if they are truly being underserved in the current marketplace.

FIGURE 5-15
Summary slide

Whether your recommendations are positive or negative, you are required to take a stand about the viability of the product you're researching. Sometimes, as in the case of Paul the movie producer, your recommendations aren't what the client wants to hear. It's just reality, and sometimes that's just how it plays out. Yet, the reason you conduct research and analyze data is to learn about the real potential of the product so that you can make empirical calls about how people will spend their time and energy. You might learn that the client's initial vision faces a lot of challenges. You might also learn that there are better alternatives to the product. It's your job to analyze the data and to present these insights with solid supporting evidence.

You are now at the end of the Competitive Analysis Findings Brief, and you understand with absolute certainty what kind of marketplace your product is facing. You are now at a crossroads:

- If you're in a red ocean, you need to ask, "Why am I creating something in a saturated marketplace?" You might need to go back to the earlier chapters to reassess your customer segment, customer problem, or competitive landscape.

- If you're in a purple or blue ocean, move on to Chapter 6. You're at the threshold of possibility—to build an innovative product! Now, you just need to resolve how to capitalize on the opportunity.

Presentation and Takeaways

It's not uncommon for the client to only glance at the spreadsheet and appreciate that the UX strategist has done his homework. Thus, include the spreadsheet as an appendix, so the client can reference the raw data as needed and when convenient. I recommend downloading an Excel version of the Google spreadsheet so that the client can look at it offline or share it with others without having to link to the cloud version. You can also include the link to the cloud version if you expect this exercise to continue and potentially become collaborative.

Recap

A thorough competitive analysis requires an organized effort to gather information about the competition. In this chapter, you learned that the competitive analysis helps you gain insight into current trends as to what is or is not working. Knowing the unknowns helps your team to not repeat mistakes but instead make good ideas better. A good analysis also exposes gaps and opportunities for your product to take advantage of in the marketplace.

In Chapter 6, you will use what you've learned to create new value through differentiation and innovation focused specifically on the UX and/or business model.

[6]

Storyboarding Value Innovation

"Reaching beyond existing demand is a key component of achieving value innovation."[*]

—W. CHAN KIM AND RENÉE MAUGBORGNE,

BLUE OCEAN STRATEGY

IF YOUR GOAL IS TO INVENT, YOU NEED TO LOOK FOR THE BENEFITS that will make your product indispensable to users. That means you need to understand how to break out the big UX moments that need to show incredible value *before* you move into a formal design phase. To get there, you need to mash up the principles of Tenet 2, Value Innovation, with Tenet 4, Killer UX (Figure 6-1).

If you're a seasoned design professional, be aware that this chapter is not about pushing pixels or making cool-looking deliverables. Instead, it's about using design hacks to focus your team sharply on identifying and maximizing your product's potential value innovation. It's about accelerating your thinking through your product's ultimate value proposition.

---

* Kim, W. Chan and Renée Mauborgne. *Blue Ocean Strategy*. Harvard Business School Press, 2005.

FIGURE 6-1
Tenet 2 and Tenet 4: Value Innovation and Killer UX

Timing Really Is Everything

In 1990, I devised an interactive animation that fused my software design skills with my love of experimental art and music for my master's thesis at the New York University Interactive Telecommunications Program. It was a mash-up of technology and art jammed onto an 800 KB floppy disk. The electronic experience was programmed for the Macintosh in HyperCard and VideoWorks. The disk featured an interactive table of contents with links to animations of poetry, games, and rants combined with an industrial noise soundtrack. After numerous sleepless nights, I succeeded in my objective—to create what was to be the world's first animated electronic magazine. It worked, played, and all fit on one disk! This was *Cyber Rag #1*, which you can get a glimpse of in Figure 6-2.

FIGURE 6-2

Cyber Rag (1990) electronic magazine on floppy disk

Sure, there were some competitors in the marketplace. For instance, there were nonanimated HyperCard stacks with tech-centric content. There was also an interactive art disk that ran on the less popular Commodore Amiga and could be downloaded from a bulletin-board service (BBS). But there was no other digital product like *Cyber Rag*, and I saw the golden opportunity to make digital content more mainstream and accessible to the masses by placing it on a Mac-based floppy disk.

However, it was one thing to create a completely original electronic magazine on a disk and quite another to get it out to the general public, have them recognize it for its originality, and buy it. Much as in Chapter 3, my younger self had to figure out who her customers were. I eventually learned that my customers weren't the computer nerds of the 1990s who might download an electronic mag for free off a BBS. Even I did not own a modem (yet). That's when I realized that my *Cyber Rag #1* wasn't just tied into the experience of a new electronic publishing medium. It also aligned with the DIY attitude of the Generation X who self-published their own fanzines about pop cultures. They just didn't do it digitally *yet*. Somehow, I had to reach my Gen X peers in independent book and record stores. This meant that besides creating the physical product, I also had to somehow package it, market it, and distribute it.

A typical Saturday in my mid-20s involved saving copies of *Cyber Rag* onto hundreds of floppy disks. I glued on labels, printed packaging, sealed the packages, and then I'd walk into independent bookstores in New York City and Los Angeles to pitch my product to the owners. Their typical reaction was bewilderment because they had no concept of my value proposition at the time. Some owners didn't even have access to a Macintosh to preview the product for themselves. How were they to know if the disks weren't empty, corrupted, or filled with hardcore porn? I learned that the best tactic was to front the product initially to the storeowners to lessen their fear of selling an unfamiliar publishing medium.

But the disks sold well. Customers were curious and willing to dole out six dollars to experience their first electronic magazine on a computer screen. Typically, a store would call me within a month after my initial pitch to ask me for more product. When I began to gain notoriety in the press, I started selling thousands of disks (*Cyber Rag #1, #2, #3* and *Electronic Hollywood I* and *II*). The disks were on sale in independent bookstores, in art galleries, and via mail order; they even sold to people all over the world. I had no business model except to keep publishing disks until "something" happened.

Then, "something" finally did happen. After two years, I came home from my job as a typesetter to find a message on my answering machine.

"Hi Jaime! This is Henry from EMI Records. We are calling on behalf of Billy Idol who just bought one of your disk magazines. He wants to see if you are interested in working with him on his new project. Can you please have *your* people call *our* people to arrange a meeting? Thanks."

I was excited but also confused. Who were "my" people? Was I going to have to ask my mom to call Billy Idol?

My mom didn't call. I did. And I got the gig.

In 1993, EMI released *Cyberpunk*, Billy Idol's new album on a CD that featured a floppy disk in a special-edition digipak, as shown in Figure 6-3.

FIGURE 6-3
Billy Idol Cyberpunk album (1993) with floppy disk

It was the first-ever commercially released interactive press kit (IPK). The floppy disk was essentially a customized version—a "Save As" in Macromedia Director—of my software, bringing my innovation score up from one to two. I was excited and thought this venture was going to make my career. From here, I would finally be able to financially support myself as an interface designer and electronic publisher. Soon everybody from David Bowie to Michael Jackson would call me for custom disk magazines for their future albums. Not just my early adopters but the entire world would finally "get" how cool this new electronic publishing medium was. The ocean seemed so blue!

Sadly, here's where I hit bumps in the road. Sure, I had successfully innovated a new digital medium, found a blue ocean for it, and pushed it into two user groups (indie bookstore customers and rock-star musicians) who loved it. The thing was, though, Billy Idol was no longer the *big* celebrity he used to be. Instead, critics slammed him, some calling the album pretentious for jumping on the cyberculture band-wagon.[†] His new songs gained little traction on MTV or the radio, and

---

† *http://en.wikipedia.org/wiki/Cyberpunk_(album)*

the album flopped. There was also a huge issue with the packaging. The digipaks were so bulky they took up almost three times as much space as a regular CD. This made it hard for record stores to stock it. The Billy Idol *Cyberpunk* album literally did not have the right product/market "fit."

I was never hired to make an IPK or custom floppy-disk project again. However, I did learn some valuable lessons.

Lessons Learned

- Timing is everything. Even if you are first-to-market with a disruptive innovation, there are no guarantees of success. In the case of electronic publishing, digital media really should be distributed digitally. But in 1993, this wasn't possible. The first web browser for the Internet was still being invented.

- Context is key. My own floppy disk magazines were "compelling" not just because of the new technology. The content on them, which featured anti–Silicon Valley rants and tips on sneaking into expensive tech tradeshows, was actually a symbiotic part of the value innovation. Billy Idol's album marketing content was perceived as more of a gimmick.

- There are many aspects to building successful digital products. Inventing them is just one small part of the fun. You also need sustainable adoption, scalability, wide distribution, revenue streams, and a team bigger than yourself. Basically, you need an innovative business model.

Techniques for Value Innovation Discovery

You have already learned that by doing competitive research your team can gain insights into what digital products and services exist in the marketplace of your value proposition. Obviously, though, this research isn't just to help your team replicate other products or improve them only marginally. Instead, you want to create new value with a superior invention.

To have a sustainable and marketable product, UX strategy requires you to balance business goals with user value. Even though you aren't creating the first electronic magazine or even the first ever website, your product should still have a unique *something* to engage customers in new and different ways. This is especially important if you're dealing with a free digital product. Your future customers need to *want* to choose your solution over any other because, a) it's significantly more efficient than what's currently out there, b) it solves a pain point they didn't know they had, and/or c) it creates an undeniable desire where none existed before. Basically, you create a leap in value by taking advantage of the uncontested blue-ocean market space through value innovation.

The value innovation in your value proposition manifests itself as a unique feature set. Features are product characteristics that deliver benefits to the user. In most cases, fewer features equals more value. Here are the top four "secret sauce" value innovation patterns of feature sets that I've observed in the digital realm:

- The product offers a new mash-up of features from competitors and relevant UX influencers. The hybrid then offers a much better existing alternative for accomplishing a task. (Meetup + a payment system = Eventbrite)

- The product provides an innovative "slice" or a twist to a value proposition from existing larger platforms. (Google Maps + crowd-sourcing = Waze)

- The product consolidates formerly disparate user experiences into one single simple and crucial solution. It becomes the one-stop shop for a user task. (Vine or Instagram with regard to simplifying how to take and share mobile videos and photos)

- The product brings two separate and distinct user segments to the table to negotiate a deal that had not been possible before, thus revolutionizing those users' world. (subletters + travelers = Airbnb)

As you can see, the patterns aren't about building replicas of existing products. Instead, you want to build on existing design conventions and take those capabilities to the next level. Great ideas are just waiting to be discovered in unexpected, unassuming places. You just need to peruse the Web like a hunter searching for prey!

The rest of this chapter examines poaching techniques for discovering new opportunities for value innovation via these four patterns. Poaching has traditionally been defined as the illegal hunting, killing, or capturing of wild animals, usually associated with land-use rights.[‡] However, there is nothing illegal about poaching features and interaction patterns that are the general approach to solving a common type of problem. You'll be borrowing these kernels from different places and putting them together in a brand-new context to create value innovation. This is how you don't just beat the competition, you make them completely irrelevant.

The four techniques you are about to learn are how to:

- Identify the key experiences
- Take advantage of UX influencers
- Do feature comparisons
- Storyboard the value innovation

Be aware that these techniques are more for your personal or your team's edification. They are not necessarily deliverables that you will present to a client.

IDENTIFY THE KEY EXPERIENCES

Generally when the word "key" precedes a term, it means that the words that follow are mission critical. We see the word used in numerous business terms such as "key leverage points," "key performance indicators" (KPIs), and "key stakeholders." The first time I saw the term "key experience" was at a Lean UX workshop presentation I co-taught with long-time UX guru Lane Halley (see Figure 6-4).

---

‡ *http://en.wikipedia.org/wiki/Poaching*

FIGURE 6-4

Key experience slide at Lean UX presentation in Los Angeles, July 2013 (with Lane Halley in the left corner pretending it's not her slide)

At the lecture, Lane showed a slide that read "A Minimum Viable Product (MVP) is just enough product to validate your key experiences (value proposition)." Even though Lane later claimed that she didn't invent the term, I took her definition as the gospel and immediately integrated it into my techniques.

For your purposes, the key experience is the feature set that defines your value innovation. It must exist in order for your product to have a competitive advantage. It defines the experience that sets your product apart from all others. It might be an exotic permutation of features, or it can be a single significant feature (as I described in the patterns earlier). For example, in his book *Microinteractions*,[§] Dan Saffer describes how "Twitter is built entirely around a single interaction: sending a 140-character message." And, as discussed in Chapter 2, Twitter has completely revolutionized the way people communicate in the world.

To get your idea juices flowing on the key experience, ask yourself these questions:

[§] Saffer, Dan. *Microinteractions*, O'Reilly, 2013.

- What will make your provisional personas (hypothesized customers) love this product?

- What moment or part of the user's journey makes this product unique?

- Based on your competitive research and analysis, what scenario or feature resolves a big shortfall?

- What kind of workarounds are your potential customers currently doing to accomplish their goals?

Your answers might just lead you to the key experience that you'll eventually deliver through a killer UX design!

However, be careful about confusing your key experience with a list of features. As is described in Chapter 4 and shown in Figure 6-5, this happened to one of my students, Ena, when she took her first pass on defining the key experience for Airbnb for Weddings.

Key Experiences (1st version)

- Search for venue with a price and number of guests

- Read reviews by brides who had their weddings at these venues

- Find updated price, available packages, inclusives, amenities, photos

- View calendar of viability for site visits and booked wedding dates

- View response rating and contact venue through the app

- Review customer service, response rate and overall venue

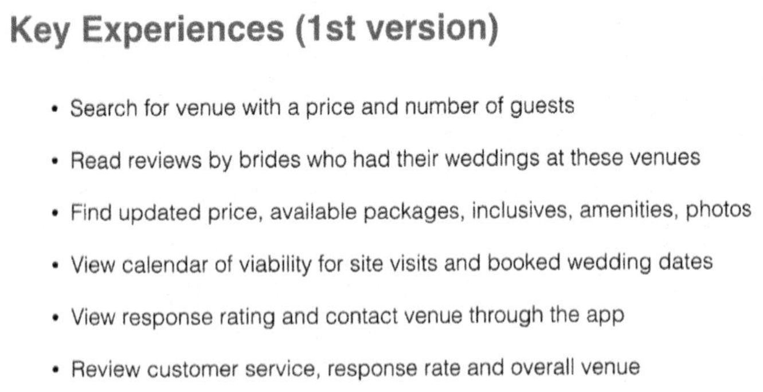

FIGURE 6-5

Ena's incorrect key experiences for Airbnb for Weddings (which I asked her to redo)

Ena identified six complex key experiences, which raises an obvious red flag. If "key" means most important, how can there be six? Instead, she created a *really important feature* list. In the fully baked 1.0 version of her product, it would probably be a good idea to include all these features because brides-to-be will probably want to perform all those functions through the site. But the purpose of the key experience is to be more minimalistic. What feature set is the most integral part of the value proposition? If you look at Twitter again, think about all the features that are part of the platform: direct messaging, the newsfeed, retweeting. Yet, the *key* experience is the 140 characters. The feature set that creates it is a text field that allows only 140 characters. It is what defines and separates Twitter's UX from all others for all its users.

So I asked Ena to take another pass at the assignment. I asked her to really think hard about what she learned from her competitive analysis. I also gave her some more specific questions to ponder:

- What is an example of the most important thing the customer can do with your product that they can't do with other competitors?

- What is the pain point that you are trying to solve that is not currently being solved by competitors?

- How would your solution be presented to the customers on a screen? Is it an interactive interface or a displayed result? Express the benefit that users will see.

- Finally, what would customers do next after they saw this screen? Would they realize the value proposition? Again, express the benefit as a scenario that the user will see.

Based on those questions, Ena came up with something better, as is demonstrated in Figure 6-6.

Key Experiences (2nd version)

- A result set of options showing affordable yet amazing wedding venues

- A turnkey solution option of a wedding package that includes a short list of vendors for the food, flowers, and valet parking

FIGURE 6-6
Ena's second attempt at the key experiences for Airbnb for Weddings (which I approved)

Yes, a lot of features were left off Ena's second version; when you are performing UX strategy, you need to carefully pick your battles. You want to ruthlessly focus your team and resources on the indispensible benefit of the product. In this case, the answer for Ena was to focus on the experiences that would separate her Airbnb for Weddings from the mothership platform Airbnb. The differentiation is what the key experience needs to express.

However, Bita and Ena (who eventually teamed up during the Airbnb for Weddings apprenticeship) realized that they could come up with an even better key experience. During the customer-discovery phase, they learned that a major pain point for both their customers was organizing all the vendors. Because weddings are supposed to be one-time events, the learning curve for a bride-to-be is really steep. It takes a lot of time and energy to learn how to book a venue, plan a menu, order flowers, arrange parking for guests, all for for a one-time deal. Bita and Ena began to wonder if they could make the planning process the key experience for their users by packaging it somehow. And they came up with their solution by utilizing their UX influencers.

TAKE ADVANTAGE OF UX INFLUENCERS

In Chapter 5, you learned about UX influencers. They are not your direct or indirect competitors; their value proposition has absolutely no relation to your own. However, their user experiences and features can provide insight into your product's value innovation. The trick is that you need to think outside of the box. Remember how one of our value innovation patterns is mixing and matching disparate feature sets? Well, that's what happens here. Sometimes by jamming pieces that don't seem to fit together, you get amazing disruption. You just need to take a leap of faith to see how a noncompetitive product or service could be bent to serve your needs.

For example, Bita and Ena found inspiration in DIRECTV and the paid bundles that it offers its users. That company has absolutely nothing to do with the Airbnb for Weddings value proposition, but the UX around the TV bundles was very well thought out. Obviously, DIRECTV takes its UX very seriously, and Bita and Ena thought this type of UX would make an excellent starting point for their key experience.

First, let's visit DIRECTV to see how it present its TV packages. Take a look at Figure 6-7; there are quite a few interesting ideas about how to group things together and allow people to customize their own TV package. You might even see a glimmer of a potential new business model. Look closely. (Hint: it's the concept of a turnkey solutions.)

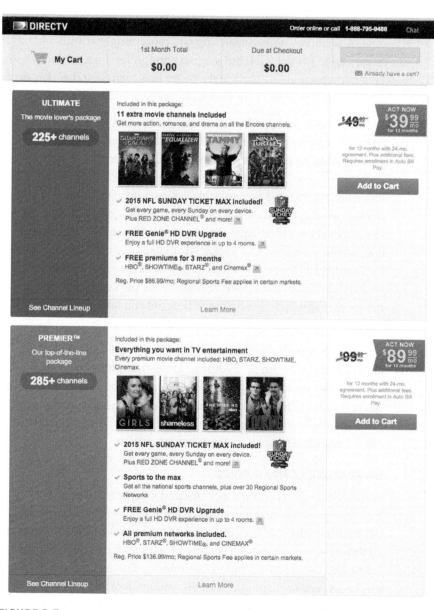

FIGURE 6-7

DIRECTV package (example of great information design)

When you visit DIRECTV, the first thing you do is type in your zip code. A result set immediately appears presenting you with a handful of packages. It's not a lot, but it's just enough for a user to work with. That gave Bita and Ena their first clue for how to present their key experience: do not present more than five packages to a bride-to-be.

Although each package has the same design and layout, they are differentiated by background color. That gave Bita and Ena a second clue: present wedding packages with an obvious differentiation mechanism. Perhaps they could use different background colors. But an even better idea might be to use a recognizable image or icon that denotes the distinction among the packages. For example, a high-end wedding package might show a limousine that says "Just Married" on the back window, whereas an economy package could show a regular compact car. Clues three and four came when they noticed how DIRECTV displayed packages by price from lowest to highest. As the user scrolls down, the more expensive packages list more benefits and take up twice as much space.

You'll catch clues by looking at all the details and figuring out how to use them for your product. Ideally, you will improve on the concepts, taking them up a notch on the design ladder for your product. But, you're not trying to design anything just now. Instead, you're aiming to pluck out the best ideas. After you have them, you'll mock them up into a storyboard to demonstrate the value innovation.

DO FEATURE COMPARISONS

Before you begin creating mock-ups and storyboards, be sure that you look for more than just one comparison reference. Research and identify multiple (three to five) instances of a similar user feature, and put all those references into one document. This way, you can compare different approaches to a single UX problem. The comparison findings can be useless or inspirational. Still, you are looking for new models, and you want to think beyond the familiar to conceive of better ways to browse, search, filter, share, and reach a user objective.

This deconstructed approach is called a feature comparison. You might find it contradictory, especially given that in Chapter 5 I agreed with Steve Blank, who deplores creating a bloated feature requirements list. Nevertheless, now that you are just using tools for discovery without necessarily showing the client, a feature comparison can be very helpful to identify opportunities for value innovation. It takes all the puzzle pieces out of the box and puts them onto the table in plain sight. Then, you can pick out the best pieces and components to build a new interaction pattern. You do whatever is necessary to poach elements and then stitch together a superior UX.

A feature comparison can even take you deeper into the research you already have. When you did your competitor research, you created and captured a short list of the most interesting features of your direct and indirect competitors, as depicted in Figure 6-8. You can return to this list to hunt out your inspiration.

Personalization Features	Community/UGC Features
save favorite venues, select available options based on the criteria you want your wedding to have (from decor, to food, to cocktail hours, drinks, etc) you have to see estimated breakdown cost for your selected venue, compare these breakdowns for up to 3 venues	reviews between hosts and guests, add comments on each blog post, review establishments, create events, create lists
Signup allows users (those looking for venues) to bookmark venues and vendors. Vendors can have direct links to website and email address, live access to an account manager for profile assistance and performance statistics, Featured listing on search results page, The ability to list services in more than one category, and extended search radius.	YouTube videos; showcases their services via video testimonials and presentations; numerous Linkedin articles

FIGURE 6-8
Features learned from the competitive research

The answer easily could be staring you in the face. Or, you might need to go a step farther to make your value innovation discovery. You might need to go back to the competitors' websites, take screenshots of the features, and really study them.

For instance, several years ago, a multinational conglomerate hired me to design the UX of an ebook reader for the iPhone. Because there were already several readers on the market (Stanza, eReader, Kindle, Nook), I did my competitive research and analysis. I downloaded them and captured my data. I captured screenshots of many different functions, features, and experiences, such as how to browse for a book, the UI of the loading screen, the navigation of the table of contents, and how to highlight and annotate. Basically, I documented any feature that touched the key experiences I had to design. I then imported all of my screenshots into iPhoto and organized them based on their relationships to one another. As my final step, I arranged them onto large canvasses in Adobe InDesign so that I could compare them visually side-by-side. Based on these comparisons, I took notes when ideas occurred to me. Figure 6-9 presents a sample of that document.

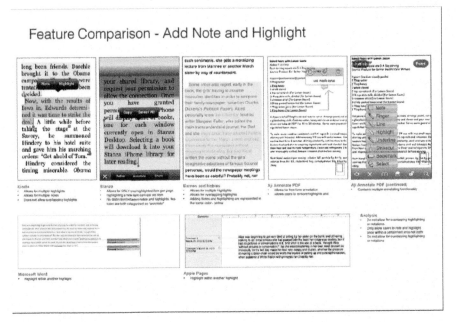

FIGURE 6-9
eBook reader feature comparison of adding a note or highlight

The process took at least four hours, and the client didn't ask me or pay me to do any of it. In the end, however, I was able to observe and quantify best practices, lame practices, and the really interesting approaches the competitors were creating for users to accomplish tasks with formal or newfangled design patterns. It also saved me endless design hours. I didn't need to design the project from scratch, because I didn't have to reinvent the wheel. Some other benefits included the following:

- Seeing the common user flows through the apps so that I could quickly make an application or site map.

- Recognizing the patterns and common ways for helping users accomplish their goal. In other words, if I wanted to lure customers over from another application to my own, I could determine user expectations in advance.

- Avoiding creating something totally new and making the UI more complicated because I now knew what my competition was already doing well.

- Dealing with insane stakeholders or a HIPPO (Highest Paid Person's Opinion) who, based on no empirical evidence, thought that he knew the best way to do my job. With my well-researched evidence, I was able to lead the UX design the way I thought best 95 percent of the time.

Using a feature comparison on competitors and UX influencers, you can compare everything from visual design, to interaction design, to feature sets, to how the content is displayed. The objective is to avoid being as clueless about your competitive environment as our friend in Figure 6-10 clearly is. Sometimes, you can capture the necessary iPhone or Android screenshots from the competition's store or you can just spend the money ($10 to $30) on the applications. Charge the client, or pay for it yourself and bill your client for an extra hour. Ultimately, the comparison will save you and your client time and money. It will open your mind, especially after the deep, focused dive you took in Chapters 4 and 5.

Personal Disruption

The big payoff of exposing yourself to new experiences outside of your comfort zone is that they make it possible for us to grow as people. You change when you disrupt habitual patterns, and it affords you new ways of doing, being, and experiencing. For example:

- When I took up ballet at age 45, I finally learned how to stand up straight.

- When I took up gardening at age 42, I finally learned how to make a tasty fresh salad.

- When I had my son at age 39, I finally learned how to slow down and just let some things happen.

Looking at everyday things with fresh eyes helps us to look beyond the obvious and unearth new mental models.

Disruption, whether in our professional or personal lives, breaks down the self-imposed walls that lock us into conceiving or designing the same thing over and over again.

FIGURE 6-10
Not being aware of your surroundings is like the old myth about an ostrich hiding from danger by burying its head in the sand.

STORYBOARD THE VALUE INNOVATION

Now that you have identified the key experience of your product, you will want to stitch those moments together into a narrative thread otherwise known as a "story." And obviously, with your emphasis on the visuals from your feature comparisons, it will be great tool to do that.

The storyboarding process has been around since German filmmaker Lotte Reiniger first drew and colored storyboards for her animated feature film, *The Adventures of Prince Achmed*, in 1926.[¶] Since then, they have become versatile tools used for advertising campaigns, comics, motion pictures, software design, and various other business pro-

---

¶ *http://meganratner.squarespace.com/lotte-reiniger-art-on-paper*

cesses. The reason is that a storyboard promotes visual thinking. Or, as the authors of the book *Game Storming: A Playbook for Innovators, Rulebreakers, and Changemakers,*** write, "[It is a] visioning exercise [that] allows participants to imagine and create possibilities."

Three steps to storyboarding value innovation

The goal of a storyboard is to tell the story of your key experience(s) visually. You want to use the format to zero in on the most important components of the experience. Say more with less, and finish with a happy ending in that the problem for your user is solved. Here is my recommended framework for building (and presenting) a storyboard:

Step 1: Create your list of panels.

Keep in mind that you do not want to demonstrate all the features of the product (as Ena incorrectly did when she first mapped out her key experiences). You are only showing the most "valuable" moments of your customer's journey through the storyboard panels. Some of these moments will impact the interface design, and other moments will actually occur offline. Show the progression of the entire experience regardless of whether the experience takes 20 minutes (such as Uber) or two months (Airbnb) in real time.

For Bita and Ena, this meant showing how their bride-to-be experienced her dream wedding coming true rather than showing how account registration on Airbnb for Weddings works. Here are the panels they stitched together:

1. Bride-to-be is looking for a beautiful and affordable venue online.

2. She finds a result set of two to three listings.

3. She sees a detail view of an awesome listing.

4. She selects a package (venue, food, flowers).

5. She receives a confirmation of venue/tour/submission.

6. She gets married on the beach!

** Gray, David, Sunni Brown, Jamews Macanufo. *Gamestorming: A Playbook for Innovators, Rulebreakers, and Changemakers.* O'Reilly, 2010.

Step 2: Decide on your visual format (digital montages versus sketching on paper).

Some people know how to draw or sketch. Others (like me) cannot even draw a meaningful stick figure. What matters the most is that you choose a format that is fast and easy for you and your team to pull your storyboard together. If you are fast in Photoshop, just mash up some interface ideas together as graphics. Do not waste time wireframing a storyboard. It's fine to use photos from Google or to slightly modify screen grabs from other sites. Create, draw, or gather all your images and make certain that they are the same approximate aspect ratio and that they fit nicely onto your canvas. There is no reason to design an entire user interface at this stage. Instead, zoom into the components of the interface that illustrate the best concept.

Ena decided to use a mix of photos she found on Google Images. She then mocked up her comps quickly in Photoshop. She also used the exact layout from DIRECTV for her results set and the detail view of the listing because it's not important for her to design something new right now. She just needs to show how the UX might work.

Step 3: Lay out your storyboard on a canvas, add captions below each panel.

Now, review your storyboard. Does it flow well? Is it concise? Is it easy to follow the customer's ideal experience? If so, you've successfully storyboarded your value innovation. Keep the captions brief and in lower-case—less than two lines. Again, less is more.

Figure 6-11 and Figure 6-12 present Bita and Ena's storyboards, respectively. Don't they give you a good sense about what the value innovation for their product will be like?

Storyboard of "Airbnb for Weddings" - Guest Experience

1. Jenny searches for a beautiful and affordable wedding venue.

2. She receives a result set showing different venues with pictures and basic pricing.

3. She selects a venue she likes and sees a detailed view of the listing.

4. She chooses a wedding package for this venue that fits her budget.

5. She gets confirmation of the details including the date of her tour.

6. Jenny and her husband after their fantasy wedding, just the way they planned!

FIGURE 6-11

Bita's storyboard showing value innovation for the bride-to-be

Storyboard of "Airbnb for Weddings" - Host Experience

List Your Space

Airbnb for Weddings lets you rent out your home for the most profit.

Home Type

⚲ Mansion ⌂ Estate Other ▾

Capacity

🐾 120 ▾

Continue

Airbnb for Weddings

Robin sent you a inquiry about "Oceanfront Villa". Reply, pre-approve, or decline by **10:53 PM PDT** on **March 15th**. Based on your rate of $40 per guest along with associated fees, your potential payout for this **July 31st** reservation is **$10,500.**

Pre-approve / Decline

Reply

1. Homeowners are looking for new ways to make money off their property.

2. They create a listing in less than 30 minutes.

3. They receive an inquiry from a prospective bride-to-be.

4. They give the couple a tour of their home and show them photos from past weddings.

5. The wedding event happens just as planned and the homeowners make a $10,000 profit.

FIGURE 6-12

Ena's storyboard showing value innovation for the host

As I mentioned at the beginning of the chapter, storyboards are not necessarily deliverables. There are cases for storyboards in other work environments where they are super helpful to pitch ideas, but for now, we just are using them to map out the key experience in a narrative context.

Business Models and Value Innovation

I've discussed how to do value innovation feature poaching in regard to the UX, but don't forget that they also can be and should apply to your business model. The reason is that value innovation is a competitive advantage that ultimately combines cost leadership with differentiation. This means that your killer UX is related to the business model, and vice versa. These two factors combined will also ultimately leave your competition in the dust and sustain your product in the dynamic marketplace.

Let's take a look at a marketplace that I wish I had less personal experience with: online dating, and three platforms that exemplify it, eHarmony, OkCupid, and Tinder.

eHarmony's business model is based on a monthly subscription service. Its value proposition relies on its matching algorithm which focuses on the core traits of its clients, such as agreeableness, spirituality, and extroversion. The onboarding requires users to answer hundreds of questions before they are sent a highly curated set of matches. To get more matches, you need to close out the ones that you have. There is no way to browse profiles on your own. It even provides tools for a more guided communication process, because the platform is designed for "marriage-minded people."

OkCupid is the polar opposite of eHarmony, even though it exists in the same marketplace. Its business model is free to customers, and over time, its revenue stream evolved from paid advertising, such as with Facebook, to a premium feature service. But the value proposition is intrinsically wrapped up in a powerful UX by which users can filter matches based on qualitative and quantitative data points. Users can also customize their own algorithm by answering highly personalized prompts in a polling feature. The customers are always completely in control of how wide or narrow they cast their nets while OkCupid reaps the benefits of the user data and premium revenue stream.

The latest and most innovative of the online dating products is Tinder. This mobile-only contender already has more than 30 million users[††] and is quickly chipping away at OkCupid's value proposition. Tinder is all about ease-of-use and immediacy. As Figure 6-13 shows, users sign in with a real or fake Facebook account, upload a few photos, maybe write a bio, and are up and running 15 minutes later.

FIGURE 6-13

My concise user profile on Tinder

No Service   2:24 PM

Done   • • • ○   Edit

Jaime, 48
less than a mile away Active just now

About Jaime
Bad ballerina (I'm awful, but keep going), software designer, author, mom, foodie, hopeless romantic. I'm 5'5". Intense, yet casual. Former New Yorker. Now live on the East Side in a big dumb house with my 9-year old son here 1/2 the time. Spend my days in the library writing. Hoping to start spending some free evenings with a cute, intelligent, funny, strong self sufficient 5'9"+

Here's where Tinder's value innovation kicks in by inverting the historical mental model of dating sites by only allowing users to interact with each other once both parties express mutual interest. With Tinder, users are constantly served up cards that are only curated by distance, age, and gender. That's key experience #1. The user swipes left if she

---

†† http://www.latimes.com/business/technology/la-fi-tn-tinder-plus-20141106-story.html

doesn't like the profile. She swipes right if she does. If both users swipe right, they can send messages to each other in a native message system. Unlike other dating sites, Tinder provides matches within a one-mile radius. That's key experience #2. If you live in a traffic-heavy city like Los Angeles or New York, you can zoom in on suitors who live within walking distance. So what started as a hookup app for millennials has now evolved into the go-to place for people of all ages to fall swiftly into an any-length relationship.

In addition to that, Tinder didn't initially launch with a identified revenue stream because its business model first required mass adoption. Now, Tinder is experimenting with revenue streams such as selling targeted advertising or a paid membership (Figure 6-14), which offers users more sophisticated functionality.

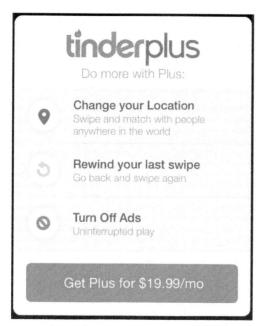

FIGURE 6-14
The new Tinder revenue stream

Here are the points that I want to make:

- All these products have completely distinct user experiences and business models.

- They all have had undeniable success competing in the same customer pool.

What makes each of them innovative is its unique way of hooking users through a permutation of features and business model components, through their finely tuned different parts.

Recap

In this chapter we covered a lot of material and concepts related to ideation and connecting ideas to your final objective: articulating your value innovation! I explained how value innovation for digital products is accomplished by focusing on the primary utility of a product. You learned about the importance of key experiences (showing the value proposition) and how creating a product that is the same or only slightly better than the competition is a waste of time. I showed you how to identify UX influencers. You learned about feature poaching, which you can use to pluck features, interaction patterns, and business model ideas from other products and then mash them up to create something new. Finally, you learned how to tell stories with storyboards that will connect your customers' journey with the value innovation.

Now, it's time to leave this fantasyland behind and see if you're innovating in reality by creating prototypes to run experiments.

[7]

Creating Prototypes for Experiments

"The premature outlay of huge amounts of money in pursuit of the wrong strategy is the thing to avoid. You need to have an experimental mindset."[*]

—CLAYTON CHRISTENSEN

THE PREMISE OF *LEAN STARTUP* IS TO GET FEEDBACK EARLY AND OFTEN in order to validate that you are on the right path, which is also the fondation of Tenet 3.[†] Eric Ries and Steve Blank insist that it's important to run experiments on your product as soon as possible. There is even a spinoff movement called Lean Startup Machine (see Figure 7-1) that holds worldwide events in which startups and product makers learn how to design, build, and test a Minimum Viable Product (MVP) experiment over a weekend.

FIGURE 7-1

Lean Startup Machine's slogan

---

[*] *http://www.christiansarkar.com/christensen.html*

[†] Ries, Eric. *Lean Startup*. HarperBusiness, 2011.

A successful UX strategy also needs this continuous testing to ensure that your product will deliver a solution that people will really, *really* want. Thus, you need to jump from your storyboard to an MVP or prototype of your product. You'll then take it into small, structured, lean experiments to learn as soon as possible if your team's latest assumptions are on the right track and to force you to confront the reality of what it would actually take to make your business model work in the real world. This kick-starts the process of blending the ingredients that make up all four tenets of my UX strategy framework, as presented in Figure 7-2.

FIGURE 7-2
The four tenets of UX strategy

Giving It Your Best Shot

Years before my dad bought the doomed hot dog stand I discuss in Chapter 4, I watched my mom start and run a successful business out of her bedroom closet of our San Fernando Valley home. It was the early 1970s, and my mom, age 35, fell hard for the sport of tennis. This was the decade of tennis in the United States. Its popularity was fueled by the televised championships at Wimbledon as well as the US Open and the French Open, with competitors like John Newcombe,

Ken Rosewall, and Chris Evert. Backyard tennis courts, country clubs with strong tennis programs, and tournaments popped up all across the country. In sunny southern California, tennis became an integral part of the upper-middle-class lifestyle. While I attended elementary school, my mom dragged my little brother in his playpen to the local park where she took lessons. She was a natural who developed a powerful slice return, and six months after starting lessons, she won her first ladies double tournament trophy (see Figure 7-3).

FIGURE 7-3

Photo of Rona Levy holding her first tennis trophy in 1972

It didn't take long before my mom began to look beyond the game. One day, while having lunch with her doubles partner, Lea Kramer, inspiration struck. The friends loved all aspects about the sport—on and off the court—but both agreed that it was almost impossible to find reasonably priced tennis clothes. A competitive audit of discount tennis clothing stores in Los Angeles assured the women they had stumbled on a blue ocean. They had found themselves a value proposition.

They each had $500 to invest. Neither of them had any retail experience. Lea knew how to do bookkeeping. My mom had only worked as a legal secretary and never attended college. But my mother was a hustler. She suggested that they experiment with their value proposition by doing a trial run. She reached out to a family friend to see if he could help them acquire some product. He worked in the "schmatta" (rag) business and knew his way around downtown Los Angeles clothing manufacturers. He also knew the movie star Elke Sommer, who agreed to sell the new business partners some of her new tennis clothing line at just over cost. With 4 dresses, 10 pastel skirts, and 12 bras, my mom and Lea just needed to find some customers.

They first started trying to acquire customers at the tennis courts, where they showed off their wares from the trunk of my mom's Chevy Nova. But people really needed a private place to try things on. So they obtained local club lists with names and numbers of players they could schmooze into coming over to their homes. I remember coming home from school to find dozens of half-naked women parading around my mom's bedroom while she urged them to try on different styles. Then, my mom and Lea were even invited to be part of a charity (donating 10 percent of sales) in a Beverly Hills home. They trucked their clothes to this wealthy customer segment, where they sold the product in a "pop-up" dressing room in the mansion's garage. These experiments eventually made them a rousing success. Their entrepreneurial scheme was even featured as one of the "Ten Biggest Bargains in L.A" in *LA Magazine.*[‡] Within their first year, they built up $10,000 of inventory and a customer base from all over, including Beverly Hills, Ojai, and Pacific Palisades. It was time to scale from their bedroom closets to a brick-and-mortar location on Ventura Boulevard. *Love Match* Tennis Shop (see Figure 7-4) was officially born!

FIGURE 7-4
Photo of Lea Kramer (left) and Rona Levy (right) in front of Love Match Tennis Shop in 1974

---

‡ Rena LeBlanc, "The Ten Biggest Bargains in L.A." *LA Magazine*, July 1973

The business was a break-even from the start, and my mom and Lea typically reinvested any profits back into purchasing more inventory. They enjoyed the discretionary income and the flexible schedule that let them raise their young children and also play tennis. After three years, they moved the store into a space three times the size in a new shopping mall. *Love Match* Tennis Shop continued its success, but after almost 10 years, my mom decided to move on. Lea bought out her share for an amount that they both agreed was fair. In accordance with the etiquette demonstrated at the end of a proper tennis match, they shook hands and thus concluded their business partnership.

Lessons Learned

- You do not need an MBA or even a college education to start a business and for it to be successful. You do need to be a go-getter.

- Start small. If you have a big idea, figure out a way to trial it. Manage risk by taking action. Place small bets fast.

- Stay in a partnership for as long as you have the stamina to pull your weight. But when it's over, leave gracefully and with a handshake.

How I Became an Experiment Addict

When Marc Andreessen coined the term "Product/Market Fit" back in 2007,[§] he said, "In a great market—a market with lots of real potential customers—the market *pulls* product out of the startup." This aligns with Steve Blank's Customer Development methodology, in which he insists that product makers begin building by understanding their customers' problems, and then tweaking the solution to the customers' needs. In a UX strategy, you do that by running experiments.

---

§   *http://web.stanford.edu/class/ee204/ProductMarketFit.html*

First, though, we need to define what exactly an experiment is. An experiment is a test of a hypothesis. The goal is to discover whether your hypothesis is right or wrong based on measurable results. After the experiment, you should be able to evaluate your results and accept or reject your original hypothesis.

Experiments are diverse and can be run in a laboratory or in the field. They can be controlled (run with a control group for comparison) or natural (run with no control groups). No matter what type, though, experiments are all about testing a variable in order to falsify a hypothesis. This variable is any item, factor, or condition that you can control or change. In observing the variables in the experiments, you look for a cause-and-effect relationship, and you conduct the experiment for a finite amount of time, because you want to measure and empirically capture observable evidence about what happens when the variable changes. It's that simple. Or so you might initially think.

In early 2011, I was working full-time as an offsite UX strategy consultant for Cisco Systems. At the same time, I was looking for smaller, get-your-hands-dirty opportunities with local tech startups in Los Angeles. In March, I met Jared Krause, a brash, hilarious, articulate entrepreneur, and a fellow NYU alumnus to boot. He had big plans to make a fully featured online platform that enabled people to easily trade all types of goods and services, and he also had initial private investment lined up. Sure, there were other bartering/trading platforms out there, but none with a sophisticated mechanism for matching users based on common interests and geolocation. Other trading platforms such as BarterQuest and Swap.com had clunky interfaces with the type of inventory you might find at a yard sale. Jared wanted to create something groundbreaking.

I started working on the project immediately in addition to my full-time enterprise job, going through a divorce, and my son starting kindergarten. About six months later, we had completed the business requirements, a project roadmap, information architecture, and about 50 percent of the UX wireframes. Jared put together an impressive team including a specialist in artificial intelligence. Our value proposition was basically that it would be the "OkCupid for barter," or in Jared's words, "a dating site for your shit." The big idea was that customers could make lists of all the things they had to offer and all the things they wanted. Then, the back-end algorithm would match up the appropriate people.

The project was ambitious and complicated. Figure 7-5 demonstrates that the transaction flow alone was complex.

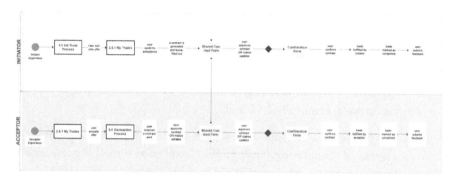

FIGURE 7-5
Transaction flow created for TradeYa

Then one day, at the beginning of a wireframe review call, Jared told me I had to stop working on the UX. Instead I had to go read the *New York Times* best seller *The Lean Startup*. Over two days I listened to the audio version while hiking the Arroyo Seco trails in Pasadena. The concepts in the book jolted me awake to two scary realities. The first was that Jared and my course of action for the product drastically needed to change. This meant I had to throw out or put aside a lot of hard UX work. The second reality was that my practice of UX strategy and design methodology based on the traditional "waterfall" software development model was now outdated.

The rules had completely changed:

- No more working on UX strategy phases geared toward a big 1.0 "launch." Now, I needed to plan for making small incremental pre-releases (MVPs) that articulated different aspects of the UX.

- No more working in isolation and then just handing off documentation to the team (stakeholders, developers, designers). Now, I needed to continuously collaborate and strategize *with* them to ensure that the product was released as quickly as possible.

- No more crossing my fingers and hoping that customers would love the product *after* it was built. Now, I needed to insist that my clients let me conduct experiments along the way that tested the UX and the value proposition.

Changing our process mid-project was very stressful. Plus, we were running out of funding, so Jared needed to bring in another round of investment. The investors wanted real evidence of a solid rationale for the potential success of our product. The big question Jared kept getting was, "Why would someone want to wait for a worthwhile trade for their old laptop when they could just sell it on Craig's List and then spend the cash on whatever they wanted?" Jared and I needed to begin experimenting immediately with an MVP to show that our utopian vision wasn't from Planet Utopia.

The challenge was to isolate a slice of the UX that would truly test the essence of the value proposition. We also needed something technically feasible that the developers could build in less than one month. Jared was confident that his own extreme marketing abilities would drive enough people to the landing page. Still, we needed a place for them to land that would make immediate sense and not feel like an empty shopping mall.

Because we didn't want to wait for a month to learn if people followed through with the actual transaction in the offline world (which was outside of our online transactional funnel), the MVP also needed to yield immediate results for any successful trades. We needed to learn a lot from this experiment. The most important things we needed to learn was whether trades were more likely to happen if the person who wanted to trade something was open to a variety of commensurable offers versus a specific "want" item. Jared had a hunch that if we spotlighted just one trade per day and made it for something highly attractive to our hypothesized customer segments, we would have a higher guarantee of a successful transaction (a trade actually happening).

The most difficult part to determine was how the experiment would work without any backend engineering. It required us to focus on the key experience that provided the most innovation. For TradeYa, it was the capability of being able to get something you wanted without having to pay money for it. We needed people to want to engage in the act of trading with strangers. To ensure that all trades actually went through without a hitch, Jared intended to manually facilitate them. This could be as easy as helping both parties with the swap logistics over email or coordinating a time for them to meet up in front of a 7-Eleven with

Jared as a mediator. Over one weekend, Jared and I sat side by side and knocked out the all the necessary UX documentation for the developers. In less than one month, "Trade of the Day" was born.

Figure 7-6 depicts the application maps of the before and after of the original TradeYa vision and the first MVP.

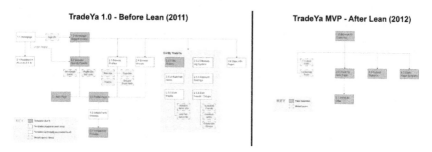

FIGURE 7-6
TradeYa's sitemap before and after we went "Lean"

Figure 7-7 shows the home page wireframes of the before and after of the original TradeYa vision and the first MVP.

FIGURE 7-7
TradeYa's home page before and after we went "Lean"

It's pretty clear from just a quick glance at the UX documentation how much the product shrank. We basically had to figure out a way to enable a rudimentary trade on the frontend (the user interface) without requiring the developers to do any backend engineering (code and database). Our thought was that if Craig's List had done perfectly fine without requiring users to even have accounts, the same could be true for the first version of TradeYa. As a result, I chopped out all the personalization and transactional wireframes—no user profiles, shopping carts, or user reviews. The MVP's experience simply didn't need it.

The product went from fat to lean; it was going to do a lot less but do it well. That was crucial, because we didn't have the time or the resources to build out the original feature-heavy version. We also had the common two-sided marketplace issue of the chicken and the egg. Without users to trade "stuff," who would come to trade with them? Thus, the age-old question: what came first, the trader or the tradee?

Here's where Jared made the experiment more intense. He insisted that everybody on the team (investors, developers, designers, all of us) had to test this by coming up with goods or services to trade until each of us had completed a successful trade. I had not planned on getting my hands *this* dirty! I didn't have any old couches or personal computers that I wanted (or needed) to trade. So I chose to trade on my UX skills. (See Figure 7-8.) My trade-of-the-day offer was two hours of my UX consulting time over Skype in exchange for either a) open to offers or b) the highly specific task of converting some old Flash animations of mine into YouTube videos.

FIGURE 7-8
My own TradeYa on TradeYa

It was scary yet fun. Moreover, it was truly like our original value proposition, a dating site for your shit. Within 24 hours, I accepted a trade offer from Edward, a digital consultant out of Portland. This was when I wholeheartedly connected the dots. I had firsthand experience that the value proposition and UX weren't quite like eBay; rather, it was much closer to OkCupid. The trade was successful. Edward put my animated cartoon series on YouTube, and I schooled him on how to begin obtaining UX work in Portland. I even hooked him up with a job interview. The entire user journey was pretty magical. Our trade was worth more than paper money because we both got so much out of the exchange of our traded skills without either of us having to file a W9. The current and potential investors liked what they saw, and more funding was raised so that we could continue experimenting and learning.

As you can see from this case study, there are lots of different types of experiments that you might run and design to determine product/market fit—ones that don't involve writing a single line of code. Here's two popular methods:

Online campaigns

Jared was confident in his ability to draw people to our new landing page through marketing, which meant that he would need to advertise TradeYa. The primary purpose of any advertisement, concierge MVP, explainer video, or Kickstarter campaign, is to measure if potential customers take action. They need to respond with that tentative first click. A positive response such as a click can track specific actions with bite-sized measurements called metrics. Metrics can tell us the following:

- How many people landed on the YouTube video page?

- Of those, how many people watched the entire video?

- How much traffic was driven from the video page to the product site?

- How many people submitted their email address for more information?

- How many people made it down the entire sales funnel and signed up for a monthly subscription?

A truly successful conversion will engage people with your product's value proposition and eventually convert them into customers. Metrics have the potential to tell us everything from the clickthrough rate (CTR) of an online campaign to customer satisfaction levels. (I discuss this in greater detail in Chapter 9.)

But online campaigns can also be used to pitch the MVP's value proposition to users to see if they'll "buy in" to the concept. This is usually a short-format "explainer" video or animation that explains the benefits of the product. You can find them on web pages, YouTube, or crowdfunding platforms such as Kickstarter and Indiegogo; and they are meant to draw investors, raise funds, test product appeal, and acquire users. Successful buy-in is indicated by customer suspects who provide their email address or other personal information. This type of feedback data is considered "currency."

One of the most famous examples occurred in 2008 when Drew Houston released a three-minute screencast recording of a product he was working on called Dropbox. The screencast showed a simulation of the product's value proposition: its functionality, ease of use, and benefits. The video went viral and almost overnight garnered Houston more than 75,000 signups[¶] from early adopters eager for a product that had not even been built. Now, that's some successful conversion results that show people want your product! This advertisement or "concierge MVP" (as Eric Ries called it in *Lean Startup*) primed the pump for startups to begin going ballistic running experiments using explainer videos. (See Mint, Crazy Egg, Dollar Shave Club, Groupon, and even Airbnb.) Figure 7-9 shows the explainer video that Jared produced for TradeYa.

¶ Ries, Eric. *Lean Startup*. HarperBusiness, 2011.

FIGURE 7-9

Jared's explainer video of the TradeYa value proposition (*https://www. youtube.com/watch?v=ENBGDRHAJN4*)

Concierge MVP

"Concierge" is a French word that essentially means doorkeeper. The job of a concierge in a hotel or residential complex is to ensure that the experience of its customers (tenants, guests, whoever) is frictionless from the moment the person enters the building (or service or product). When I speak about Concierge MVPs, I'm referring to an attempt to simulate an aspect of the customer's experience without the interface and to do it with as little friction as possible. You are simply de-risking your product by simulating as many of the frontend key experiences as possible without the interface backend to see what goes wrong and what goes right. When you don't have the time or resources to build a backend, creating a Concierge MVP is the next best thing.

This is exactly what Jared did while we worked on cutting off a lot of feature weight. He personally facilitated trades between users—by phone, by email, and in person—without the use of the backend to do it automatically. There are many other examples and articles that describe twenty-first-century concierge experiments concocted to test value propositions of products such as Car's Direct, Zappos, Food on the Table, and even Airbnb. My take is that early adopters are simply fascinated by technological innovation and open to experiencing something new, even if there is some trickery involved.

But this isn't anything new; innovators having been "faking it," and users have been "falling for it" for a long time. In 1769, an inventor named Wolfgang von Kempelen performed a demonstration of his automaton chess-playing machine for the empress of Austria. The Mechanical Turk, or "The Turk," toured Europe for decades playing chess and defeating challengers including statesmen such as Napoleon Bonaparte and Benjamin Franklin.[**] Even Edger Allen Poe published a theory speculating that the chess moves were actually determined by a legless war veteran who could fit in the tiny space inside the cabinet. What users didn't know was that it actually was a chess master hidden inside the machine, but in a much larger secret compartment concealed by folding partitions (see Figure 7-10). Users were playing *him* rather than *it*.

** Standage, Tom. *The Mechanical Turk*. The Penguin Press, 2002.

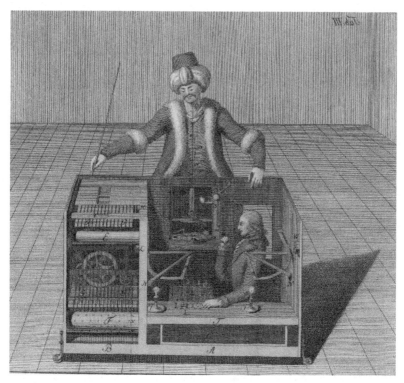

FIGURE 7-10
Engraving of a replica of "The Turk" by Joseph Racknitz (licensed under Creative Commons)

But the illusion really got people to think. It got mathematicians thinking about mechanical computers. It also gave audiences at the dawn of the industrial revolution a taste of the value proposition of the supercomputer. Today, it's feasible for any aspiring entrepreneur to manually simulate a complex digital product. Amazon's Mechanical Turk[††] offers a crowd-sourcing marketplace with which businesses can outsource microtasks to individuals. The platform provides on-demand access to a diverse and scalable workforce that takes advantage of human intelligence to mimic backend technology. This is the same as how Jared personally enabled the transactions behind the scenes of TradeYa before

---

†† *https://www.mturk.com*

the larger product was reworked to align with our new vision. Whatever magic you decide to perform, concierge experiments are less risky than building out the entire product and then seeing what happens.

Wizard of OZing It

Digital product simulation actually dates back to a 1983 experiment done at IBM by J.F. Kelley. In his whitepaper titled "An Empirical Methodology for Writing User-Friendly Natural Language Computer Applications,"[*] he unveils a methodology he calls the "OZ Paradigm."

Kelley describes his test as "an experimental simulation in which participants are given the impression that they are interacting with a program that understands English as well as another human would. In fact, at least in the earlier stages of development, the program is limping along, only partly implemented. The experimenter, acting as 'Wizard,' surreptitiously intercepts communications between participant and program, supplying answers and new inputs as needed."

We all know this famous "wizard" character that Kelley was referring to from *The Wonderful Wizard of Oz*. In this classic children's story, the wizard convinces Dorothy that he is "great and powerful" by using magic tricks and props. His incredible simulations lead her to believe that he is the only man capable of solving her problem and those of her companions.[†]

The concept of creating simulations of new technologies to test out innovative concepts is core to gaining early validation. Essentially, J.F. Kelley was doing Build-Measure-Learn feedback loops, exposing many users to his product who had never even used a computer before without completely building out the entire, complicated interface. He gained validated user research by using humans instead of machines to simulate just enough artificial intelligence to make his system seem real.

---

[*] Kelley, J.F. "An empirical methodology for writing user-friendly natural language computer applications." *Proceedings of ACM SIG-CHI '83 Human Factors in Computing Systems* (Boston, December 12-15, 1983). New York; ACM: pp 193-6.

[†] Baum, L. Frank. *The Wonderful Wizard of Oz*. George M. Hill Company, 1900.

Testing Product/Market Fit by Using Prototypes

TradeYa already had a digital presence when Jared and I decided to backtrack and build an MVP. But, what if you don't have an actual website yet? What if you just have a storyboard and an idea? That's when a prototype comes in handy. The goal of a prototype is to avoid coding and designing until you have true validation that your solution is desired and can be sustained by your hypothetical customer segment.

A prototype is anything that serves to familiarize the user with the ultimate experience you are trying to create. These can be low-fidelity paper prototypes or high-fidelity mockups. In the tech industry today, prototyping is a big deal. Digital teams create highly detailed ones in programs such as Axure or OmniGraffle. These prototypes can be useful for tactical usability testing and conveying functionality to the development teams. Conversely, they can easily become resource overkill just making something "clickable" to convey a strategic concept. In fact, you might have noticed how I haven't mentioned wireframing (the typical UX deliverable) at all as something to do for strategy. Most customers and stakeholders can't look at a wireframe and truly "get" the experience. If you leave important ideas up to their imaginations, you risk some customers' disapproval because they can't understand it.

I believe a prototype that you don't learn from is a waste of time. In Chapter 6, I talk about the reasons you needed to focus on key experiences. Now, you'll use your storyboard as the starting point for creating a *solution prototype* so that you can run an experiment. You will use it to show proof-of-concept to users for when your team goes out to do guerrilla user research, which we look at in the Chapter 8.

THREE STEPS TO DESIGN HACKING THE SOLUTION PROTOTYPE

I used to call a solution prototype the five-screen MVP, but I have moved away from that because, honestly, a prototype is certainly not "viable" or a "product." Its sole purpose is to force your team to create the minimum amount of screens necessary to demonstrate the key experience of the interface, the value proposition, and a sneak peek of the potential business model of the product. It pushes your team to take your innovative storyboard to the next level.

However, like the storyboards, solution prototypes are not meant to be pixel-perfect for development. The interfaces and artwork can be cut and pasted from other existing websites, thus requiring minor typesetting of the content. You are using the output to conduct an experiment to get customer validation. The prototype is not the final product, although it might inform, inspire, or annoy the future designers of it.

Here is the general framework of the solution prototype screens and their content. The order and amount of the middle screens is flexible based on how many key experiences you need to show.

1. **Setup**   Typically the landing page or user dashboard.

2. **Key UX 1**   Typically in one to three screens, shows the crucial interactions that show value innovation.

3. **Key UX 2**   Typically in one to three screens, shows the crucial interactions that show value innovation.

4. **Value proposition**   This is the final result of a successful transaction.

5. **Pricing strategy (if applicable)**   This shows the cost of the app, monthly fees, package costs, and so on. If the revenue stream of the product is advertising, then you should consider putting examples of how ads might look on the prior screens.

Let's return to Bita and Ena, my students whom I introduced in Chapter 3, to see how to make a successful solution prototype.

Step 1

Write a simple list or an outline of the screens you are going to show. It's going to potentially include one or two key experiences. As with the storyboard, you want to really distill out the details that you need to show.

Bita and Ena wanted to show the screens from their storyboard but with more details. This was the list they wrote:

1. The landing page with the user's query entered

2. The result set with the listing and the maps and the filters exposed

3. A filtered result set with the listing and the maps and the filters closed

4. A result detailed screen

5. A photo gallery featuring images of a home, specific to the wedding

6. The package options with pricing

7. The tour setup screen

8. The confirmation screen with final pricing, including cost of service

Notice how all the steps of the solution prototype refer to the experience online. That's because this is what Bita and Ena need to test: does the digital product solve the customer's problem?

Step 2

Start ~~creating~~ mashing up the images that tell the story.

Chapter 6 points out that there are lots of well-thought-out UX and UI design patterns that you can safely reference at this stage in your process instead of building them from scratch. However, try as hard as you can to make your prototype *seem* real, which as I mentioned earlier with the Mechanical Turk is key to making a simulation of a machine pass muster.

Figures 7-11 through 7-18 show what Bita and Ena's ultimate solution prototype looked like. If you look closely, you will see that most of the ideas were borrowed from competitors and influencers.

FIGURE 7-11

Airbnb for Weddings prototype screen 1

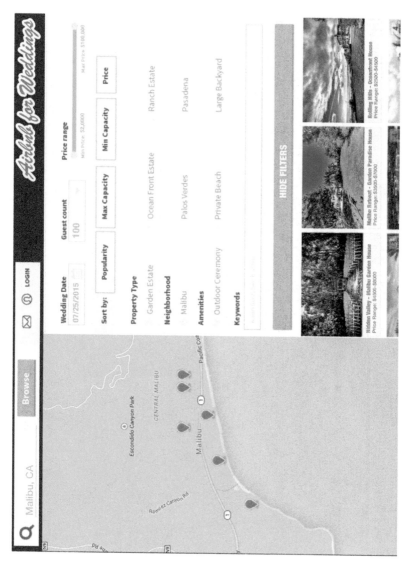

FIGURE 7-12

Airbnb for Weddings prototype screen 2

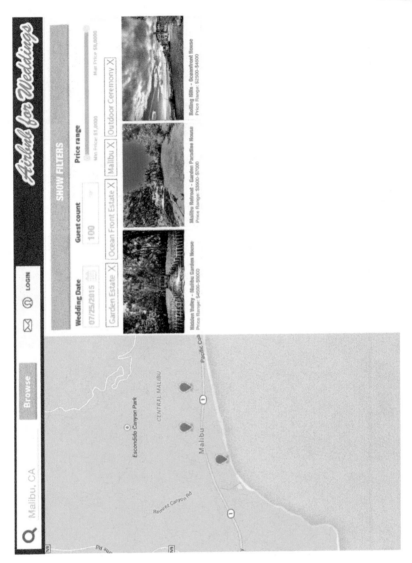

FIGURE 7-13

Airbnb for Weddings prototype screen 3

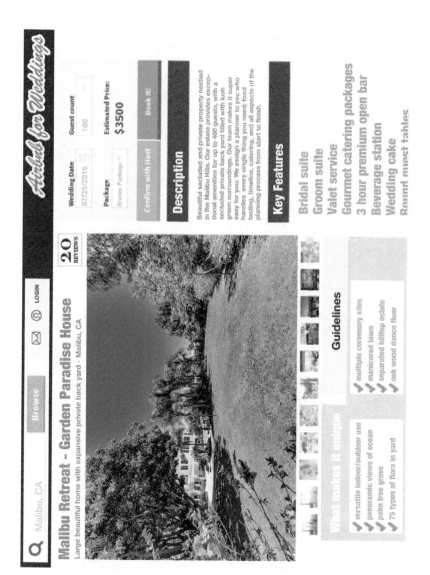

FIGURE 7-14

Airbnb for Weddings prototype screen 4

FIGURE 7-15
Airbnb for Weddings prototype screen 5

FIGURE 7-16

Airbnb for Weddings prototype screen 6

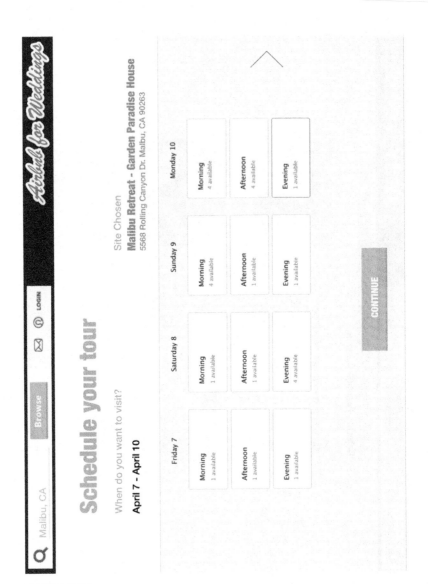

FIGURE 7-17

Airbnb for Weddings prototype screen 7

Wedding Itinerary

Confirmation Code: 2DJNE4

Email Itinerary   Print Itinerary   View Receipt

SITE

Malibu Retreat - Garden Paradise House
5568 Rolling Canyon Dr. Malibu, CA 90263

DATE

Saturday July 25, 2015

GUESTS

100 guests

COST

Venue	$3000
Catering	$1100
Flowers	$1000
Valet Parking	$265
Entertainment	$875
TOTAL	**$6240**

FOOD PACKAGE

Gold Package

FIGURE 7-18
Airbnb for Weddings prototype screen 8

Screens 1 through 5 are Airbnb concepts reworked with content.

Screen 6 is the DIRECTV package retooled for a wedding package.

Screen 7 is the appointment booking system lifted from Apple's Genius bar.

Screen 8 was custom designed.

Feel free to create the first version using whatever tool (pencil, white-board, Photoshop, or whatever works for you) will help you and your team work the fastest. When you know what's going on in the entire solution prototype, it's time for you or the visual designers to get to work.

Step 3
Paste all the screenshots into the presentation tool.

If I am working on my own, I do mockups in Photoshop. If I am work-ing with a team of designers, I advocate building the prototype by using Google Presentation. This helps the team easily collaborate as we build out different screens. The Google Presentation prototype also outputs perfectly to PDF format, as well, so it's easy to distribute. Bita and Ena decided to build their linear solution prototype in Photoshop and then exported the final product to PDF.

This is an important step, because the point of the presentation isn't to show the solution prototype to stakeholders. It's to show it to custom-ers. The users need to feel like they are *using* the interface even if it isn't interactive. Having a PDF on a pretty color screen like an iPad can be very effective in guerrilla user research (I discuss this in more detail in Chapter 8). The participant can swipe the screen at her own pace. She can move forward and back so she understands the narrative linearity of the key experience. Based on this minimal interaction, you will get great feedback. For instance, when Bita showed the solution prototype to a bride-to-be and her groom, they loved the idea of being able to have a fancy wedding in an affordable home. They had used Airbnb and understood the way private subletting worked. However, they noticed that they couldn't set up a tour in the home through the solution proto-type interface. Bita and Ena hadn't thought of that. Consequently, they adjusted it to include a calendar function with which users could pick tour dates, as illustrated in Figure 7-17. They then ran another round of experiments to show their new prototype to five more targeted custom-ers to validate that the feature was more than just a "nice to have" add.

Cool Tools for Interactive Prototypes (If You Decide to Go That Route)

Adobe Acrobat (*http://www.adobe.com/products/acrobat/create-inter-active-pdf-files.html*) Create interactive PDFs by importing images into Adobe Acrobat and making them interactive.

Balsamiq Mock-Up (*https://balsamiq.com*) A rapid wireframing tool that comes with hundreds of interaction patterns and icons for quickly creating mockup websites, desktop apps, and mobile apps.

Invision (*http://www.invisionapp.com*) Invision allows you to make high-fidelity comps in whatever tool you like, upload the .pngs, and easily share them on a mobile device for validation with customers. It's easy to capture comments and versions, too.

UXPin (*http://www.uxpin.com*) Using UXPin, you can import from Photoshop and serve up your demo on a URL where people can try out a demonstration of it.

Prott (*https://prottapp.com*) Using Prott, you can easily stitch together images, add hotspots, and output interactive prototypes that work great for testing concepts on multiple devices.

SOLUTION PROTOTYPE REALITY CHECK: WHY USER EXPERIENCES AND BUSINESS MODELS MUST GO HAND IN HAND

Remember the Business Model Canvas in Chapter 2? Let's zoom into the left side of the canvas and take a look at Figure 7-19. We need to consider how those components—key partnerships, key activities, and key resources—might affect the composition of your solution prototype.

The Business Model Canvas

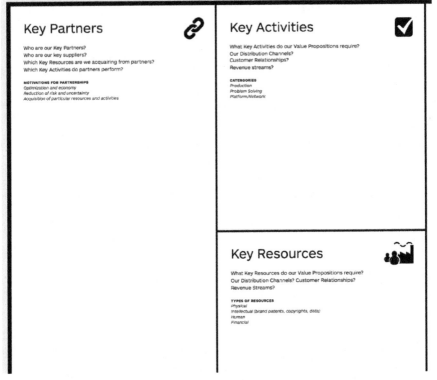

Key Partners 🔗

Who are our Key Partners?
Who are our key suppliers?
Which Key Resources are we acquiring from partners?
Which Key Activities do partners perform?

MOTIVATIONS FOR PARTNERSHIPS
Optimization and economy
Reduction of risk and uncertainty
Acquisition of particular resources and activities

Key Activities ✔️

What Key Activities do our Value Propositions require?
Our Distribution Channels?
Customer Relationships?
Revenue streams?

CATEGORIES
Production
Problem Solving
Platform/Network

Key Resources 🏭

What Key Resources do our Value Propositions require?
Our Distribution Channels? Customer Relationships?
Revenue Streams?

TYPES OF RESOURCES
Physical
Intellectual (brand patents, copyrights, data)
Human
Financial

FIGURE 7-19
Key components behind the scenes of our solution

You need to keep your team honest about the logistics behind your prototype concept. If this is the simulated digital solution of your interface, are you hyperaware of all the things that need to make it work behind the scenes? Moreover, are those things feasible and sustainable? In the case of TradeYa, obviously our concierge model was not sustainable. If we wanted to scale, we couldn't rely on Jared personally facilitating each and every transaction. He couldn't hand-hold every new user through the anxiety of making their first successful trade. So, we had to come up with a better option. (More on that in Chapter 9.)

In the case of Bita and Ena, before they showed their prototype to real users, they created a list of questions and issues that were specific to each step. Among the questions they asked themselves were who the key partners are. What are the key activities? And what and from where would they get the key resources? To get those answers, they asked these questions:

Screens 1 through 5

Where would we get the initial inventory of big houses to make it work? Can we initially build our inventory of houses by contacting people on Airbnb or other sublet listing sites?

Screen 5

How are we going to get the photography good enough to entice customers to book a private home? Can we (like Airbnb) hire a photographer to shoot the backyards and rooms?

Screen 6

How are we going to select the party vendors for the food, valet, and flowers? Should we go with fewer than a dozen to begin? How will we establish those partnerships? Is it better to focus on local, small franchises who already cater to specific areas?

Screen 7

What are the most likely time-slot breakdowns that hosts and guests will choose for private tours? Is what is shown the best breakdown or can it be limited to weekends?

Screen 8

Is it even possible to generate this type of total cost for a wedding package? Is putting the word "estimate" in there a better safeguard or will it turn off the guests who have a certain budget? What is the reality of creating packages with so many variables?

Overall prototype questions

What would make this solution easier to trial? What if we zoomed into a specific segment of the market, such as just Santa Monica or beach areas in Los Angeles? How many people would it take to truly organize this major event when it actually occurs? Do we potentially need a wedding planner who will orchestrate everything? Or, is this platform to cut out the middle man (wedding planners) and to create a turnkey solutions to save costs to the brides?

The answers to these questions change over time. For instance, where do Bita and Ena get the homes to showcase on the site? Initially, they would probably need to solicit hosts personally—much as my mother and her partner Lea did for their first clientele. As they begin to scale, Bita and Ena would need to use online advertising to bring users to the first iteration of their digital interface. They would need to sell those users the value proposition, which would cause them to join the service.

Before I get into conversion (Chapter 9), it's time to learn how to test drive your solution prototype by running face-to-face experiments on customers. It's time to engage your potential users in a guerrilla user research attack.

Recap

The moral of this chapter is: don't burn your time, money, or efforts on a product no one may want to use. Instead, concoct ways to develop and run small, structured experiments to gain validated user learnings. Do something to concierge the experience of a new product, even if it means selling it out of your own bedroom closet.

Most experiments fail, so just think through the outcomes and focus on the worthwhile takeaways. Sometimes, the results will not be black and white. Thus, you will need to interpret them by having collaborative team-debriefing discussions following each experiment.

[8]

Conducting Guerrilla User Research

Take a chance and step outside.
Lose some sleep and say you tried.
Meet frustration face to face.
A point of view creates more waves.
   —JOY DIVISION (1979)

BY RUNNING SMALL, STRUCTURED EXPERIMENTS, THIS QUALITATIVE
fieldwork will help you to immediately validate assumptions about the
value proposition and innovative key experience from the users themselves. In this chapter, you will focus on harvesting actionable takeaways from your potential customer segment through guerrilla user
research. You will use the prototype from Chapter 7 to get closer to the
truth with an open heart and mind to really hear what your potential
customers feel and think about your product's core experience. This
chapter focuses on Tenet 3, Validated User Research (Figure 8-1), and
makes use of the UX Strategy Toolkit.

FIGURE 8-1
Tenet 3: Validated User Research

Guerrilla User Research: Operation Silver Lake Café

On September 23, 2013, an unarmed team of UX vigilantes launched an organized attack on the value proposition of the software engineer I introduced in Chapter 1. The treatment center operation lasted 8 hours and involved 10 participants in two hipster café locations in Silver Lake, California. The entire team of vigilantes (team lead, UX researcher, and event coordinator) and interview participants walked away unscathed. Neither café location was compromised, and all interviews were conducted without major incident. However, the client left the scene emotionally exhausted because the result from the research falsified his hypothesis that his desired customer segment—everybody—would be willing to pay for this solution, which left his business model in shambles.

Here is how the events played out:

1:10 p.m.

A UX researcher arrives at Café Location One. She buys a coffee and leaves a large tip. She then walks to the upper level to find an isolated area, out of view from café workers. The area has about six square tables. All the seats are taken, so she waits for a table to clear.

1:30 p.m.

A table clears with two seats; the UX researcher grabs the table and throws her extra jacket over the one seat. She takes out her laptop to test the WiFi connection and AC power outlets. While she sets up, Jaime (team lead) and the client (the software engineer) enter the café. They buy coffee, leave a large tip, and make their way upstairs. They make eye contact with the UX researcher and scan the area for a possible primary interview table for three.

1:45 p.m.

A table for three clears that is near an AC outlet and also has a view of the staircase. Jaime sits at the seat facing the stairs. The client sits opposite from her. Jaime texts the event coordinator: *The interview location is ready.* The event coordinator takes his position in front of the café and pulls out his clipboard to look official. His job is to catch participants before they enter the café.

1:55 p.m.

Participant One shows up at the cafe. The event coordinator greets him at the door. The coordinator walks Participant One into the café and up the stairs to the primary interview table. He introduces him to the team lead and client. Before he leaves, the event coordinator takes Participant One's order for coffee.

2:05 p.m.

Participant Two shows up five minutes late. The event coordinator greets her at the door. He walks her upstairs to the secondary interview table with the UX researcher, who greets her in a respectful and professional manner. He then takes her order for coffee and goes downstairs to buy the beverages; he leaves a large tip. The event coordinator returns upstairs with the beverage orders for both participants. It's at this time that he also gives them their cash payments. While the interviews commence, he then goes back outside and waits for the next set of participants to arrive.

2:10 p.m. to 2:45 p.m.

The team lead and UX researcher conduct 30-minute interviews and wrap them up on time (Figure 8-2). The client listens to the interviews and takes notes in real time that are saved in the cloud for the team to view. When concluded, the team lead and UX researcher quickly discuss if any changes need to be made to the interview questions. They make those edits and then text the event coordinator to bring up the next participants.

FIGURE 8-2
Guerrilla research interview in session at Café Location One: team lead on left;
participant faces the wall; client on the right

2:55 p.m to 4:59 p.m.

During this block of time, Participant Three arrives. Participant
Four ends up being a no show, and Participants Five and Six arrive
as planned. The event coordinator greets each participant at the
door, takes them upstairs to the appropriate interview table, takes
their drink order, delivers it, and pays them. The team lead and
UX researcher conduct and conclude the remaining interviews on
time while the client continues to observe and take notes.

4:45 p.m.

After the last scheduled participant arrives, the event coordinator
heads down to Sunset Boulevard to Café Location Two. He orders a
sandwich and beverage and then finds a table near an AC adaptor
to prepare the next location.

5:00 p.m.

The interviews at Café Location One wrap up after three hours. A
total of five participants have been interviewed. The UX researcher,
team lead, and the client discuss their findings, capture their
insights, and tweak the interview questions for the second set of

participants at Café Location Two. The UX researcher goes home; she's not needed for any more interviews. Jaime and the client head down the block to the second location. They meet the event coordinator and order dinner. By 5:20 p.m., the event coordinator takes his position at the door with his clipboard.

5:30 p.m.

Participant Seven arrives. The event coordinator greets him at the door. He takes the participant to the table.

6:00 p.m.

Participant Eight arrives 30 minutes early through a back door in the café. She heads directly to the interview table and interrupts the interview in session. Jaime takes Participant Eight over to the event coordinator who deftly handles the situation. Jaime finishes up the interrupted interview.

6:30 p.m. to 8:30 p.m.

Two more interviews are conducted without issue. One participant who was intentionally double-booked at the halfway point shows up, is paid, and is excused after 30 minutes.

8:30 p.m.

The interviews at Café Location Two wrap up after three hours. A total of three more participants have been interviewed at this location.

9:00 p.m.

The client, Jaime, and event coordinator discuss their findings and capture their insights. The debriefing session concludes, and all parties go home.

After a long day, a week of planning, and a $5,000 research budget, we didn't even need to look at the notes afterward or analyze what we found. It was clear the participants consistently admired and applauded the solution prototype. They loved the value innovation and key experiences demonstrated through the UX in the prototype. But, the stakeholder knew in his heart that he had a major pivot on his hands. Even though the customers were enthusiastic about the solution, they continually invalidated his business model—channels, revenue stream, and cost structure. (See the business model canvas in Chapter 2.) Without it, his product wasn't sustainable. He had to go back to the drawing board, pivot, or make a tough choice about whether to continue or not.

Lessons Learned

- When you put key stakeholders in front of a real customer, they will learn the good or bad news sooner rather than later, directly from the source.

- An organized, well-coordinated, and mobile team effort is essential to successful field research.

- To get validated learnings, you don't need to invest in an expensive or time-consuming endeavor.

User Research versus Guerrilla User Research

The purpose of conducting user research is to understand the needs and goals of your target audience in order to inform the value proposition of the product. There are many traditional techniques for understanding users' perceptions including card-sorting, contextual inquiries, focus groups, and surveys. There are hundreds of books that you can buy to learn user-research techniques. The two recent ones that I like are *UX for Lean Startups* by Laura Klein[*] and *The User Experience Team of One* by Leah Buley.[†]

User research usually involves usability testing and/or ethnographic research. Each has advantages and disadvantages, and it's important to know the difference so that you can decide what kind of research is best for your product and process.

Usability testing focuses on whether your products work by discovering how people use the product in real time. Data points tested in a usability study include the following:

- Does the user perform the required tasks using the interface?

- How many clicks does it take for users to perform them?

---

[*] Klein, Laura. *UX For Lean Startups*. O'Reilly Media, 2013.

[†] Buley, Lean. *The User Experience Team of One*. Rosenfeld Media, 2013.

- How long does it take for the user to figure out your product?

The answers to these kinds of questions can validate whether your product's calls to action are positioned correctly, whether the user can find important information, or if the nomenclature of the navigation is clear. Traditionally, usability testing is conducted in special usability labs with two-way mirrors or on the premises of large corporations. Nowadays, it can be conducted remotely by using online services (such as *Usertesting.com*) that provide quick, reasonably priced screencast videos that record how people use your product or prototype while speaking their thoughts. However, usability testing generally is to interaction design what quality control is to physical product design. This means that it's typically conducted after the product is completed but before it's released to the general public.

In contrast, ethnographic research—the study of people in their natural environment—is all about getting to the deep, dark places much like the qualitative personas Alan Cooper advocated in Chapter 3. To get an idea of how in-depth it can be, let's look at one of my heroes, anthropologist Dr. Genevieve Bell from Intel. In 2005, I saw her give an inspiring keynote speech about a project she conducted in Asia to learn how people use technology. The research was meant to gather insights from developing countries to inform Intel on future chip designs. Over two years, Dr. Bell visited hundreds of households in 19 cities in 7 countries. She described one story about how she tracked down a woman in a remote village. Even though the woman didn't have water or electricity or even a computer, she still regularly corresponded by email with her son who was away at college. So how did that happen? The woman walked dozens of miles to a family's home, and the family helped her with all email transmissions. The woman never used the computer at all!

That kind of user research takes some hardcore contextual inquiry. And although I admire Dr. Bell, her intense fieldwork, and her comprehensive and thought-provoking analysis, most of us don't work for Intel or have the time and money to spend on that kind of research. When I try to estimate the expenses myself—more than 200,000 air

otels, guides, per diem, 19 field notebooks[‡]—my mind
you're working for a big-budget client, large enterprise,
sion with long-term initiatives for product strategy, it's
ikely that you're dealing with a research-averse stake-
a big rush to "get something out there." In this case,
to perform any user research whatsoever can be a chal-
you need to have faster ways of conducting qualitative
user research that will deliver immediate feedback with testing budgets closer to $5,000, rather than $500,000. So, what do you do?

The answer is guerrilla user research, which can be thought of as a
nonlethal form of guerrilla warfare. Guerrilla warfare is a strategic
form of confronting the enemy using a small mobile force to perform
ambushes and hit-and-run tactics. Who is "the enemy," you might wonder? The main enemies for your team are probably time, money, and
resources, because if you run out of them, you might never know if
you've actually created an innovative but sustainable digital product.
For clients with little time or no budgets, traditional user research such
as ethnographic studies would take too much time, and usability testing just isn't relevant to help determine if your value proposition is on
target or your key user experiences provide value innovation. That's
where guerrilla user research comes in—it's cost-effective and the
mobile tactics should help you to validate the following quickly:

- Are you targeting the correct customer segment?

- Are you solving a common pain point the customer has?

- Is the solution you are proposing (demonstrated in the prototype of
  key experiences) something they would seriously consider using?

- Would they pay for the product, and, if not, what are the other
  potential revenue models?

- Does the business model work?

Even clients with fat budgets should consider performing guerril-
la-style research. That's because doing this form of "lean" research is
not just about saving money, it's about saving valuable time. The tech

---

‡ http://www.nytimes.com/2004/05/06/technology/for-technology-no-small-world-after-all.
   html

industry moves at a rapid pace and innovation is a moving target. As I've talked about in many chapters, your window of opportunity to do something unique is either closing or shifting. Guerrilla user research assures you that your team's "operation" will deliver immediate, useful, and pointed knowledge.

Guerrilla Warfare: A Spotlight on Juana Galán

One of the most famous female guerrilla fighters of all time was Juana Galán (see Figure 8-3). She became known in 1808 during the Peninsular War when Napoleon Bonaparte's Grande Armée attacked Spain.* His formidable army consisted of hundreds of thousands of well-drilled and disciplined professional soldiers. To defend her home, Juana Galán organized the women in her village to fight back. She led them through highly improvisational tactics such as pouring boiling oil on roads and throwing scalding water out of windows against the French soldiers. These mobile combatants not only saved their own village but also played a part in the French army's decision to abandon the entire province of La Mancha.

FIGURE 8-3

Portrait of the Spanish heroine guerrilla fighter Juana Galán (1787–1812). Licensed under Creative Commons

---

* Rudorff, Raymond. *War to the Death: The Siege of Saragossa.* Hamilton, 1974.

THE THREE MAIN PHASES OF GUERRILLA USER RESEARCH

Guerrilla user research is different from traditional user research methods because it is fast, is lean, aligns the team vision, and provides immediate transparency with the stakeholders. But it requires a lot of coordination. Unlike a sterile research room with recording devices, you can't control your environment in the wild. So, your team needs to think through every step in the process and have several back-up plans in place. Lives might not be at stake, but cost and time must be contained!

Let's begin with a high-level review of the three phases to understand the basic breakdown of time and expense involved. Then, I will explain each phase in detail using the treatment center operation as the case study.

Planning phase (one to two weeks depending on team size and number of participants)

The planning phase is the most complicated of all three phases because it involves everything from finalizing your solution prototype to scheduling the participants. Everything must be thought through, timed, and rehearsed. Everyone involved must know their respective roles and where to stand or sit. As in a guerrilla warfare action, you need to get in, do the *thing*, and then get out quickly without being "captured" (in other words, thrown out by the café owners).

The five steps that I will teach you to ensure a successful planning phase include the following:

Step 1: Determining the objectives of the research study. Define which aspects of the value proposition and UX are being examined.

Step 2: Preparing the questions to be asked that will get us validating. Then, rehearse the entire interview along with giving the prototype demonstration.

Step 3: Scouting out the venue(s) and mapping out logistics.

Step 4: Advertising for participants.

Step 5: Screening the participants and scheduling time slots.

Interview phase (one day)

The interview phase can be the most nerve-wracking and exhilarating of all three phases, because you must prep the location, coordinate the sessions, and conduct the interviews.

The interview phase involves:

- Prepping the venue

- Participant payments, café etiquette, and tipping

- Conducting the interviews

- Taking succinct notes

Analysis phase (two to four hours)

The analysis phase is the least complicated of the three phases but is still essential. Don't get sloppy on this phase, because you need to aggregate the data captured during the interviews, debrief team members who sat in on the interviews, get the client's feedback if the clients was present, synthesize all of these inputs quickly, and ultimately decide if the interviews were effective in getting the right kind of evidence. The last step is making decisions on the best way to move forward based on your analysis.

PLANNING PHASE (ONE TO TWO WEEKS)

Step 1: Determine the objectives

In this first phase, you need to establish the objectives of the research study and define which aspects of the value proposition and UX was being examined.

Ask yourself, "What is the most important thing I need to learn to determine if this product really has any purpose, marketability, and viability?" What this means is that you need to ask what is the riskiest assumption(s) still on the table at this point in your process. In the case of the software engineer, the value proposition was still up in the air. If I use the formula introduced in Chapter 3, I can tell you that the value proposition before the guerrilla user research was basically Hotels.com for people seeking treatment for their loved ones. The software engineer's interface provided a matching system similar to Hotels.com, in which users enter a price that they want to pay. The system then offers matches in the specified price range. As in Hotels.com, the name of the rehabilitation center would be withheld until after the user booked it. A big concern was that my team didn't know if this reverse-auction business model was desirable for that user segment.

Because the business model was innately tied to the UX, this uncertainty paralyzed our ability to make any other decisions about the product. We could not move forward until we could determine the success or failure of the value proposition. This also meant that we had to decide as a team along with the client how many times we would hear the word no before heading back to the drawing table, versus how many times we would need to hear yes before moving forward. At the end of the entire operation, what would be our success criteria? That of course depended very much on the feedback from the participants we would interview.

Step 2: Preparing the interview questions

Chapter 5 discusses the distinction between quantitative and qualitative data points via a Starbucks latte (16 ounces and 90 degrees Fahrenheit versus comforting and yummy). There is also a distinction between quantitative and qualitative user research that goes beyond data points, because often we will collect both in either type. Quantitative user research generally relies on a large sample size of users. More users means more numbers. In contrast, qualitative user research will rely on a smaller selection of customers—quality over quantity. This is the main difference, and qualitative user research is the kind of research your team will conduct.

In guerrilla user research, your goal is not to place the prototype in front of 1,000 users in one day. Instead, it is to interact with 5 to 10 handpicked users to gain intensive and pointed insights. The Nielsen Norman Group believes that testing up to 5 users in a usability study is enough people before you begin to hear the same things back over and over again.[§] If you show your product to 10 users and discover that none of them likes the idea, you might have your baseline for whether the product is a success or failure. However, if you want to keep pursuing

---

§ http://www.nngroup.com/articles/how-many-test-users/

your value innovation, you need to learn information beyond the user's like or dislike. You need to persist and discover exactly why, how, and what you can change to make the product better.

Remember, these are *not* usability tests in which you just observe how the user accomplishes the task with the actual product. These are demonstrations (and not necessarily clickable) that are meant to help the participant visualize the future product clearly enough to give useful feedback on whether they can achieve their goals. You will guide the user through a key experience, and the feedback you receive will predominantly be verbal, real, raw, and in your face.

To get that kind of qualitative response, you need to really think about your interview questions. The right kind of open-ended and follow-up questions can lead to discovering opportunities for value creation you might not have previously considered.

I recommend creating your interview around two great approaches: the *problem interview*, which you learned about in Chapter 3, and the *solution interview*, which comes by way of lean guru Ash Maurya.[¶] You must carefully construct all questions; they should relate to your product and your expected UX. They shouldn't lead the participant. The questions you ask also need to be flexible enough to be easily rephrased for each participant's personal situation. For example, in the treatment center operation, some participants booked themselves into rehabilitation, whereas others booked a loved one.

Here is the general structure that I like to use when building my interview questions. You can access a copy of this format in one of the templates in the UX Strategy Toolkit online. You can also use it to capture your questions online. Share them with your team. Discuss them. Brainstorm about them. Really look at each of them to create the best interview possible.

Set up, recap/verify screener input (three minutes)

Before the participants come to the interview, you need to prescreen them through a phone call or other means, which I'll discuss in Step 5 of Phase 1. However, when they arrive onsite, you want to kick off the face-to-face interview by verifying what you already know. These

---

[¶] Maurya, Ash. *Running Lean: Iterate from Plan A to a Plan That Works*. O'Reilly Media, 2012.

questions also warm the participant up to the questions in the problem interview. To make the participants more comfortable, you might repeat back information you learned when you screened them. You might want to have them expand on any aspects that will help you understand their experience.

Here are some of the setup questions that my team asked on the treatment center operation:

- Can you tell us how many times you have booked your loved one into a rehabilitation center?

- How long was each stay and did the facility offer you discounts to prolong the stay?

- How did you find out about individual rehabilitation centers (word-of-mouth recommendation, the Internet, a list provided by a specialist, and so on)?

- If you used the Internet, how did you find the facilities (for instance, Google), and which sites did you use for finding them and learning about the specific details?

Notice how the questions would seem nonintrusive to the participants. They aren't shocked by them, because they know (based on the advertisement and screener questions) that that's why they're here. However, the questions have a second purpose, and that is to set up the context for the next part of the operation: the problem interview.

Problem interview (10 minutes)

The problem interview is set up similarly to the problem interview described in Chapter 3. The difference is that you are probably going to ask more questions and in greater detail. You want to get deeper insights about the problem, too. In these questions, ask the participants how they solved the problem in the past. Try to fully understand what their experience is like. Have them recite the timeline of problem-solving events they undertake in a linear format.

During the problem interview portion of the treatment center guerrilla user research, my team focused on payment. Who paid cash for a treatment center as opposed to using Medicare? Here are some more examples we asked in this line of questioning:

- For those rehabilitation centers for which you paid yours
  process different in terms of your options for making a

- Did the center negotiate the price with you? Do you
  received fair value for what you paid? What do you think n
  cost of the facility worth the price?

- Do you remember how long in terms of time from when you decided
  upon the treatment center and the patient actually went in? (Prompt:
  What is urgent? How long did the selection process take?)

- Was there anything specific you remember that was really great or
  really horrible about the process of finding the treatment center?

In total, we prepared 10 problem questions, and the answers definitely
gave us a lot of insight into our participants' pain points. In addition,
the questions also helped get the participants back into the mindset
of what it was like to experience those problems. In this way, we could
contextually prepare them for the solution interview.

Solution demonstration plus interview (15 minutes)

The problem interview sets the stage for the solution interview, in
which you reveal your product solution and learn if it solves the customer's problem. You might need to create several solution concepts and
a set of questions for each key experience you need to present. In the
case of the treatment center operation, my team presented three solution demonstrations for three key experiences, as shown in Figure 8-4.
If you find yourself in that scenario, schedule your time accordingly.

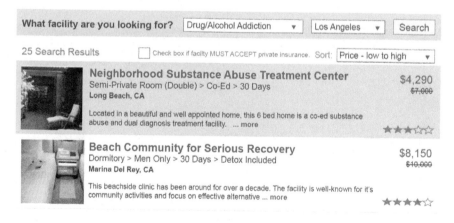

FIGURE 8-4

Portion of prototype screen from the rehabilitation study

create solution-interview questions that will encourage participants to think through your solutions and other alternatives; they might have insight into making your product better. Again, don't create or ask leading questions. Conversely, don't put participants on the spot by forcing them to brainstorm in front of you. Give them options of familiar mental models that will give the solution prototype context. Be open-ended initially with the questions, and then give enough hints and prompts to validate the solution.

Following are the solution questions for one of the key experiences (see also Figure 8-5). You might also have to contextualize the screen for the users before asking them any questions.

- Screen 1: What do you think is going on in this screen?

- Screen 2: What do you think all these pull-down options mean? (Go through each one.)

- Screen 2: What do you think the ratings are based on?

- Screen 3: This is the listing page with information about the rehabilitation center. What do you think is going on here?

- Screen 3: What do you think of the "Apply Now" button? Where do you think it will take you?

- Screen 3: You might have noticed that we don't display the treatment centers' actual names. Would that be an issue for you?

- Screen 3: Would you be comfortable applying to this facility without contacting it first?

Story 1 - Apply to a Treatment Center - 10 mins		
Screen 1 - What do you think is going on on this screen?	i like that it gives the city and price, that's important for me. It seems like as easy way to find treatment facilities and get a sense of the prices and options.	i think the prices seems really intimidating. i don't understand what the stars represent, (she assumes they are based on reviews left by past residents as opposed to expert reviews).
Screen 2 - Show dropdown/filtering in search. What do you think all these pull-down options mean? (Go thru each one)	i guess you can look for drug and alcohol or just drug or just alcohol dependence or dual diagnosis (lots of addicts mental illness and requires special place). you can sort by price, and rating, and distance, and deals (do they have deals like airplanes do?)	they are self explanatory, curious what deals means like buy 30 days get 15 free? i'm not sure what it means. i find the check box appealing because it's crucial for me to know which centers accept private insurance or not.

FIGURE 8-5

Solution demonstration interview questions from the rehabilitation study

Final thoughts (two minutes)

At the conclusion of the interview, be sure to thank the participants by name. Share with them a tidbit of the knowledge you gained from the screener interviews to make it personal, and tell them how much you value their honest feedback. Ask if they might be open for you to follow up with them in the future when you are further along with the product.

Now, your team must rehearse the entire interview using a colleague or friend to play the participant role, asking her the questions and walking her through the prototype demonstration to verify that the questions and solutions make sense.

Step 3: Finding the venue(s) and mapping out team logistics

It's important that everyone—stakeholders, the product team, and anyone else—take advantage of this opportunity to interact one-on-one with your intended customer. So work with them to ensure that they will attend.

Determine how many people are going to be part of each interview. No matter if you are running multiple interviews simultaneously or one at a time, try always to have one note taker (ideally the client or stakeholder) and one researcher doing the interview. Taking notes and trying to ask questions at the same time consumes valuable time, and it's important for the interviewer to focus on the participant.

If you plan to schedule multiple interviews, add an event coordinator to your team who can screen participants as they come and go, handle money, and deal with any other issues that might arise. Before the interview dates, your guerrilla user research team should definitely meet and go over all their roles. In the case of the treatment center operation, my team had three preparatory meetings to go over logistics, location, and scheduling.

A big question I always hear is why a café; why not my office, or a lab? Here's why:

- You want the participants to feel like this is an informal meeting. They should be comfortable enough to not feel judged, unlike when being watched through a two-way mirror in a lab.

- The participant will be in a somewhat familiar environment around other people as opposed to a sterile lab or private office in a large building or a coworking space. Your team is the minority; the participant is not.

- Cafés are free locations! There's no need to rent a lab or a coworking space. (A hotel lobby can be okay, too, but these locations can be more difficult to access and even harder to find free or nearby parking.)

- The clients or product stakeholders also can interact with their potential customer in this informal setting. Instead of being separated by a mirror, or surrounded by colleagues, it's just them, their product, and a person telling them to their face whether they like it or not. It's hard for any stakeholder to remain on Fantasy Island after that.

Here's a list of the most important rules for choosing your café:

- Find and spend some time at a café you like at the exact time of day that you plan to do your study. Ensure that it's not loud, difficult to find, or insanely busy on the days you want to conduct your interview. I tend to gravitate toward sole-proprietor cafés and away from busy franchises such as Starbucks. Find the café that fits your needs best.

- Test the WiFi connection. Ensure that there are multiple tables that can comfortably seat three people with nearby AC power outlets.

- Ensure that the tables are not in line-of-sight of café workers or near an entrance. You want to be tucked out of the way.

- You'll need to camp out for three to four hours on interview day so choose a counter-service type café or coffee shop without table service. You'll want to avoid being disrupted or asked to leave before all interviews are done.

On Not Using Recording Devices

Note-takers are vital components to my interviews because I don't use recording devices. I capture data in real time and then debrief with the stakeholders immediately afterward. I used to use devices but have since abandoned them for the following reasons:

* Recording devices make people more self-conscious. Some participants are concerned about sounding stupid, and others fear the recordings could make their way to a more public place like the Internet. In the case of the treatment center project, this was an important issue because the participants were talking about very personal experiences.

* It's more efficient and cheaper to bring a person who can type fast notes straight into a spreadsheet or any text document than spending the time transcribing them after the fact.

* When conducting an interview, it's better to be in the moment and fully engaged in the conversation as opposed to playing around with recording devices or notes. I pay far more attention to what participants are saying and doing when I know that I won't have a second chance to listen to the interviews.

* When you debrief with the stakeholder and your team immediately after the interview, you can instantly make decisions and take action on whether to abandon, refine, or move forward with your solution.

Step 4: Advertising for participants

In certain cases, researchers recommend finding unpaid volunteers because they believe money influences the participants' answers. Still, you can't stop people from lying, whether they are paid or not. There is a fine balance between compensating people fairly for their time and extracting the right information from the right people. I recommend compensating participants, because at this point during your strategic endeavor, *they* are helping *us*.

Payment amounts also depend on whom you are targeting and how much they value their own time. Seemingly, if you need to speak with busy professionals, you'll have to pay a lot more then you might to other customer segments. Make your payment high enough to recruit worthwhile participants but low enough to keep your study affordable.

ıe advertisement that participants will be paid in
If you're not sure where to start, try a payment of
minutes. During the initial screening calls with
probe them to ensure that they have the insights
end up paying the people who will really help your

ıter operation, my team initially advertised for par-
ıist. Here are some other ways:

- Facebook friends (if you have a lot, ask your network for introductions to their friends).

- LinkedIn Special Interest Groups (post to specific relevant groups).

- Meetup Groups (attend meet-up groups in your area or post to them).

- Twitter (use # [hashtags] for casting a wide net or @ profiles for hopefully gaining a retweet among a specific group of followers).

- Get referrals of friends of friends who fit your customer segment.

- Canvas an area where there is a high concentration of your target customer segment. For instance, my students at the University of Southern California (USC) were able to recruit participants for their field study by setting up a table in a highly trafficked area on campus and offering free sodas (to those who passed their screener questions) in exchange for making an appointment to be part of the research study.

Just be aware of the implicit bias if you recruit from family and friends.

My team opted for Craig's List because we assumed it would cast the widest net and get us the fastest responses possible. And it did. Within two days, we had about 75 responses. (I will discuss how to screen through candidates in Step 5 of Phase 1.) However, when we learned after the Silver Lake operation that we needed to target a more affluent customer segment, we opted for another method (see Chapter 9).

When advertising for participants, keep the copy of the advertisement simple. Here is a basic framework of a Craig's List ad for you to build off of:

Title: Paid Research Study: Looking for <customer type> who have experience with <problem type>

Body: Market research firm in <city> is looking for <more specific customer type> participants to join an upcoming paid research study.

The study is going to be on <day and date of the week> during the hours of <# - #> at a café in the <part of town> area. Please let us know the ideal time that works for you.

The study will last for <#> minutes and the compensation is $<##.00>. (optional) The study will not be recorded on audio or video.

Please respond with your contact information and the best time to reach you.

(optional) Link to survey here:

The framework can change based on the requirements of the study, as is evidenced by the advertisement we used for the treatment center operation shown in Figure 8-6.

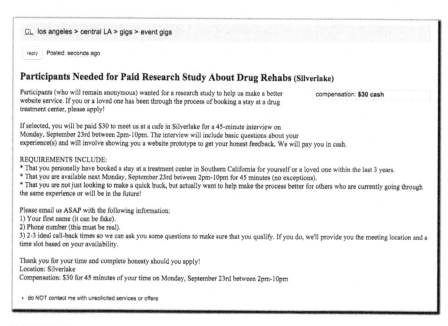

FIGURE 8-6

Craig's List advertisement for participant recruiting for the treatment center project

No matter the advertisement, make it clear whom you are looking for and why you need their help. The copy should hook your potential customer segment so that they do respond with genuine interest. Date, location, and time will depend on your customer segment. For example, in the treatment center operation, my team needed to schedule interviews on a business day, starting in the late afternoon and running into the evening to accommodate people's work day. In contrast, Bita and Ena (my former students whom I introduce in Chapter 3) ran their guerrilla user research on a Saturday because that's when busy brides-to-be tended to be free.

When posting your advertisement on Craig's List, you have the option of two kinds of ads: free or paid, with some cost variance by city. For example, it's more expensive to run job ads in San Francisco than Los Angeles, and whether you choose a paid ad will depend on which category you think your customer segment will visit. The two most common sections for running research study ads on Craig's List Los Angeles are in the "et cetera" and "general labor" sections. If you are not in a hurry and don't want to pay people, you can try the "volunteer" section, too.

Step 5: Screening participants and scheduling time slots

When you post an advertisement on Craig's List or elsewhere, you are likely to get responses. But how do you know if the respondents are the people you actually want to interview? This is why screening participants is the most critical part of the planning phase. You must choose participants who match your hypothesized target customers to ascertain if you are validating the correct problem with your solution. This is where thoughtful construction of screening questions comes into play. Look at your provisional persona and think about the critical characteristics needed. Don't fill your interview with friends or family. By doing so, your study is no longer a "controlled" experiment.

As is discussed in Chapter 3, good screener questions help you to weed-out the wrong people. Yet, whereas you conducted them in person in Chapter 3, you can do it digitally now. You might ask respondents to your advertisement to answer questions that you know are deal breakers. You could send them to a tool such as Survey Monkey or even a Google document. For the treatment center operation, we needed a subject matter expert (SME) to screen our candidates. Whenever a person responded to our ad, that person's information was captured in a document available to the entire digital team and client. You can see an example of this template in Figure 8-7.

USER RESEARCH STUDY (SCREENER): Silverlake - September 23, 2013				
Name	Phone Number	Time Booked	High-level Details	Rating 1-3 If we should choose them (3=yes, 2=maybe, 1= no).
Sarah	323-398-4789	2pm @ Vita	Has a son who is now an attorney who is a recovering cocaine addict. He went to three different paid treatment centers.	2+
Mark	323-527-6213	2pm @ Vita	Has a 42 year-old heroin addicted daughter. Just went through booking treatment at a rehab in OC. Very sharp and nice. He will be great for us.	3
Julie	310-631-0084	3pm @ Vita	Very articulate. Has been in recovery for 7 years and glad to be of service. Paid for own treatment at Promises. Went in for addiction to meth.	3
Steve	818-495-6893	3pm @ Vita	Has a lot of experience being in treatment. Last stay was 3 yrs ago for alcoholism. Sounds very educated and knows the drill.	3
Ben	619-548-3496	4pm @ Vita	Self. But also has helped numerous people enter treatment. very knowledgeable of the process from a - z. wants to help. also in silverlake area.	2

FIGURE 8-7
Participant screener and schedule

Because the respondent sent her phone number in their initial contact, the SME was able to call her back. He always began the conversation by double-checking the initial information and documenting any changes. He asked for the participant's name, phone number, and times and dates she'd be available. Then, he asked her the screener questions, such as the following:

- Were you the person seeking treatment or were you seeking treatment for someone else?

- Do you mind telling me how much you paid? Where and when did you go? (To confirm it was residential and for how long.)

We needed people who had paid for themselves or loved ones to go to a treatment center, which is why we asked the first question. We needed their experience to be recent (within three years), and we needed to ensure that they could afford paying a certain amount for a rehabilitation, which is why we asked the second question. We also ensured that the ad didn't reveal that potential participants would be grilled with screener questions as a means to help cut out respondents who just wanted to make money.

After we had this data, the SME gave each participant a rating of 1 (no), 2 (maybe), or 3 (yes). After the SME's debrief, my team called all the "3" participants to officially schedule them for an interview. Because people's schedules change, ensure that you try to get them in within 5 to 10 days later.

INTERVIEW PHASE (ONE DAY)

In this second phase, your team is now executing the planning phase. Everything needs to run like clockwork, like the choreography of a ballet. If something goes wrong, the action cannot stop. Everybody must know their places and how to react and adjust if something unexpected happens. The show *must* go on.

Prepping the venue

Arrange for each researcher to arrive at the café to find a good table at least 30 minutes before the interviews begin. Before the interview day, you should instruct them on where and how to set up in the quietest area possible; you probably observed where this should be when you found the location. As mentioned previously, it should be out-of-view from café workers and away from major walkways, such as entrances or exits. All devices and laptops should also be charged before arrival. But to be safe, find tables near an AC power outlet, especially if you're going to be there for a while. Try to avoid sitting by a window or in an outdoor area where there might be glare on the computer or device screen.

There should be one researcher for each table you need. The researchers should each bring a jacket to throw over an extra chair to save it. You don't want another patron to interrupt an interview or distract the researcher by asking if it's free. The researcher should do what she can to limit the participant's visual distraction, too. For example, the researcher can sit facing out toward the main café while the participant sits facing the researcher and only the wall. The table should be clean—food and beverages should be limited. Your team should always have eaten beforehand, and participants should receive at least one beverage of their choice.

Ideally, your team will play your solution prototype on a tablet device because it's easier to pass to participants, and unlike a laptop screen, it won't block the participant's face from you. Ensure that all devices work properly before the interviews begin. Is your demonstration functioning properly on it? Can each device connect to WiFi? If a stakeholder or note-taker joins the researcher, they should sit directly across from each other; this way the participants will sit in between them, providing an optimal view of their reactions and interactions with the demonstration.

Participant compensation, café etiquette, and tipping

Designate a team member to pay the participants upfront. In our Silver Lake scenario, the event coordinator was in charge of this, but it could just as easily be the stakeholder, team lead, or UX researchers. Get the money out of the way early so that the participants don't wonder about it. Pass it to them in an unsealed envelope as opposed to handing it to them under the table like it's a drug deal.

Sometimes, participants are concerned about what the compensation means—will this interview be used against them somehow? In the case of the treatment center operation, this was a real concern because we were documenting personal and emotional experiences. Because you've screened them beforehand, however, you know that they have a personal interest in helping you; it's just a matter of reassuring them to participate sincerely. Pay them upfront, and be genuine. Explain that you are paying for their honest feedback. Tell them that you're not here to pitch the product. This isn't a "beta-test." This is just the concept of a new potential product. My team even sometimes says they're not the people designing it (even though we are) to put some participants at ease.

Because you are using this café or eatery location for free, be cognizant that it is a place of business; don't be a cheapskate. Spend some money on beverages and food, and most importantly overtip. The team lead or event coordinator should bring a big wad of bills broken into smaller denominations. I have on several occasions put $10 in the tip jar while making eye contact with a barista to ask if it was possible to turn down the music.

Conducting the interviews

Conducting a good interview for gaining worthwhile insights is an art form to be mastered with practice. To learn more, check out a book called *Interviewing Users* by Steve Portigal.[**] It is an outstanding primer focused specifically on interviewing techniques for conducting user research out in the wild. If you are shy or new to talking to customers, practice with team members and friends beforehand.

Here are my basic guidelines for conducting your guerrilla user research interviews:

- Always greet people with a warm smile. I typically stand up to shake hands and immediately thank them for coming.

- Do not begin interviews with small talk. Be professional. You want to quickly build a rapport with them and avoid dwelling on how cool the café is or how difficult it was to find parking.

- Quickly state the reason why they are there and that you looking to them for their brutal honesty. Then, launch into your setup questions.

- Stick to the script. Ask additional follow-up questions if needed to probe deeper into specifics about how they currently solve the problem. Find out how, if, and why your solution would work or not work for them.

- Have the note-taker set his phone as an alarm to keep your pace (typically 15 minutes). The ringer should be on silent so that the phone vibrates to indicate to the researcher at the table that it's time to move on to the solution portion of the interview, even if there are more questions to go.

- Ensure that you schedule buffer time between participants in case an interview does go longer than planned or a participant shows up late.

- At the end, thank the participants for their time and tell them how helpful their insights were.

** Portigal, Steve. *Interviewing Users*, Rosenfeld Media, 2013.

You also should be able to make slight changes to questions and the solution prototype throughout the day. This is another benefit for your team to conduct, collaborate, and capture data in the cloud. You can update questions in real time and keep all researchers abreast of the changes. However, don't do anything more than small changes to the demonstration. Your researcher or team member will need to make the change and share the update to all interview groups before the next round of participants arrive. Also, you don't want to change the demonstration and questions too much; otherwise, you'll disrupt the baseline for your control group.

Extracting succinct notes

The reason you conduct guerrilla user research is that at the end of the day, 90 percent of the work is done, the information is organized, and your team has some action items to do. So, your note-taker is a very important component on this day. He should ideally be typing notes into a computer document during each interview. You can even have him type it directly into the UX Strategy Toolkit so that the information is viewable by the team in real time. If he is taking notes on paper, he had better be fast; immediately after the interviews he'll need to transcribe notes into the cloud or into a document that is shareable with the team.

During the interview, the note-taker should not worry about spelling. She can go back and fix it later. She should try to distill participants' responses into short sentences that encapsulate the essence of their responses. She should focus on capturing answers (see Figure 8-8) to script questions without noting additional insights—that can come later when there is a lull between interviews and team members can talk. Or, it can come at the end of the day when the note-taker can clean up the data a little and provide insight into how to fine-tune a solution or pivot.

FIGURE 8-8
Team members Bita (middle) and Ena (far right) during the Solution demo portion of the interview at a Culver City café. Participant on the left.

During or after the interviews, the note-taker or you can also color code the spreadsheet to help make the analysis quicker (just as in Chapter 5 when you analyzed the competition.) A major pain point would be color-coded red. If a key experience or product concept received an easily fixable response, the note-taker could color-code it green. Feel free to develop your own system.

ANALYSIS PHASE (TWO TO FOUR HOURS)

As I described at the beginning of the chapter, my team and the software engineer didn't need to analyze our findings after the guerrilla user research. It was clear that the business model didn't work. The users we interviewed were interested in the value proposition, but they couldn't afford or were not willing to put down a large enough sum of money Hotels.com-style to sustain the business model. The product, as it was, needed a direct channel to an affluent customer segment.

However, if it's not that obvious, the analysis phase involves synthesizing all the feedback from the interviews to determine your team's next action. Did the guerrilla user research validate or invalidate your assumptions? Was the experiment a failure because the execution was sloppy? Or, did something unforeseen occur such as in the case of the treatment center operation, in which we learned the business model did not work? Your goal is to use the analysis as a decision point to pivot in a different direction or double-down on further experiments that actualize the value proposition.

At the bottom of the template is a row called "Validated Learnings." This is where you can put your high-level findings for each participant and track which participants either validated or invalidated your solution hypothesis, as shown in Figure 8-9.

Validated Learnings

Liked the overall design of the prototype. However, would doubtfully book a treatment center online for his daugher without knowing the name of the facility and getting a personal tour of it. Invalidated the business model.

FIGURE 8-9
Validated Learnings sample cell

To do the analysis, you need to take a step back as you did in Chapter 5. Zoom out from all the details that you were just bombarded with and think carefully about the big picture. You might find yourself doing one of these things:

- Assess to determine if the correct customer segment was reached, by looking at your provisional personas or initial customer discovery research. If it was not the correct customer segment, begin making new assumptions about the right one.

- Assess if the problem that your product is trying to solve is an actual problem based on the feedback that you heard. Was it a small problem or a big problem?

- Assess if the solution that you showed was on target. If people were not truly excited about the value proposed in the solution prototype, think through possible ways to improve it.

- If the value proposition was validated, congratulations! However, don't stop there. Determine if there are any easy fixes that can be made to improve the user experience.

- If the value proposition was not validated, assess why immediately. Was it because you had the wrong customer, problem, and or solution? Is it fixable? How can you change the product or user experience?

- Listen to the signal. If the experiment was an abysmal failure, resolve to take a break while you reset your entrepreneurial or intrapreneurial clock.

- If you have a client or stakeholder who does not believe in your research and wants to build the product regardless, you face an existential challenge wherein you are trying to balance your principles and your pocket book. Only you (and your spouse) can answer this one.

Enter your insights, answers, and conclusions into a spreadsheet in the UX Strategy Toolkit at the bottom of each participant's column quickly. You want to make the turnaround on your team's decisions fast.

You are now at the end of your guerrilla user research, and you are once again at a crossroads:

- You invalidated your value proposition. If you are wrong about your original customer segment, go back to Chapter 3 (customer discovery).

- You invalidated your value proposition. If you are wrong about your solution, go back to Chapter 4, Chapter 5, Chapter 6, and Chapter 7

- You validated that you have product/market fit. Go build a functional MVP and move on to Chapter 9

Recap

Conducting guerrilla user research (especially with stakeholders present) can feel intimidating at first, but the more you do it, the less scary it becomes. It has the benefits of immediacy and transparency. Plus, your entire team and the stakeholder will be better off learning sooner rather than later if your solution works. Plus, you do it as a team; everyone is equally invested in the outcome. They have the benefit of really seeing how users will experience the product.

[9]

Designing for Conversion

*You can't play in the man's game, you can't close them—go home
and tell your wife your troubles. Because only one thing counts
in this life: Get them to sign on the line which is dotted.
A-B-C. A-Always, B-Be, C-Closing.*

**BLAKE FROM THE DAVID MAMET SCREENPLAY, *GLENGARRY
GLEN ROSS***

IF YOU WANT TO BE A CLOSER, YOU MUST CONSTANTLY TWEAK YOUR UX
strategy to increase successful outcomes for user engagement and customer acquisition. You need to design efficient funnels that do everything from engage first-time visitors to eventually convert them to
repeat customers. Customers include anybody and everybody that you
need to engage for your value proposition and business model to work.
And yes, users who don't pay for your service are customers, too. As
people begin entering from the top of the funnel, you must immediately track and measure all the crucial data points along the way so that
you can validate your product's success.

This is known as *designing for conversion* or *optimizing your product*. The
process ties together all the tenets, as depicted in Figure 9-1. In this
chapter, I'll demonstrate how successful UX strategy uses analytics to
optimize the UX design from the user's first impression of the value
prop to the user becoming happily addicted to the product. A tool called
the Funnel Matrix will demonstrate how to align your entire team on
different stages of customer acquisition by identifying measurable
metrics for them to take action on to pull the customer into a deeper
level of engagement.

FIGURE 9-1

The four tenets of UX strategy all need to be served up right now

Seeding Growth Hackers

Growth hacking is a term coined in 2010 by Sean Ellis, a marketing blogger and entrepreneur.* The concept behind it is for product teams to come up with extremely clever, cost-efficient ways to increase customer growth. Facebook, Twitter, LinkedIn, Airbnb, and Dropbox are companies that have all used growth hacking techniques to become successful. Hardcore growth hackers are a crossbreed of marketers, coders, and analytics experts. They are masters of analytics tools, traffic generation, and product optimization with a deep understanding of the innards of search-engine optimization (SEO), ad platforms, and social media tools. They are called hackers because they are ruthlessly focused on growing the business by any means necessary. They push the limits of traditional marketing using techniques such as A/B tests, landing pages, viral factors, email deliverability, and social media integration. The goal of growth hacking is to tie viral and paid ad campaigns to user engagement metrics so that you can identify the most

---

* *http://en.wikipedia.org/wiki/Growth_hacking*

valuable marketing channels. Growth hacking entails continuous tinkering with the product's sales funnel so that it is fully optimized for acquiring new users and getting them more deeply engaged.

In the case of TradeYa, our core team knew we were out of our depth. We could design, strategize, and develop the MVP. We could fill out the Funnel Matrix—we knew what kind of answers we needed. What we didn't have was the expertise to get those answers from the metrics and analytics reports in front of us. We didn't know how all the tools and dashboards worked, but we had to run hardcore tests to refine and perfect our MVP to relaunch in 30 days. It was the Christmas holidays, and we were pretty sure it was a fantasy to hope for a highly advanced growth hacker with usability testing and design skills to end up at our door. Plus, we had a budget of only about $5,000. So, we decided to hack together some growth hackers of our own.

That's how the TradeYa MVP Apprentice Program was born. Jared and I wanted to diversify our budget with as many fresh minds as possible who would work collaboratively on connecting all the analytical tools we needed to update the existing MVP. They would use the Funnel Matrix to plug in the feedback data from each other of their initiatives so that we could validate all the assumptions the core team had made about the levels of user engagement. Figure 9-2 shows the blog post we used to attract the talent we needed.

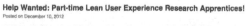

FIGURE 9-2

Help wanted: experimenters for testing the TradeYa MVP

Within 72 hours of JLR Interactive's "Help Wanted: Lean UX Apprentices" post blasting through the Twitterverse and LinkedIn, all 8 spots were filled with qualified individuals, hand-picked for this challenge. They came from all over Los Angeles and included professionals with advanced skills in architecture, marketing, engineering, and psychology, with degrees from MIT, Cornell, NYU, and UCLA. Although some of the apprentices already had an understanding of UX design and the Lean Startup approach, the intent was to take advantage of the cross-pollinating catalyst effect of their diverse expertise and backgrounds from outside of UX by throwing them into the deep end of hands-on MVP testing and optimization.

We were really lucky. Our apprentices were eager and focused when they met for the first time in an intensive workshop on January 2, 2013. During a whirlwind three hours, the eight apprentices were brought up to speed (see Figure 9-3) with the history, philosophy, and MVP of TradeYa. First they learned about the principles of conversion-centric design for customer acquisition. Then we discussed how they would stay aligned through collaboration and task delegation using a cloud-based tool that I devised called The Funnel Matrix.

FIGURE 9-3
Jaime (on left) and Jared (on right) talking about funnels while instructing the eight TradeYa Lean UX apprentices

TradeYa's testing phase ran from January 1, 2013 to February 28, 2013. Over the course of the first 30 days, the apprentices learned about analytics tools, set up those tools for TradeYa, and then acted as users themselves—trading and bidding on one another's items—to test the product's transaction funnel. They would then verify whether the tools were capturing the key metrics accurately. Any changes in hypotheses were also continually updated in the Funnel Matrix, which the entire team could view and track. For our measuring tools, we ended up using Google Analytics and KISSmetrics—the development team added JavaScript code to all HTML pages.

Jared and I closely watched and guided the development to ensure that we got the data points we needed. This way, when we launched the MVP, we would be able to track all the desired actions required for users to successfully trade.

Lessons Learned

- To design for conversion, you really need to bring together a cross-functional team including designers, developers, product managers, *and* marketers. The marketing and sales team creates a list of initiatives and must be able to act quickly on it. The development team also has a list of metrics that they need to track and measure.

- The output of the Funnel Matrix technique directly informs the user flow, feature list, and a short list of wireframes to be designed or redesigned that are optimized for a desired user action.

- The data and metrics help with every stage in the sales funnel to make continual improvements and give insights into your customers' actions.

Using the Funnel Matrix Tool

A funnel is a cone-shaped utensil with a tube at the apex for conducting liquid or another substance through a small opening. When I put oil into my car's engine, I use a funnel to increase the success rate that oil will make it directly to where it's supposed to go. The funnel is the mechanism I use to avoid waste.

In the ecommerce world, waste happens when potential customers aren't funneled into the engine of a product. Somewhere along the way, the customers did not sign up, activate their accounts, initiate a transaction, complete a transaction, or some other reason. In other terms, the customer did not experience the value proposition correctly and might have clicked away without satisfying his needs. The design of the ecommerce or digital product funnel didn't convert him into an engaged customer.

In the book *The Entrepreneur's Guide to Customer Development*,[†] authors Brant Cooper and Patrick Vlaskovits use a Funnel Matrix to represent how a prospective customer goes "from Internet 'Googler' to satisfied user." I was inspired to expand the concept and create my own tool for dialing in the metrics directly correlated to UX strategy.

The purpose of filling out the Funnel Matrix, which you can see in Figure 9-4, is to force the entire team involved with the product—stakeholders, product managers, marketers, visual designers, developers, and everybody else involved—to think through all the required actions potential users and customers must make as they progress down the funnel to become repeat users. The Funnel Matrix's other purpose is to validate, measure, and learn ways to better optimize the user's experience to increase conversion rates. After I began experimenting with, using, and tweaking this tool, I quickly discovered that it allowed me to be more empirical and less precious with my own UX strategy process.

FUNNEL MATRIX: <Your Product Name Goes Here><Month(s)/Year>								
Funnel Stage	Stage Definition (customize your own)	User's Process	Desired Action	Business Task	Metrics	Required Functionality	Validated Learnings	
SUSPECT	A suspect is user that might possibly require your product or service.							
LEAD	A lead is a potential sales contact -- an individual or organization that expresses an interest (i.e. by providing their email address) in your product or services.							
PROSPECT	A prospect is anyone who is demonstrating a desire for a particular product/service by engaging with in a valuable (to the business) way.							
CUSTOMER	A customer is a person or organization that pays to use a product or service.							
REPEAT USER	Repeat users are customers who "regularly" use your product or service.							
REFERENCE	A user who refers others (evangelizes) on behalf of your product.							

FIGURE 9-4
Funnel Matrix tool empty template

The Funnel Matrix tool shows different stages of user engagement and acquisition as well as the criteria to evaluate for each stage. I created this Funnel Matrix using Google Spreadsheets so that my team could collaborate and work on it simultaneously. (A copy of the template is available in the UX Strategy Toolkit.)

---

† Cooper, Brant and Patrick Vlaskovits. *The Entrepreneur's Guide to Customer Development.* Cooper-Vlaskovits, 2010.

Note that how you use the Funnel Matrix will depend on where you are in your product development cycle:

- If you have an existing product or MVP like Jared had with TradeYa, your team can use the entire matrix to optimize it. Tweak and measure your metrics until you get it right.

- If you are designing wireframes for your first functional MVP, use the Funnel Matrix to speculate on the levels of user engagement and the key metrics you might use. Then, you will test the top (suspect) level with something like a landing page test, which I'll discuss later in the chapter.

- If you are still in the conceptual part (storyboards, prototypes, and so on) of your UX strategy, take this as opportunity to get an overview of where you will end up when your team is ready to design for conversion. I'll also teach you what to do when you're ready to validate the top of your funnel.

WHY A MATRIX AND NOT A MAP?

At this point, a few UX strategists might scratch their heads and wonder why I'm not advocating for a *journey map* (also called an *experience map*). A journey map looks like a flowchart and shows all touch points. It's a visual representation of the user's journey and interaction through the UX of your product. It is generally created from output following a collaborative brainstorming session with product stakeholders. Sometimes these maps are quite complex to decipher, especially if you were not a participant during the session. If you haven't seen one of these maps, do a keyword search for them on Google Images.

When used effectively, a journey map can aid the UX strategist and stakeholders in envisioning cross-channel experiences through digital and nondigital touch points. Personally, I find that the map takes too darn long to create and lacks accountability because it is rarely benchmarked to the product's reality after it begins to be released. Here's what I've seen happen all too often: the key stakeholders, internal UX team, or both are called together for a consensus-building session. They break into groups, jot down ideas on sticky notes, and then post them on a wall or board. Everybody stands back while the most assertive participants reorganize the concepts into clusters. At the end of the session, someone takes photos of the lovely yellow papers. The designer turns these concept clusters into what often appear to be zany circuitous informational diagrams that would potentially give Edward Tufte‡ a stroke. The posters are then hung or stored somewhere in the office to hopefully influence employees on their way to the bathroom.

If you strive to be more empirical in your strategic process, you need to develop this approach and deliverable into a system of disciplined procedures that are gauged and updated throughout the product ideation phase and development cycle. That's why I prefer using a cloud-based matrix as a centralized data depository. With this customizable tool, everybody on a team can work collaboratively and even from multiple locations. You can usually do the first pass in two to four hours, and afterward it is easily accessible for everyone to update. The output is easy to interpret, and, more important, the matrix can serve as a central data depository for metric reports after the product is released and iterated upon. When, in his book *The Lean Startup*,§ Eric Ries talks about lean accounting with real-world metrics, this Funnel Matrix is how you can harness it for the UX. So please put your sticky notes away (at least, for now). Let's begin to explore and fill out the Funnel Matrix tool. (For a different opinion on journey maps, check out what Experience Strategist veteran Holly North has to say about them in Chapter 10.)

ROCKING THE FUNNEL MATRIX

The first time I tested the Funnel Matrix tool was on TradeYa with Jared. For months, we had been sifting through analytics reports that measured hundreds of user actions and trying to make big-picture decisions based on them. But we figured it would be more efficient to try to make smaller decisions based on validated data output from singular user actions. We needed to focus our time, energy, and money on being able to make meaningful changes to our MVP in order to answer questions coming in from our investors. Thus, Jared, the developers (who Skyped in from India), and I spent an intense four-hour period filling out the exercise.

In the UX Funnel Matrix tool, you have rows and columns made up of cells that need to be populated with your team's carefully considered input. This input is driven by your user's story, a narrative told over a specific period of time. If Jane discovers your online product (for the

‡ *http://www.edwardtufte.com*
§ Ries, Eric. *Lean Startup*. HarperBusiness, 2011.

purposes of this example, TradeYa) while cruising her Facebook feed, what stages must she go through to become an active user? She's probably not going to go from "suspect" to "repeat user" in one giant leap. Instead, she needs to be effortlessly funneled to this deeper level of interaction with your product. Therefore, each row conveys a snapshot of her story as she moves through the stages from first-time exposure to a dedicated user who eventually helps you to market your product.

You also want to set a time limit for your experiment, because it gives your team deadlines for measuring expected outcomes for different hypotheses. For TradeYa, we capped our length at 60 days. We wanted this limit because we wanted to know what it would take to have a user transition from a customer who doesn't pay to one who does. We believed that if we could not make the users convert in this amount of time, we would be at a point of diminishing returns.

THE VERTICAL AXIS

The rows in the Funnel Matrix contain the stages of user engagement for your online product. These stage labels should be directly correlated to the business model of your product, as illustrated in Figure 9-5. Different products require different engines for growth. There is a great table in the book *Lean Analytics*[¶] that I like to refer to while I go through each of the rows.

Business model						
Company stage	E-commerce	Two-sided marketplace	Software as a Service	Free mobile app	Media	User-generated content
Will it grow?	Will they find you and tell others?		Will they sign up, stick around, and tell others?		Can you grow traffic to a level that can be profitably monetized?	
Stickiness stage: Achieving a minimum viable product that engages customers in a meaningful, valuable way.	Conversion, shopping cart size. For acquisition: cost of finding new buyers. For loyalty: percent of buyers who return in 90 days.	Rate of inventory creation, search type and frequency, price elasticity, listing quality, fraud rates.	Engagement, churn, visitor/user/customer funnel, capacity tiers, feature utilization (or neglect).	Onboarding; adoption; ease of play; time to "hooks"; day-, week-, and month-long churn; launches; abandonment; time played; regional testing.	Traffic, visits, returns; segmenting business metrics by topic, category, author; RSS, email, Twitter followers and click-throughs.	Content creation, engagement funnel, spam rates, content and word-of-mouth sharing, primary acquisition channels.
Virality stage: Growing adoption through inherent, artificial, and word-of-mouth virality; optimizing viral coefficient and cycle time.	Acquisition-mode: customer acquisition costs, volume of sharing. Loyalty model: ability to reactivate, volume of buyers who return.	Acquisition of sellers, acquisition of buyers, inherent and word-of-mouth sharing. Account creation and configuration.	Inherent virality, customer acquisition cost.	App store ratings, sharing, invites, rankings.	Content, virality, search engine marketing and optimization; promoting long time on page.	Content invites, user invites, in-site messaging, off-site sharing.

FIGURE 9-5

Business model stages from *Lean Analytics*

I recommend that you start the Funnel Matrix exercise with the generic stage definitions provided but take time to customize them as the content and the data for the other cells falls into place. You might not need

---

¶ Croll, Alistair and Benjamin Yoskovitz. *Lean Analytics*. O'Reilly Media, 2013.

the exact stage labels shown in Figure 9-6, because there will be known and unknown exceptions about how people will engage with your product. But these generic labels will get you started. What is crucial about the stages is that they flow as a linear and measurable progression down the funnel of the product.

Funnel Stage	Stage Definition (customize your own)
SUSPECT	A suspect is user that might possibly require your product or service.
LEAD	A lead is a potential sales contact -- an individual or organization that expresses an interest (i.e. by providing their email address) in your product or services.
PROSPECT	A prospect is anyone who is demonstating a desire for a particular product/service by engaging with in a valuable (to the business) way.
CUSTOMER	A customer is a person or organization that pays to use a product or service.
REPEAT USER	Repeat users are customers who "regularly" use your product or service.
REFERENCE	A user who refers others (evangalizes) on behalf of your product.

FIGURE 9-6

The vertical axis of the Funnel Matrix

Start by trying to make it across the first row before defining the other stages, especially if you are new to customer development techniques. As the desired actions come into focus, you will understand that the definitions are directly tied to your actual user engagement strategy as users first begin to discover your product. Then, you work your way down. The column headings are the different factors that you need to discuss and debate with your team. I'll explain these in more detail later in the chapter.

For each stage, I will first give a generic description and then an example of what specifically we put into a cell for TradeYa. For this chapter, I will also modify the definition given at the beginning of the book in which the term "user" is interchangeable with the term "customer." For the Funnel Matrix, a user will be defined as someone who moves from the beginning of the funnel to the end and then becomes an engaged (and paying) customer.

Suspect stage

A suspect is a user who might possibly require your product or service. For TradeYa's Funnel Matrix, a Suspect was anybody who had or ever wanted goods or services. Yes, this sounds like everybody because, in fact, it means everybody. Therein lies a problem; a horizontal marketplace containing everybody is too wide. To zoom into your suspect, you need to narrow the categories to the types of goods or services that your specific segment would want. As depicted in Figure 9-7, the TradeYa Suspect is also somebody who thinks it would be cool to trade things for social reasons. We knew this type of user existed because of clothing swaps, collector clubs, and other trading sites. We felt like we were looking for a Suspect who was similar to a user who might use the bartering section on Craig's List.

Stage Definition

SUSPECT	A suspect is somebody who wants something they can not afford (or prefers not to pay for). Or somebody who has something of value (good or service) that they would be happy to sell or exchange for something else.

FIGURE 9-7
Zoomed into the Suspect stage of the TradeYa Funnel Matrix

Lead stage

A lead is a potential sales contact, an individual, or an organization that expresses an interest in your product or services by providing you with some personal contact information, generally via email. You want to have a means to contact them. This begins your official relationship with the user.

For TradeYa, a Lead is somebody who landed on a TradeYa page, regardless of how she gets there, and then signs up for the site. She could come from various touch points: social media, word-of-mouth, or an organic search.

Prospect stage

A prospect is anyone who has a need and strongly wants this need met through the purchase or consumption of your particular product. He is now in the negotiation phase toward becoming either a paid customer or engaged user (to be defined in the next stage).

For TradeYa, a Prospect is somebody who sees something he specifically wants or has something specific he wants to trade; he posts something to trade or he bids on a trade already posted on the site. This user takes the first action possible on the MVP interface toward engaging in an actual transaction of our key experience.

Customer stage

A customer is a person or organization that is valuable to your business model. Customers either pay to use the product or they contribute something that is valuable to other users. In a two-sided market and in the freemium economy of the Web, this could be content, a listing, or request.

For TradeYa, a Customer is a user who engages in and completes a successful trade. This means that after bidding, she wins the trade and successfully completes the transaction, or vice versa.

Repeat User stage

Repeat users are customers who "regularly" use your product or service.

For TradeYa, a Repeat User is somebody who is involved in multiple transactions. He trades something and then continues to offer or bid on items or services to trade.

Reference User stage

A reference user is somebody who refers others to the site based purely on her initial or continued experience. She brings other suspects to your product by spreading the word. This is called *virality* and feeds that engine of growth (refer to Figure 9-5).

The reference user can refer people to your product regardless of what stage she is in the funnel. References are crucial to improving your sales funnel because they bring new users to the site through their own personal recommendations. You must love these people and work diligently at making them insanely happy with your product.

For TradeYa, a Reference User is somebody who shares a TradeYa page, whether it is one that she was promoting or just a page she found interesting.

THE HORIZONTAL AXIS

User's Process

The User's Process (see Figure 9-8) describes the types of activities that users will be engaging in at each stage as they experience your product. Where are they exactly? What task are they trying to complete? For the UX designer on your team, the User's Process is probably going to be the easiest step in the Funnel Matrix to articulate.

For the TradeYa example, let's begin with the first level of user engagement—the Suspect. What if I were to walk outside of my house and begin screaming at the top of my lungs, "Stop spending money. Use TradeYa!" For the neighbors who hear me, this action would trigger their first impression of TradeYa as a product. A new neighbor across the street—one who doesn't know me—might either ignore me or call the police. However, my friendly next-door neighbor might overhear these words and want to learn more.

User's Process
They see an item or hear about TradeYa somehow (i.e. press, word-of-mouth, social networks, etc.) that attracts them to the site.

FIGURE 9-8

User's Process cell in the TradeYa Funnel Matrix

Consequently, for the Suspect's user process, you must think, "What are my initial touch points with potential customers?" The phrase "touch point" is business jargon for however you first "touch" or engage with your customer. A Suspect might discover TradeYa on social media. Or, instead of discovering a product through a neighbor's yells, maybe he sees a friend's tweet or Facebook post with a shared TradeYa link: "Check out this surfboard that I'm trading!" Suspects also might discover TradeYa or a TradeYa item listing through an organic search.

Ultimately, what should go in this column cell is what your team thinks are the most likely ways users will initially discover the product. These "ways" are your sales channels and tactics for acquiring customers. Discover, explore, and experiment with all of them.

Desired Action

The Desired Action for the Funnel Matrix (see Figure 9-9) is what you hope users do in response to the "process" they just experienced. It is the action that you want them to take. This could be anything from favoriting a tweet, downloading your app, or clicking a link to a web page.

Desired Action
(1) Lands on TradeYa homepage and is presented with the multiple TradeYa items and is not required to "Onboard" or log-in until they click a required logged-in action. (2) Lands on TradeYa item page because user is coming from a direct referal link

FIGURE 9-9

Desired Action cell in the TradeYa Funnel Matrix

Let's go back to my TradeYa example on the residential street. If my new hypothetical neighbor hasn't called the police, she potentially a) whipped out her smartphone and googled TradeYa, b) searched for TradeYa on her computer later at home or work, or c) shared the strange experience with her social network or at the office with her coworkers around the espresso machine.

But joking about yelling aside, the desired response for the Suspect stage is for your user to have a positive reaction to her first exposure to your project. Obviously, bad first impressions equal very bad UX. You must ensure that the suspect reacts in the way that you want. Think about what happens next for her in terms of the type of content/messaging/experience that she encounters. Are there one or more scenarios or technology contexts (for example, mobile versus desktop) that need to be addressed? Do all new users come through the front door (your product's home page) or can they also come through various side doors (a Facebook link from a friend's feed that goes to a product-level page)? In each case, you'd better ensure that the value proposition is conveyed clearly.

To fill out the Desired Action cell in your Funnel Matrix, think about what your primary goal is for that user to perform. It could be any type of activity, ranging from getting the user to enter his email address, to signing in with his Facebook account, to clicking the "Place your order" button. If your product's revenue stream is from selling banner or video advertising, the goal is to make the content pages more compelling with plenty of "Read More" links to keep customers clicking and swiping. If you want to increase the Time on Site (ToS), you probably want plenty of related onsite articles to keep users bouncing around your pages like an endless game of pinball.

The desired response can be different depending on the user's level of engagement. A suspect just needs to have a positive experience, but a Customer might need to respond by clicking a Submit or Buy button. Think on a granular level about the shortest path of required actions to get your users happily down the funnel.

Business Task

Now take off your UX strategy hat and put on your marketing cap. It's time to look at the Funnel Matrix from the standpoint of your business goals, as illustrated in Figure 9-10. This is where you need to address what must happen behind the scenes to enable the user's process. This includes both tried-and-true online advertising campaigns and new forms of growth hacking. The basic concept is to build marketing organically into the product, as opposed to piling it on top of the completed product and then tying it back with metrics. This is absolutely critical to the UX strategy. Business strategy and interaction design must go hand-in-hand.

Business Task

SEO / Social Media campaigns / Publicity outreach / Paid advertising traffic

FIGURE 9-10

Business Task cell in the TradeYa Funnel Matrix

Thus, the business task at the Suspect stage for you and your team is to find new channels and try lots of experiments to reach your potential customers and grab their attention. This requires consideration of the different touch points and contexts in which users might discover your product—on Facebook, on their mobile devices, on their computers at work, or simply overheard at the espresso machine.

Fill your Business Task cell in the Funnel Matrix with creative and rational expectations for your business to meet, such as buying Facebook advertising to increase traffic or clever social media campaigns. You want to get users to promote your product because it makes them look cool. Just know that whatever you place in this cell needs to be truly supported by the business to obtain your desired actions.

Metrics

As sales and marketing people know too well, success is determined by the numbers. Your Funnel Matrix metrics are your units of measurement for how well (among other things) your users have performed your desired action. They can also tell you things such as how many users came from Facebook versus LinkedIn, or which of the top three major cities in the US sent the most traffic volume to the site. Metrics can be powerful indicators of success or failure if you choose to measure the right items and if that data is accurate. For each stage of user engagement, there will be one particular metric that really matters. Focus on that one like an obsessed "closer" who wants to keep his target customers engaged.

In the case of the TradeYa Suspects, this meant being able to analyze data about the behavior of new visitors, as shown in Figure 9-11. If the Suspect didn't come to TradeYa through the home page, what therefore were the most trafficked pages? What was the bounce rate? How many minutes did she interact with the site? Analytics tools provide a lot of data, but it's up to us as savvy and smart UX strategists to know which data represents the key metrics at each stage.

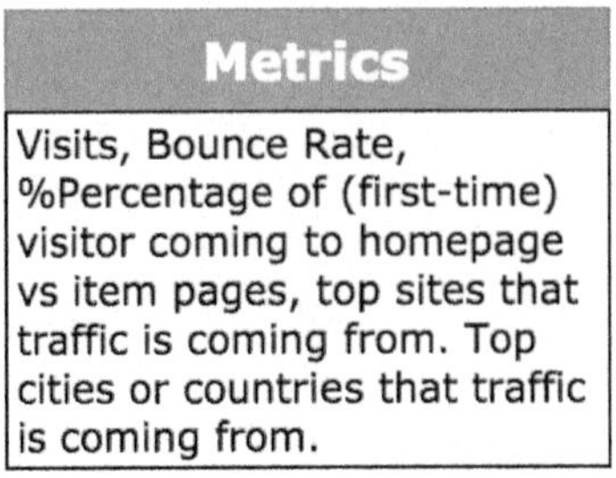

Metrics
Visits, Bounce Rate, %Percentage of (first-time) visitor coming to homepage vs item pages, top sites that traffic is coming from. Top cities or countries that traffic is coming from.

FIGURE 9-11
Metrics cell in the TradeYa Funnel Matrix

What goes in metrics columns are those quantifiable "things" you plan to measure at each stage that specifically tie a user's action to a level of engagement. Metrics are shown as totals, percentages, and ratios. Marketing people, stakeholders, and your design/development team should all become familiar with what the metrics mean. For example, a common metric is the "Average Visit Duration" (see Figure 9-12), which represents the time a user spends on the site and is measured in minutes and seconds. But this metric is more relevant for certain business models such as media sites trying to sell advertising. For ecommerce sites we should be looking at transactions. For SaaS, we dread "churn," which is the number of customers lost over a given time period. A primary goal in SaaS is customer retention. Retention = stickiness = habitual use = returning customers.

Figure 9-12 presents the Average Visit Duration metrics for a page on TradeYa.

Visits: 288,282

Unique Visitors: 181,734

Pageviews: 615,315

Pages / Visit: 2.13

Avg. Visit Duration: 00:02:04

Bounce Rate: 50.35%

% New Visits: 62.99%

FIGURE 9-12

TradeYa monthly metrics from 2013

Lean Startup guru Eric Ries states that the real metrics are "actionable metrics that either confirm or refute a previously stated hypothesis (stated in customer discovery)." This means that you want to measure things that demonstrate your product is actually *working* and that the users are engaged. However, investors and stakeholders like totals and percentages, so a common trap is to look at page views or other vanity metrics that don't represent anything more than your ability to buy or drive traffic to your landing pages. Vanity metrics only represent how many people have come to your front door. What really matters more is what percentage of those people opened it and began snooping around. It's easy to get lost in all the data that can be captured or to measure the wrong things that mean nothing at all. Your focus needs to be on measuring true indicators or "key metrics" that signify that your value proposition is working. Investors and stakeholders want to know about percentages.

Required Functionality

The required functionality are the features and platforms (i.e., Twitter) that your team must enable and integrate for that level of the funnel to work from a UX perspective. Filling out this column is a shortcut to distilling the feature set for an MVP or beta version of a product. This feature set must work for an entire user journey and is absolutely critical to the product itself working.

Each feature needs to be something that will make the product better and easier to use rather than more complicated. Focus on the features that enable the product to work well and that are carefully considered from these multiple perspectives: user value, level of effort to build, and business value. Balance the level of effort it will take to build the feature set against the impact it could have on the product. How many people will actually use it or have requested it? Is it a unique feature to your product that will set it apart from competitors, or will it just be a neat gimmick that people will try once and never use again? The Funnel Matrix tool will help you to measure the impact by tying it to specific engagement metrics. After you have traction, you can experiment with more risky features.

For TradeYa, the features that were absolutely crucial were the ability to bid on an existing trade and the ability to post a specific item to trade (see Figure 9-13). Account creation was circumvented by requiring users to have and sign-in via a Facebook account. We also needed a polling feature to learn what our customers were interested in trading. As discussed in Chapter 7, we chose to hold off on user profiles and a transactional system because they were not critical to our first goal: get people to trade something on TradeYa with the lowest barrier to entry.

Required Functionality
TradeYa landing page with Google Analytics set up. TradeYa Twitter profile. TradeYa Facebook profile.

FIGURE 9-13
Required Functionality cell in the TradeYa Funnel Matrix

Validated Learnings

At this point, we take heed and inspiration from Thomas Dolby and his song "She Blinded Me With Science": "She blinded me with science and hit me with technology." Yes, it's time for you to put on your lab coat and think like scientists, logically and without emotion. The entire purpose of this Funnel Matrix is to help you answer qualitative questions about your product using verified data for comparative benchmarking. These questions that you ask are to keep your team honest about your customer's behavior and business tasks throughout each level of engagement. Like scientists, you must ask tough questions, analyze your data, and not be blinded by your own hopes for the outcome. Keep it real.

For TradeYa, the big question at the Suspect stage was "Where were our customers coming from who would become long-term customers?" We wanted to know which of our channels (Twitter, Facebook, Google Ads, or organic search) was the most effective. We needed to do more of whatever was working. After our suspect landed on a TradeYa page, the validated learning became more specific to the suspect's actions. What types of goods or services had the most people bidding to trade? For goods, was it laptops or furniture? For services, was it web consulting or day laborers? Were people trading more goods than services? We wanted answers to help us fine-tune the site and match the enthusiasm demonstrated by early adopters when Jared was providing concierge service. We needed to understand at a granular level who they were, where they came from, and what things they were most interested in trading.

The things you expect and need to learn about your customers go here (Figure 9-14). You are trying to devise a predictable and scalable methodology for generating engaged and evangelistic users. To get there you need repeatable outcomes from your experiments and metrics. You will notice that the questions become more specific about your customer's behavior as their engagement with your product progresses down the funnel.

Validated Learnings
What percentage of users are coming through the front door (homepage) versus a TradeYa item page? What sites are they coming from (i.e. Facebook?) What are the highest populates of cities/countries coming to the site? Do we see spikes in traffic tied to a specific marketing campaign?

FIGURE 9-14
Validated Learnings cell in the TradeYa Funnel Matrix

You need to use every logic circuit in your brain to ensure that these questions are answerable and measurable. How much traffic has come to the top-level home page from organic search compared to an item page from social media? This is a measurable question. How intrigued were these users when they got to the landing page? This is not measurable.

In his book *Programmed or be Programmed*,** Douglas Rushkoff writes: "[Not] everything is a data point. Yes, thanks to the digital archive we can retrieve any piece of data on our terms, but we do so at the risk of losing its context." What Rushkoff is talking about is the ability to look at data with a discerning eye. Or, if possible, find a way to cross-reference the validated hypothesis against other data points. So show another team member your logic for tracking metrics that validate or disprove any meaningful customer discoveries. Make sure you all agree your learnings are correct.

By now the funnel matrix exercise might feel like a science experiment. That's because it is. You are conducting a methodical procedure with the goal of validating or falsifying your hypothesis—your product's unique value proposition to your perceived customers. You are using metrics to give insight into whether the cause (user process + business task) will generate a positive user effect (desired action). The outcomes (success or failure) are basically your validated learnings. The Funnel Matrix you develop will become a Build, Measure, Learn device that you deploy, rinse, and repeat throughout the weeks or months of your testing phase or even the entire life cycle of the product. It can be the reference point (see Figure 9-15) as the business makes continuous improvements. The UX person on your team can even lead the Funnel Matrix development.

Remember, though, this tool requires a balanced and involved team to solve the many problems and puzzles of your user's experience. The UX designer shouldn't and can't realistically work alone. The main reason is that so much of what will make the Funnel Matrix indispensible to your team is tied up in the analytics and metrics of your product. Instead, this is a chance for a savvy marketing team member to shine by growth hacking the Funnel Matrix to possible customer acquisition initiatives, as I explained in the beginning of the chapter with the TradeYa Apprentice Program.

** Rushkoff, Douglass. *Program or be Programmed*. Soft Skull Press, 2011.

Funnel Stage	Stage Definition	User's Process	Desired Action	Business Task	Metrics
SUSPECT	A suspect is somebody who wants something they can not afford (or prefers not to pay for). Or somebody who has something of value (good or service) that they would be happy to sell or exchange for something else.	They see an item or hear about TradeYa somehow (i.e. press, word-of-mouth, social networks, etc.) that attracts them to the site.	(1) Lands on TradeYa homepage and is presented with the multiple TradeYa items and is not required to "Onboard" or log-in until they click a required logged-in action. (2) Lands on TradeYa item page because user is coming from a direct referral link	SEO / Social Media campaigns / Publicity outreach / Paid advertising traffic	Visits, Bounce Rate, %Percentage of (first-ti visitor coming to home vs item pages, top sites traffic is coming from. cities or countries that is coming from.
LEAD	A lead is a person who on first impression finds the site's value proposition compelling enough to enter their real email address or sign up using their Facebook account.	Lands on any TradeYa page with the "Welcome Gate" up which prompts them to enter their email address or to log in with Facebook. Once they do, they have the option of going thru the Onboarding experience which they can choose to opt out anytime.	Views onboarding message and signs in with Facebook or email address. Goes through (does not opt out or bail out of onboarding). If we decide that onboarding is not required until before or after submission of a TradeYa, then the goal is to get them to browse the site effectively to a desired TradeYa page.	Increase inventory, sharing, and messaging/promting to users on the value of creating a personalized profile.	Conversion Rate, Rate up, Email Address vs Fl signups, Welcome Ema Open Rate, Email Verifi

FIGURE 9-15

Top portion of the TradeYa Funnel Matrix filled out

Analytics Tools for UX Dummies

Let's take a short break to briefly examine some useful analytics tools available today for tracking the right metrics for improving the UX. You must measure your experiments to know if you are converting users as your team releases new iterations. Specifically with the UX strategy, you need to know if your layout tweaks are helping to increase user acquisition, engagement, and successful transactions. The danger of talking about specific tools is that the best tools *du jour* constantly change. So I broke them into the following three categories.

Enterprise-oriented analytics reporting tools

Popular tools: Google Analytics, Adobe Analytics

High-level description: Reporting tools are focused on generating detailed statistics about an app or website's traffic and traffic sources. Google Analytics is the most widely used service and offers both a free basic service and a premium version. Adobe Analytics (formerly Omniture) is another tool that is focused on the enterprise market. These tools require a developer or analytics specialist for both implementation and monitoring.

Dashboards, funnel conversion, A/B testing

Popular Tools: KISSmetrics, Optimizely, Geckoboard, Mixpanel, Totango, Chartbeat

High-level description: Dashboard and conversion tools give you one visual place to watch all your metrics in real time from numerous services (for example, Google Analytics and Facebook). You can use them to measure customer engagement and retention by reporting on specific actions. They also focus on segmentation, so you can see who your users are and where they are coming from, and break them up into cohorts for conducting A/B and multivariate testing.

Email delivery/tracking services

Popular Tools: SendGrid, MailChimp, iContact, Constant Contact

High-level description: Email service providers are used for sending out highly targeted messages to website visitors or mobile app users based on what they do (and don't do) while they are using the product. "Deliverability" is the measure, usually expressed as a percentage of how many emails actually make it into the inbox of your user. Successful campaigns are based on a solid marketing strategy for sending the right amount of timely and relevant content to keep users engaged with the product and not opting out.

Conducting Suspect Stage Experiments with Landing Pages

What if you don't have a product or MVP at this stage in the game? Well, you still have a funnel to work with, but it will just all be hypothetical. You can't really connect any metrics to any of the levels yet, except for one: the Suspect.

You can potentially growth-hack the Suspect stage of your funnel with Landing Page experiments. But, before I get into that, let's begin with a few basics. A landing page is a web page that is not the home page of your product. Landing pages are designed to specifically elicit one key action from users. They are also sometimes called lead capture pages, squeeze pages, and destination pages. Users are driven to landing pages from multiple touch points—organic search results, advertising, and social network campaigns. The pages are basically specifically designed to suck potential customers into the top of your funnel.

There are many different ways in which you can use landing pages on unwary suspects to validate a value proposition. I will use case studies to illustrate how.

CASE STUDY 1: WHEN A VALUE PROPOSITION NEEDS TO PIVOT

Chapter 8 recounts how the software engineer who conceived the idea for a Hotels.com-type website for rehabilitation centers found himself in a pretty tough spot. Figure 9-16 shows what the Book Your Care original home page looked like.

Book. Save. Recover. Call Today: Toll Free 1-855-GO-BOOK-YOUR-CARE or 1-855-462-6659

book
your
care

Free Registration >   Log In >

Welcome to the safest way to book residential addiction treatment ever.

- Search best rated residential drug and alcohol rehabs in California in all price ranges.
- Read reviews, check ratings, and tour rehabs online.
- See our 100 point onsite CareCheck®.
- Get matched to the best rehabs for you.
- Not in CA? Other states coming soon so check back!

Search Now   >

One Bed One Time Exclusive Deals			
Rehab	Treatment Program	Savings	You Pay
The Lake House	30-day coed program	40% Off	$13,500
Simple Recovery	30-day coed program	35% Off	$12,000

FIGURE 9-16

The Book Your Care original home page

The guerrilla user research that we conducted on his behalf had invalidated his business model. The current website was not working, and he knew that spending money on a redesign without proper validation was going to be wasteful. So what could he do?

He needed to know if the affluent customer segment would be as enthusiastic about his value innovation as the control group from the user research. My team and stakeholders hustled to find a channel to this user group. We ran ads on Craig's List. We took out advertising in glossy magazines in Beverly Hills. The client and I even went to Alcoholics Anonymous meetings where we posed as loved ones of addicts to learn more about our elusive customer. That's when we decided to run a Landing Page experiment as a last-ditch effort. We knew we needed to run this online advertising campaign to target the affluent customer segment. But treatment centers spend millions of dollars targeting this group on Google and Facebook. So not only would the campaign be expensive, but our ocean was going to be bloody red.

We decided to use a product called Unbounce to quickly build out variations of the value proposition and test them by using targeted online advertising campaigns through Google and Facebook. This effectively put the current site on hold. We wouldn't disrupt any of the complex backend. The developers wouldn't have to waste any time, energy, or money on fixing it for the experiment. Instead, if any suspects did go through our Landing Page experiment, we would concierge them (as Jared did, as described in Chapter 7) through the process of booking a treatment center.

Figure 9-17 shows what the test landing page looked like.

To drive traffic to our landing page, we did targeted advertising on Facebook. We ran ads to users who lived in wealthy neighborhoods in Los Angeles. Here is where you want to be careful, because it's easy to spend more money than you want or need to for a small trial. That's why we came up with the following boundaries:

- We decided on an initial budget of $500.

- We determined the key words for the campaign.

- We finalized the advertisement copy to ensure that the messaging would be strong enough to drive suspects to the landing page.

- We established the customer demographics (such as education, city, and age).

- We decided on when exactly the campaign should start.

- We placed the campaign, which you can see in Figure 9-18, and then we waited!

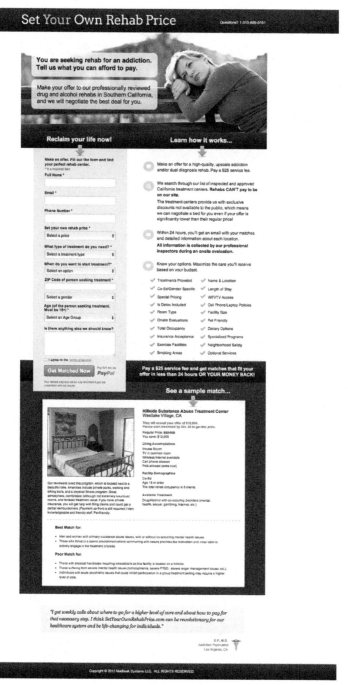

FIGURE 9-17

The Set Your Own Rehab Price landing page

Set Your Own Rehab Price

We'll negotiate with SoCal drug/alcohol rehabs to get you the best treatment. Why wait?

Set Your Own Rehab Price
www.setyourownrehabprice.com
You are seeking rehab for an addiction. Tell us what you can afford to pay. We will help you every step of the way. We'll even help get the most insurance coverage your plan allows.

FIGURE 9-18

The Facebook ad campaign

Because my team used a robust tool like Unbounce, we were able to run two variants of the landing page simultaneously from one Facebook campaign. Unbounce automatically directed half of our traffic to each page. The two landing pages tested two different pricing strategies, as depicted in Figure 9-19. This is called A/B testing.

A/B Test Centre			Reset Stats	Preview Variants	Add Variant		
Current Champion		Weight	Visitors	Views	Conversions	Conversion Rate	
SetYourPricePullDown Updated about a year ago	Edit	100%	1209	1425	5	**0.41%**	
Discarded Page Variants							
SetYourPriceOpenField Updated about a year ago	Edit	0%	0	0	0	0.00%	

FIGURE 9-19

A/B Testing Centre dashboard

In this experiment, our key metrics were the number of visitors who clicked the Facebook advertisement (suspects) and then the conversions that we got—how many users would buy into the value proposition and give us their contact information (leads). In Figure 9-19, you can see that out of 1,000-plus visitors, only 5 users were converted successfully into Leads. Half of them were representatives from other treatment centers trying to do some research on the competition. The one person whom we did manage to concierge was for a food addiction.

CASE STUDY 2: WHEN A VALUE PROPOSITION NEEDS TO ACQUIRE LEADS

Another reason to experiment with landing pages is lead generation. The goal is to acquire as many email addresses as possible of real people who have had some level of exposure to your value proposition. In Chapter 7, I explain how Jared created an explainer video to articulate the benefits of trading. This occurred before our MVP testing phase, and it's a good example of customer acquisition through landing pages.

First, Jared ran an ad campaign on Facebook. He specifically targeted Facebook users who lived in the US who had "liked" the Beats by Dre electronics page. He ran two different ads, one of which you can see in Figure 9-20.

FIGURE 9-20
TradeYa Facebook online ad campaign

Users who clicked on either campaign were directed to the landing page shown in Figure 9-21, which had the explainer video on it. Basically, Jared used the giveaway to drive traffic to the landing page. When users arrived on the landing page, they could not simply submit their email address for the contest and leave. Instead, they had to watch the video and answer at least one qualitative response to a question. This meant that suspects had to watch at least five seconds of the explainer video, which in turn meant that they were exposed to the value proposition. Jared didn't want a suspect's email address unless the suspect got the gist of TradeYa's value proposition.

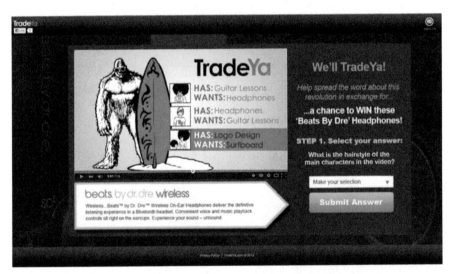

FIGURE 9-21
TradeYa landing page to enter giveaway contest

Jared spent $2,000 running the campaign, which went out to millions of users. Of those, 6,700 people clicked the Facebook advertisement, which directed them to the landing page. Of those, 5,000 people entered the contest, which meant 5,000 people were exposed to the value proposition, turning them from suspects to leads. This meant he had 74% conversion. In terms of cost for conversion, Jared paid 33 cents for the click, and 41 cents for the email address.

Some people might still say, "So what? The guy has a bunch of emails of people who just want free headphones." Well, Jared has the metrics to answer that, thanks to his very carefully thought out Landing Page experiment. More than 5 percent of the people who entered the contest started sharing TradeYa on their social networks. That made them references—they were evangelizing the value proposition to other potential suspects. When our MVP launched, Jared had 5,000 people to directly send email to, induce them to activate their accounts and be ready to engage in trading on the site. Presented in those terms, I'd call the conversion achieved by his Landing Page experiment a success.

How to concoct a Landing Page experiment

If you decide to use a Landing Page experiment for your value proposition, you're in luck; there are many WSYWIG tools for landing page testing available. They vary from simple and free to robust and expensive.

What is important when choosing a tool is that you pick one that allows you to easily:

- Add plug-and-play widgets and form modules as needed

- Assign your own domain name

- Track the conversion of your pages

To create your Landing Page experiment, you can follow this simple framework, which is basically how we ran the case studies I just described:

1. Define the experiment and determine what part of the customer experience is being tested and how it corresponds to the value proposition.

   You are testing your value proposition, a pivot, or trying to acquire users. As you read in the case studies earlier, it's really important that you try to figure out how to correspond the quantifiable results you get from your landing page to the questions for which you need answers.

2. Design/build your landing page.

   The primary function of a landing page is to convert the suspects who have landed there deeper into your experience/product by exposing them to your value proposition. This conversion must happen as fast as a 30-second commercial. You need to convey to potential customers what your product does, using whatever media does the trick. This is when you want to bring the content or brand strategists into the conversation if they are available, because you need to distill your product into something digestible by using text, photos, and video. In Chapter 3, I discuss the "pitch" aspect of the value proposition. That's the *thing* the landing page needs to communicate.

You might also need to think through the experience after the user submits the form. Ideally, it will just be a Thank You page that explains the next steps. In the case of the software engineer's product, we also included a phone number in case users were nervous and wanted to talk to us, as shown in Figure 9-22.

FIGURE 9-22
The Thank You page

3. Design/build the secondary pages.

   You'll want to run variants of your landing pages to test different value props, features, copy, and UI design patterns.

4. Run a "controlled" online campaign for a set amount of time.

   Typically, ad campaigns run less than a week. But it all depends on your budget.

5. Measure the metrics for validate learnings.

   Everything comes back to your funnel. If you aren't collecting or looking at the numbers that matter, you can't make the decisions that will make your product the disruptive invention you've always dreamed it could be.

Recap

In this chapter, I showed you how a successful UX strategy uses analytics to optimize the UX design, demonstrated the use of a tool called the Funnel Matrix and its different stages of customer acquisition, and discussed how metrics prove that the customer is progressing into deeper engagement. You also learned how to design for conversion with landing pages and bring together a cross-functional team including designers, developers, product managers, and, most important, marketers.

This concludes all the techniques I will be sharing for conducting UX strategy. Now it's time to hear from other strategists to see what their perspectives are.

Strategists in the Wild

Gotta stop drifting around
Kill this ugly duckling
We've got the power
And must not misuse it
Cuz life is short and full of thought
I use the power.
　　—THE FALL (1979)

UNTIL RECENTLY, THERE HAVE BEEN FEW OPPORTUNITIES FOR PEOPLE who practice some flavor of UX strategy to huddle together and compare notes. For this reason, I decided to hunt down some of these strategists in the wild to interview for this book. They range from business strategists to design executives and have worked on everything from shoestring to big-budget projects. My goal was for them to share their perspectives and techniques even if their strategic practices were different from my own. They were all asked the same 10 questions. Here is what they had to say.

Holly North

Born: Cuckfield, England

Currently resides: London, England

Education: BA in Sociology from the University of Sussex (England)

FIGURE 10-1
Holly North

1. How did you become a strategist and/or get into doing strategy as part of your work?

Well, I started out in television, working on the production side, and I think it was around the mid-'90s when I began hearing conversations about email and "the Web" but it wasn't until I saw a web address on an ad in the London Underground that I thought things were really beginning to shift. I wanted to understand these new digital channels better so I made the jump to digital or "multimedia" as it was called back then.

I worked with a big creative agency in London and experienced a great variety of projects, technologies, and clients. It felt great to be at the beginning of something. Then, with the rise of interactive television, I saw an opportunity combine my television experience with my digital experience. Broadcasters were looking for ways to further engage and entertain audiences amidst increasing competition. Many interactive services were conceived after the show had been produced and felt very much like add-ons or an afterthought. We realized that we had to think more strategically about the integration of interactivity and television programming, not just in relation to a particular show but how it would complement a broadcaster's business strategy. This meant stepping back and looking at the business and media strategies in the context of the market and what these technological changes were enabling. We were looking for trends, gaps, and opportunities and then develop a digital roadmap accordingly. We looked beyond just *who* the audience was and asked what they *wanted* to do and what they *needed* and within the context of use.

I studied sociology, which, looking back, was invaluable in preparing me for what I do now. Sociology requires you look systematically at human society; to examine the relationships between the individual and society and to better understand people's motives, occupations, traditions, and cultures. As it turns out, this is great training for a UX strategist.

I didn't set out to be a strategist—certainly not a UX strategist. I do think that in order to be successful one needs a level of strategic thinking, a strategic framework. For me, this means seeking out fact-based information, not relying on generalized theories, questioning assumptions.

It involves compromise, understanding our competencies, challenging our thinking. More important, perhaps, it means determining what the right questions to ask are.

2. What does UX strategy mean to you? Is it a bogus job title?

Oh, I do think there's a difference between strategy and design. A strategy sets out the plan and approach, and design is the tactical implementation of that strategy.

Honestly, I prefer the term *experience strategy* to *user experience strategy*. User experience strategy implies that it's set apart from, say the business strategy, or the marketing strategy, or even the product strategy. And it shouldn't be. Developing a product or service strategy requires that you understand the various touch points within the business: who is involved and the associated tasks or activities. This means talking to business stakeholders, sales and marketing, engineering but also to those you wouldn't necessarily expect, like the office manager, the mailroom guy, or sales assistant. Strategy comes from this collective vision of the business and its customers. Perhaps it's a matter of semantics, but when I hear people talking about a user experience strategy it's often about the user experience vision, principles, and design objectives for a particular product or service. This is certainly a part of an experience strategy but should not be limited to it.

So no, it's not a bogus title. But I do think we need to stop umming and aahring about our titles and our places in business. UX isn't an emerging discipline anymore: it has emerged. Business recognizes the importance of UX. If we are still struggling to define ourselves, perhaps we not being strategic enough about demonstrating the value we bring to business.

So, as far as what I call myself...sometimes, I call myself an experience strategist and sometimes I call myself an *interaction designer*, because I am and do both of these things.

3. How did you learn about business strategy?

I have no formal training. I learned the fundamentals of business strategy on the job, over the years. I understood fairly quickly that to be successful I had to have a really good grasp of an organization's business model and strategy, not just its customers or end users. I wasn't simply the voice of the customer, although that was my role when I was starting out.

For the longest time, UX was in its own department, usually off somewhere with visual design. Technology sat somewhere else, as did the business folks. There were few integrated teams, so we were designing in a bubble. How can you possibly design a solution for a business if you have no understanding of what that business wants to achieve?

Not everything we do supports business priorities; we have to balance it with the needs and priorities of the customer or end user. Nonetheless, to support business priorities we need to understand them. Typically, they're about increasing revenues, driving costs savings, and increasing market share. If you're not supporting those, you're not designing the right solution.

I've worked with some outstanding business strategists from whom I've learned a great deal, and I'm very grateful for that.

4. Do you think it's helpful for UX designers who are aspiring strategists to get an MBA or have a business degree?

I didn't go to business school, so I'm not entirely sure. I do wonder, however, if the time and financial investment is really worth it.

Honestly, I'm not sure if business school would have the same impact on the careers of aspiring UX strategists as it would on the careers of management consultants or investment bankers. If you are doing it for the big paycheck, go into banking or finance. If you want to gain the specialized knowledge and skills required to be a UX strategist, you won't find it in business school, you'll find it in the workplace and working with other UX professionals.

There's also a plethora of UX-centric resources out there: free online resources, books (like this one, for example), conferences, master classes, as well as university degrees, which certainly weren't available when I started out.

5. What types of products have you done the strategy for that were the most exciting or fun to work on?

Being involved in the development of a truly innovative product or service is certainly a lot of fun. But honestly, given the time, the budgets, or the aversion that many organizations have to risk-taking, it can be a challenge to create truly innovative products.

I was lucky enough to work with the Google Glass team helping to think about the customer experience strategy for part of the business, not that of the device itself. I enjoyed working with new or emerging technologies because they provide such great learning opportunities, and Glass was no exception.

Projects where I've developed a strategy that leads to the creation of value for both the client's business and its customers are really rewarding. Or projects I've done that in some way had an impact on the industry, like when I was working with the first interactive TV service provider in the UK.

Frankly, most of the time it's the client and the people I work with that makes an engagement fun.

6. What are some of the challenges of conducting strategy in different work environments (for example, startups versus agencies versus enterprises)?

Much of what we do is about aligning people, processes, and expectations, and this is challenging. I'd say people management can be a challenge within some organizations. I spend a good deal of time thinking about whom I am talking to and shaping my conversations accordingly—being aware of organizational politics. Organizational politics is another challenge. It influences what we do and how we do it, which could have an impact the quality of the work. I usually try to find out who the project decision makers are and what factors tend to influence them so I am better prepared. Adaptability is another key skill and being adept at building trust amongst those you work with.

Although exciting, startups pose their own set of challenges. There might not have been a UX designer or strategist in the organization before you, so a large part of what you do might be educating those around you on the value of user-centered design. Decisions about a product or service might already have been made before your arrival, which can make any change hard to negotiate, especially given that business owners are often product owners and feel a very strong sense of ownership in the product. People often wear multiple hats in start-ups, jumping in where needed which can cause some confusion regarding your role. Clearly communicating what you do and the value you bring to a project or solution, as a UX strategist, is key.

Time can also be a challenge. Startups often move at breakneck speeds to get a product to market, so you can be pushed to deliver quicker than you're comfortable. It's important to step back, slow down for a bit, and review where you are. Is the product or service supporting business priorities? Is it supporting the needs of the end users? Are you able to explain what the product or service is, in a way that your grandmother would understand?

7. Have you ever conducted any form of experiments on your product or UX strategy, whether it be trying to get market validation on a value proposition or testing prototypes on target customers? How do you get closer to the truth while you are conducting strategy?

Do we ever get closer to truth? What *is* the truth, Jaime?! To answer, yes I have conducted evaluations. The type of evaluation depends very much on the available budget, the available time, what is being evaluated, what point in the process we're at, and who the end users are.

I think it's vitally important that we evaluate our work as UX strategists and designers. We're tasked with crafting an experience that other people will use. The amount of time and effort we put into this means objectivity might be a hard thing to maintain. We are often not the target audience either, so we're not best placed to see the good, the bad, and the ugly. That's why we need to put our work out there, at different stages of its development, for others to evaluate. And it's not just end users you turn to for evaluation: it's important that you regularly invite the business to evaluate your work because they ultimately own the experience.

I love user testing. I love sitting down with people and seeing how they react to something we've designed. No matter what stage of the process or what form the evaluation materials take. The outcome of these sessions helps make me and design teams more effective. And it can be feedback that comes from sitting down with friends, to more a formal response from a group of users in a usability lab. I don't think I've ever conducted any testing or any research where I haven't been surprised by something. No matter how good we are, we're designing something for people, other people, so it's inevitable that we'll be surprised with how some people end up using the product…or not.

It's important to spend time *with* people while they test something. This might be as close as we can get to "the truth." For example, how do you know what people are looking at on a page before clicking, without watching them? You won't find out what they are thinking, without asking them, and you won't know to ask them unless you've seen them pause.

8. What is your secret weapon or go-to technique for devising strategies or building consensus on a shared vision?

I would like to share what is called a *user journey*, or *customer experience map* (see Figure 10-2).

Customer Experience Map

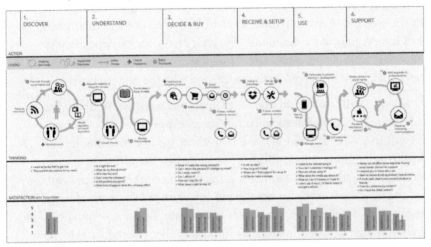

FIGURE 10-2
A customer experience map

An experience map is a strategic tool, rooted in user research, for capturing the complete experience a person might have with a product or service. It documents the experience from the customer's perspective. What they're doing. How they are doing it. How they feel about it. I use experience maps to help me understand the end-to-end experience a customer has with a brand. It helps me to see where the brand is creating value for the customer and where it is not. Ultimately, it's a tool that helps determine the best strategy for delivering a seamless customer experience across multiple touch points.

I use customer experience maps to help focus a client on the customer. I bring stakeholders from across the business together and take them through the map. It's a great tool for helping them understand the experience from the customer's perspective and can be used to help build consensus on how to best serve customers at each touch point.

Depending on the nature of the engagement, I also might create a service map. It's similar to a user experience map but from the business's perspective. It captures how the business services the customer at each touch point. I layer this over the customer experience map to help understand what the business is doing, as a way of contextualizing the customer experience.

Each map tends to be a little different because they're based on research, the results of which can vary significantly from one project to another. Maps are similar in that they're visual representations of the user journey and tend to have similar phases within them. They often don't represent a linear process, because customers tend to move back and forth through phases interacting with some touch points and not others.

The experience map in Figure 10-2 was part of an engagement with a retail client looking to refresh its brand and improve its overall customer experience, across its digital channels.

As you move from left to right across the map, you can see the six phases of the customer journey. These are the behavioral stages customers experience when discovering and interacting with a brand's product. There is often continuity across experience maps with regard to these phases, but as I start amassing data about the purchase journey, I often refine or add to these.

For each phase, I ask customers what their goals are; what were their motivations. And then I try to discover the trigger or moment that moves them to the next phase. I jot down questions they ask themselves as they describe the journey, which helps me identify whether a brand is answering those effectively, or at all. I ask customers to describe their activities, interactions, and how long they take. I also ask them to rank their satisfaction of each activity on a scale of one to five, one being negative. Obviously, measuring customer experiences isn't an exact science, because we're trying to quantify a feeling, but it's useful nonetheless. I often collect quotes from customers to accompany the rankings to help clients understand why customers ranked something in such a way.

There's no right way to design an experience map. As I've mentioned, it depends on the nature of the engagement. I don't treat it as a deliverable as such; rather, it's a tool to move forward, leading to the development of strategy or design.

9. What is a business case or anecdotal story that you can share that walk us through the steps you have to go through when conducting strategy specifically for an innovative product?

I think it's really hard to innovate and it's something many clients want to do. It's hard because it can require organizational or procedural change. Intellectually, clients understand this needs to happen, but emotionally it's hard to commit to.

But it's not Google Glass all the time. Innovation can happen in small, incremental steps. You can innovate around a feature or an interface or in phases, and ultimately it builds up to this really extraordinary, meaningful, hard-to-replicate experience.

I'm not sure that the steps I've gone through—when working on what were considered innovative products or services—have been wildly different from those on other products or services.

My process follows a similar pattern. I ask a series of questions.

I look at the business. Figure out what problem we're trying to solve Determine the business objectives. Determine the measurements of success. Look at where the business is now and where it wants to be.

I determine who the intended users are. Without doing this, we'll be designing for ourselves.

I look at the target market for the product. Who is or might be the competition? Is there a similar product on the market? What are the gaps and opportunities? What are the industry trends?

I look at the business capabilities and core competencies. Can the business achieve and maintain a competitive advantage based on its current capabilities and competencies? Do we have the capababilities to support the product now and in the future?

I often go back and refine what I've found with each new interview and with answers to the questions gathered, I review, analyze, and strategize. Gaps and opportunities will become apparent, creative solutions can be devised. Then, in collaboration with business stakeholders, priorities can be applied and an action plan developed.

10. What are important skills or mindsets for a strategist to have? Or what makes you good at your job?

You need a healthy dose of emotional intelligence. Nurturing relationships, building trust, and the ability to inspire people are what UX strategists do on a daily basis.

Be a critical thinker. Ask "why" questions and if you don't get answers, reframe, and ask again. Don't rely on the thinking of others and don't assume. Challenge the existing opinions and beliefs of those around you...and your own.

Base your point of view on facts you've gathered from multiple sources. Evaluate and reevaluate to make sure your approach, decision, or design is still relevant.

Listen to those you don't agree with. Are they making sense? Have you overlooked something? Seek opinions from people with different areas of expertise to gain different perspectives.

Own your decisions. Be prepared to be wrong. Be prepared to compromise.

Peter Merholz

Born: Santa Monica, California

Currently resides: Oakland, California, US

Education: BA in Anthropology from University of California, Berkeley

FIGURE 10-3

Peter Merholz

1. How did you become a strategist and/or get into doing strategy as part of your work?

I taught myself multimedia design in the '90s. My first formal role in software design was as a web developer, and then I transitioned from a web developer to being an interaction designer, and then from an interaction designer to a UX designer. Along the way, I realized that I needed answers to strategic questions, and that I needed to augment my "UX toolkit" to allow for more strategic thinking.

I truly became a "strategist" sometime around 2001 when I was at Adaptive Path. Adaptive Path was a very straightforward, very user-experience, design-oriented company. We were doing interaction design, information architecture, user research, and usability testing. However, to do the best design work that we could for our clients, we did more: we would ask them questions, so we understood the context in which the design work took place. We didn't want to make a design for the sake of designing. We wanted to make the design deliver on some common interest, goal, or objective. And what we found was often our clients didn't know the answers to our questions. They had never bothered to ask the questions themselves, and they didn't understand how important those answers were to the shared design vision. So, we found ourselves moving upstream, doing what is essentially strategy work, to answer those questions. That's how I became a strategist; to simply find the answers to the questions that I needed in order to do the best design work.

2. What does UX strategy mean to you? Is it a bogus job title?

You know, it's funny. I just wrote a blog post about how there's no such thing as UX design. And my point in that post was the design part of what we call UX design is typically just *interaction design* or *information architecture*. And the rest of what we call UX design is really just strategy and product management. However, at Adaptive Path, we talked a lot about defining what experience strategy and/or UX strategy was, so I think there's validity to this concept. There is such a thing as UX strategy because product strategy and business strategy have failed in the prior decades to account for the user needs and awareness. To make sure that the user and the user experience was appropriately beneficial, we had to develop this thing called UX strategy.

In an ideal world you wouldn't need UX strategy, because it would just be a component of your product or business strategy. We're moving into this ideal world, I think. We're seeing more and more often that UX is considered a part of a broader strategy. But, I think the separate and distinct concept of UX strategy was necessary for us—at least so we could focus on it—to shine a light on it and develop a toolkit to then wrap up in product strategy.

So, "UX strategy" is not bogus or overblown, but I do think that it's a temporary artifact or a moment in time that we are in. If I think what UX strategy means to me, it is addressing those questions you need to answer and the answers to those questions that help inform your design. It's not sufficient to simply have a business strategy or product strategy in the classical way of understanding your audience or total addressable market. You need to have a deeper understanding of your users, audiences, customers—whatever you want to call them—who they are, what they want, how they behave, and what they're looking for. Traditional strategy methods, even if they talked about customers, didn't really embrace deep customer understanding and empathy. So I think, what UX strategy does is it goes deeper into customer understanding. Again, what we're seeing develop is a business strategy that is starting to appreciate that more directly.

3. How did you learn about business strategy?

I had no formal training or business strategy education. But something happened while I was at Adaptive Path. I was trying to understand how to do better UX design just after the dot-com bust happened. It was 2002 and there was a lot of soul searching going on in the UX community about proving our value. A common theme that we felt we needed to prove was the Return On Investment (ROI) of user experience. One of the opportunities we had at Adaptive Path was to explore these types of questions. I started digging into MBA-ish literature and then we got into contact with a professor at Berkeley's Haas School of Business, Sara L. Beckman (PhD, Industrial Engineering and Engineering Management, Stanford University).

She was one of first people who were trying to understand that design provides an interesting categorical advantage within business. One of her MBA students, Scott Hirsch, partnered with Adaptive Path to write a business paper on business value and how ROI drives user experience. With their advisement, we attempted to apply some real business thinking to our UX process. And so it was through these kinds of exposures that I was able to learn about business strategy and the kinds of things businesses tend to care about.

Honestly, business strategy is pretty straightforward: money in, money out. How do you reduce costs? How do you increase profits? At the heart of all businesses, that's what it's all about. If you can talk to a CEO or C-level people about how they can reduce or manage costs and increase revenues, or if they're going to increase costs, increase revenue, whatever it is, that's still business strategy. Tah dah! It's not a black art.

One of the ways that I've been most informed about business strategy happened in 2005 when Adaptive Path hired Brandon Schauer, who has a master's in Design and an MBA. Brandon ended up running Adaptive Path before it was acquired by Cap One. By working with him and being exposed to his methods, I was better able to understand the opportunity that design and UX has within a business context. In the '80s and '90s, we had already squeezed as much efficiency out of every value chain we could find. It was a lot about just-in-time manufacturing, process engineering; just squeezing, squeezing, squeezing, until the point of diminishing returns, and continuing to do that work. And so the opportunity was, well, how do we realize whole new value propositions. And that's where good design comes in to point the way to whole new opportunities or differentiation within a space.

4. Do you think it's helpful for UX designers who are aspiring strategists to get an MBA or have a business degree?

It's not hurtful. Maybe it is moderately helpful. I've seen people who've gone through that experience and it's been beneficial for them. But, you can also earn while you learn and come out in a very similar place. An MBA or business degree could be good for folks who are really transitioning from a craft form of a UX practice into something more strategic and need help making that shift. I feel like if you're already doing it, even if it's self-taught, an MBA isn't going to get you much more. It could be useful depending on the school for making connections and meeting new people. Having a Harvard MBA or Stanford GSB certainly is not going to look bad on your resume. But that type of education is going to be a big financial investment too.

5. What types of products have you done the strategy for that were most exciting or fun to work on?

A transformative experience for me was working with Brandon Schauer at Adaptive Path on a project for a financial services client (not Capital One). It was in 2005, just when he joined our company. This project was meant to be a simple website redesign. But because we had a really savvy client, we were also able to do some strategic work, financial analysis, and modeling. This strategic work gave us a deeper understanding of the user research so that we could tie all these things together to help inform a potential strategic overhaul of the client's entire service offering. However, as it turned out, they were not able to realize our vision because their organization was not set up to take on such a big shift.

What I learned on that project and some subsequent projects is that even if we delivered an amazing strategy to an organization, if the corporation is not shaped and its cultural values are not set to embrace that strategy, the strategy is meaningless.

The most fun strategy projects that I've worked on were vision projects. We did two for companies in South Korea, one that was the future of media, and one that was the future of commerce. These vision projects are awesome and they're fun, especially when you're working as a designer in a design firm. For one project we did a ton of trend analysis, trying to understand where these technologies were going, user behavior, and how that was evolving. That involved a lot of secondary research, which I'd say is not a typical method or UX practice. We read blogs, articles, and academic papers. We really just tried to soak in the space. We interviewed experts in media, we interviewed people who worked at YouTube, people who worked at product companies, people who worked in academia, looking at this stuff, trying to figure out— you know, where the future was going.

In digging through the trend research, we identified specific concepts, which we placed on blue stickies (see Figure 10-4). Then, we grouped those concepts around themes, which were yellow stickies. And we used red whiteboard marker to provide context and narrative for the concepts and themes. When we felt good about the map for a year, we took a picture of the whiteboard. Then, we erased all the marker lines and moved the stickies around (and added and removed stickies) to tell a story for the next year, and when we felt good about that, took that picture. So, the photos of the whiteboard became a time series of our trend forecasting, and fed into the Trend Map poster that we created (see Figure 10-5).

Building the Trend Map

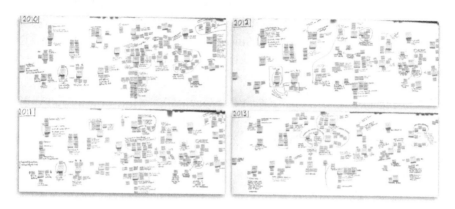

FIGURE 10-4
Trend analysis working session output

Process Overview

Trend Forecasting

Through interviews and secondary research, identifying trends and their implications.

Secondary research
Analyst reports, news articles, industry blogs

Expert interviews
8 conversations with thought leaders from MIT, YouTube, Google, Nokia, *The Wall Street Journal*, T-Mobile, and Intel

Fringe User Interviews
6 conversations with future-forward users, addressing different aspects of extreme media consumption — TV, games, movies, music, sports, and news.

FIGURE 10-5
Trend forecasting slide

When those understandings paired with our design creativity and forecast of media experience in the midterm (three to five years), it was super fun. I learned a ton from that project and opportunity.

That's a lot of the challenges for a lot of UX strategy work, particularly agency-based, where the impact of the UX strategy work is often unclear. I've not seen a lot of real organizational evolution. Since I've left the consulting world, one of the things that have been intriguing to me is how little interest Silicon Valley has in the word "strategy." It's almost like it's a bad word, because I think it's believed to mean a lot of chin stroking and not a lot of shipping, and there's some truth to that.

The Lean Startup movement was responding to the same Silicon Valley mindset that is also kind of minimizing the value of strategy. The companies that practice strategy very seriously, such as Intuit, I don't know what they have to show for it. So I'm kind of sympathetic to it. I think that there's a role for strategy to play and explicit strategic efforts to play, in-house and within these tech companies, but there's a struggle to find a right amount of strategy. You don't want to feel as if it's overwhelming, or it's a waste of time and energy, or it's too grand for us to realize, or that it's just "Why did we bother?" Hitting that happy medium is an interesting challenge.

6. What are some challenges of conducting strategy in different work environments (for example, startups versus agencies versus enterprises)?

Within an agency context, it depends on the agency. At Adaptive Path, if you came to us, you were going to be embracing strategy. We weren't the type of design agency that if we were to begin talking strategic concerns to you, you wouldn't be, "Wait, what? No just push some pixels, will ya?!"

Some agencies have those challenges of moving upstream. But, I think for an agency, you have to set yourself up as a strategic provider, and if you attract clients, you're doing strategy work. That's relatively easy. Within that agency environment, and because of the way the projects tend to be structured, you can kind of create the safe space for strategy to be done. Now, the challenge for an agency, which I was referring to before, is that strategy can often feel irrelevant, by the time you go deliver it, or months later when you follow up on it, you're like, "So what are you doing?" "Oh well, we had a reorg or this person left, or that person left, or what it is. We shifted this, that, and the other thing." So the work you did just kind of doesn't get used. So that's the challenge for an agency.

The challenges for doing it in-house, at an enterprise, are for strategy to remain relevant. One method is to connect the strategic work to the production work, because those two functions tend to be owned by two different parts of an organization. So, the challenge is how do you make sure that your strategy feels actionable and operable so that your teams can draw and act on it. I think in an enterprise, you might get a lot of rich, deep, thoughtful strategy, but you might find that the market has changed by the time you've come up with all your strategic insight.

In the startup environment, the primary challenge for strategy is that there's often no time to do it. To do strategy of any significant complexity correctly, it takes time, effort, and energy. In a startup you often don't have that available excess time because you're still trying to prove yourself, and just get a toehold. The strategic orientation within a startup has to come from the founders, as opposed to it being an explicitly separate activity that a UX strategist is conducting on his own. Having a UX Strategy and making sure you're thinking properly about your UX as part of the broader product strategy is important. The companies that succeed are the ones that understand this, even if they haven't practiced it explicitly.

The primary challenge is to embrace a meaningful and appropriate UX strategy, regardless of environment. The secondary challenge is making sure that strategic effort is operating at the appropriate cadence that your environment requires.

I'm now at a product company, Jawbone, which makes hardware. We can actually be more explicitly strategic than I've been able to be elsewhere. This is because for us to do a hardware product, it's a huge investment. To mitigate the risk of that investment, we have to be strategic or we are going to be flushing a lot of money down the toilet. And so we have some room to be more thoughtful and mindful of our strategy.

7. Have you ever conducted any form of experiments on your product or UX strategy, whether it be trying to get market validation on a value proposition or testing prototypes on target customers? How do you get closer to the truth while you are conducting strategy?

The short answer to that question is "not really." I see us doing that more here [at Jawbone] because of the risk, the up-front capital that it takes to launch hardware, you need to make sure you feel pretty good about it. So, because I'm new to this company, I need to validate earlier strategies before implementing them.

8. What is your secret weapon or go-to technique for devising strategies or building consensus on a shared vision?

Doing the right research, talking to the right kinds of folks, asking them the right kinds of questions, and observing the right kinds of behavior that can be analyzed and appropriately inform strategy and delivery. It's hardly a secret weapon; a lot of people do it. Are you identifying your prospective audience appropriately so that your research participants are the kind of people who are going to engage once you have a product in the market? Are you asking the right questions? Observing the right behaviors? Probing them appropriately? You're not just asking dumb questions. You're allowing them to be who they are, but also recognizing you can't do a purely anthropological study that can take months. So, to the degree that you're forcing things, you're forcing things appropriately, you're getting the right stuff out of it. Are you then analyzing the results in meaningful ways so that you can develop appropriate insights?

I'm a fan of personas as developed by Alan Cooper (see Chapter 3). I don't use them all the time, but when I do I like to study a full spectrum of user behavior. When I have the opportunity to look at the data from numerous user research interviews, I can identify the salient behaviors that stand out.

9. What is a business case or anecdotal story that you can share that walk us through the steps you have to go through when conducting strategy specifically for an innovative product?

For my last Adaptive Path project, we worked for a big global media brand client. We worked on its ecommerce platform—its online store. So, the strategy process began with research. This was a children's media brand, so the research involved mainly moms. We did a lot of in-home interviews, talked to moms about buying stuff for their children, and focused mostly on gifting because of the nature of this brand. It wasn't bought everyday. It was bought for special occasions. So we took that research and analyzed it.

We didn't create personas for this project; we created profiles, very similar to personas but different. A persona is a face with a name you give it, and it's meant to be a specific individual. Profiles are more categorical. We broke up these moms into four or five profile types. We had the mom who's still a kid at heart and loves the stuff herself as much as the kids love it; we had the mom who's more of the "I want to be an educator. I'm buying this stuff so I can create this world that my child can then succeed in"; then there was the mom that might be the kind of working mom who feels guilty working, so they're spoiling these kids because they want to connect with them. So you come up with these profiles. From these profiles, we then told a series of stories and scenarios. The way we structured these scenarios was to focus on different technological platforms.

We had one mom that was all web, one mom who was all mobile smartphone, one mom who was all tablet, and then we actually used a grandmother who was kind of a spoiler; well, actually more of an indulger, who crossed all these streams. And we wrote scenarios of use. The grandmother one was actually, for the sake of this story, the one who ended up being the most interesting. We did talk to a couple of these grandma types. The grandma often doesn't live near the grandchildren. Their children have moved away and have a family in another city, away from the grandparent. So, as we were writing this scenario, we have the grandparent in one city, the grandchildren in another city, and that was really interesting.

Okay, what can we do about that? Well, we write this story that's around Christmas. The grandparent wants to get the grandchild something for Christmas. The grandparent can't be there when the grandchild opens the present. So as we're writing this story, what we realize is, well, what if you open this present, here's a short form URL you can easily type into a web browser and you can get a video message from your grandma. There she is, Christmas morning, even though she can't really be there. And so, that all came out of a strategic endeavor, research analysis, scenario development, essentially product design and development, leading to this particular feature that the client loved. They fell all over themselves and built the technology to realize it because they thought it was so appropriate for them. The client has a very clear brand, a brand personality, and this hit right at the heart of who the client is as a business brand. So that's a story of from research to delivered feature where I feel that we had quite a bit of success.

You really want an understanding of what's going on in the broader market. Now, that said, I think too often organizations look at what others are doing and feel they have to match that. But you don't want to get caught in competition. Be at par. Parity is a red-ocean strategy; you're just trying to line yourself up with everyone else there. You want to find that blue ocean. Now, I would argue that you wouldn't want to find that blue ocean for the sake of finding the blue ocean. That is still being too cognizant of what your competition is doing. What you need to do is understand who you are as an organization, who you are as a business, and who you are as the people within that business so that you can see through to delivery.

I can see another company doing the same strategy that would perfectly fit its brand. But I don't know if it's what we should be doing, because it doesn't seem to fit who we are. So, again, this is where I feel UX doesn't really often embrace enough brand strategy. I think that there's a reasonable antipathy to brand and branding within UX because I feel often branding is handled poorly. It's very superficial. But, if you dig, you can appropriate brand strategy, issues of personality, issues of values that the company holds, issues of those characteristics that companies hold dear, and those elements of brand. UX needs to be very informed by that because releasing a product is hard. And if the people within the organization aren't interested by the product they're building, aren't passionate about the product that they're building, they're only building something because they think that there's a market for it, they're not really going to dig in and do all the hard work needed to get that product to market as best as they could. It's got to be a product the people that work there want to feel like they would use.

10. What are important skills or mindsets for a strategist to have? Or what makes you good at your job?

It is about a kind of mindset that you should possess where you can understand the parts and see how these parts fit within the whole. I became a strategist because I can't help but think about design in a systems context, a design within a broader context. I have a systems mindset whenever I approach anything. And it was in order to satisfy my systems mindset that I realized I needed to embrace strategy, because I needed to understand how the context of the work that I was doing fit within this broader system.

A strategist also needs to be able to be persuasive, so you need to have good story-telling, communication, and presentation skills. You need to be able to bring people along in a story of engagement. Strategy tends to be abstract, so you need to be able to make that concrete so that other people can have a visceral response to it. Strategies that remain abstract tend not to take root, so another skill for a strategist is the ability to tell the story. To shape a narrative; to connect with an audience.

Milana Sobol

Born: Kazan (Tatarstan), Russia

Currently resides: New York City, US

Education: BA in Neuroscience and Economics from Brandeis University, MA in International Finance from Brandeis International Business School

FIGURE 10-6
Milana Sobol

1. How did you become a strategist and/or get into doing strategy as part of your work?

I had a startup right after business school where I had to do basically everything and wear many hats. We built a product from the ground up, so it became clear to me very early on that without a proper vision and a strategy to get there, we would be going around in circles. So I really learned about strategy on the job.

The startup was an online music distribution platform for unsigned musicians. It happened just as the music business started to unravel and everyone wanted to challenge the ways that the record labels did business. The strategy focused on understanding our audience (musicians) and their unmet needs online in the context of what was possible to do with the technology at the moment. We had to think about ways we could facilitate the digital tools for this new era so that these musicians could have more control over their art and the product they were making. But at the same time, we had to do that in a way that the business could make money. Strategy is not just about the product vision. It's also the practical roadmap to get there; you have to think about both the end user and the supporting and sustainable business model.

When I started out, I wasn't initially very good at balancing all the pieces. I didn't understand how all the parts, business, design, and technology, came together so my planning and decision-making had holes in it. But I learned from my mistakes and was eager to try that role again in a more structured environment with better resources. So as I was exploring what to do next after the startup, I specifically sought out a position involving strategy in an interactive firm because I wanted to solve problems and build real products but in a creative environment.

2. What does UX strategy mean to you? Is it a bogus job title?

No, absolutely not. Over the years in both agencies and startups, I worked with many different types of UX strategists. There are some who think more like designers, and others who are focused on the business side of things. I consider myself more of a business strategist, and I really work the best with a solid UX strategist or very experienced designer. We need to work together to realize what the product does for the user and how do we make a business out of it. I tend to have some very basic ideas about how the product functions and the overall interaction experience, but I can never really think everything through at that granular level the way UX strategists and designers do it. So for me now, as a business owner and business strategist, the UX strategy is the core of everything we do, because in our case, the service is the product. It's not like we are just a touch point for the customers along their experience with our business. Our product *is* the digital product. It *is* the service. It *is* the business. So we have to get it right, and it has to be delightful, and people will have to want to use it, and not just need to use it.

3. How did you learn about business strategy?

I learned most of what I know about business strategy in the first seven years after school just by constantly putting myself in the environment where I actually didn't know anything about anything and had to learn about it. I had some academic credentials to get into it, but it didn't mean that I really knew how to do it in a creative agency environment. I had gone to business school and took a lot of challenging courses at a good university, so on paper I seemed qualified for a strategy position. But to be honest, when I first walked into a professional environment, I didn't really even know how to do the competitive analysis properly at the level required in product thinking. My training was more in finance.

When you are fresh out of business school, you want to do things in a very business school-y, academic kind of way. Basically, I had to learn from scratch. It was probably by the time I had done my twentieth business analysis/strategy presentation that I felt like I finally got it. It took some time before I truly understood how to put together a good story that was going to inform both the business goals and the design. But what I learned was not how to think analytically. That I already had. I learned how to tell a story. In a creative business, business strategy has to add up to a simple story about the product opportunity.

4. Do you think it's helpful for UX designers who are aspiring strategists to get an MBA or have a business degree?

No, absolutely not. I think what is required is that they spend time with their colleagues in generative meetings. They really need to learn how to talk to clients and sincerely listen to their business problems. Being a good listener is absolutely essential. So, a degree in psychology might be more helpful than an MBA. I do think it is helpful to take a couple of business classes to learn and practice systems thinking and a framework approach to problem solving. Strategy is mainly about simplifying the chaotic and the complex into a simple diagram or a statement that everyone on your team can understand and get behind. Some people are naturally better at that kind of thinking and others are better at creative thinking. I find it's very rare to find people who are super creative and analytical at the same time. Those people are very unique.

In my experience, business school is only a requirement if you want to get a really big corporate job. Having an MBA at a Fortune 500 company might be environmental requirement, but I don't think it's necessary for the creative world. I learned a lot by looking at the decks of strategists whom I respected and saw how they told the "business stories." As I mentioned before, that type of storytelling is not something you would perfect in school.

5. What types of products have you done the strategy for that were the most exciting or fun to work on?

What I'm working on right now is probably the most engaging for me. But again, that's because I'm the product owner who has a lot at stake. I think you have to have a different level of commitment not just when your name is on the line, but also all your finances and everything else. Perhaps that risk factor is what makes it very engaging.

In the agency world, you often do the strategy and sometimes you see through design, and in rare cases, you see it all the way through the build, but almost never do you then interact with the clients day-to-day to see how it really affects their businesses. With working in client services, sometimes you get feedback after delivery and you do postmortems. But it's after your work has been delivered to your clients and the project is over. When the strategy is out of your hands, then it really becomes *their* baby. And the outcomes depend on what they do with it and how they market the product. And by that point, it's really hard to isolate what worked or did not work. Was it the strategy or the design or the technology or the marketing? If the strategist is not involved throughout the process, she can't really be held accountable. For me, that's a bad thing because being able to be involved in the final outcomes is what motivates me.

So, right now I am building a product that we just put out on the market and I could immediately see how people reacted and how they use it. We spent nine months making assumptions and building a product based on our best thinking, and then, in a matter of days, we finally get some real feedback from real users. That is very satisfying, even if the feedback is not always positive. And believe me, it is not always positive. Through this direct learning, I get to iterate on the original idea with real people. The complete feedback loop is what makes it the most interesting product.

6. What are the some challenges of conducting strategy in different work environments (for example, startups versus agencies versus enterprises)?

Politics are always tough, and politics always come with the territory of any business that has more than three people. So with all kinds of enterprises and large clients, politics play a big role. You often deal with the budget that comes from a marketing department, and they have their own agenda. Often you are really building a product that's informed by the business/product group, but then the business group is not actually involved in the strategy conversations. In that case, the challenge is to navigate all of that to make everybody play together.

A startup can have its own issues. It can be a little lonely. If you start small, there are only a handful of people you see and work with, 24/7. It can become too focused and sometimes you just wish, "Oh maybe we are tired and just need a fresh opinion." Ultimately, until you start making a profit or get funded, the resources are always constrained. You don't have people focusing on what they are best at, only. We all wear many hats.

I think that's why agencies have the best balance. If you're in the right group of people where you have the diverse and qualified team, you have feedback from the UX strategist, the business analyst, and all the different types of people that make your team well-rounded. When there is proper time to think and enough different perspectives, it fosters an environment where you are able to have enough points of view to really bring out great ideas.

7. Have you ever conducted any form of experiments on your product or UX strategy, whether it be trying to get market validation on a value proposition or testing prototypes on target customers? How do you get closer to the truth while you are conducting strategy?

The best example I can talk about is what I'm working on now, which is a mobile productivity app. I've done a number of tests with focus groups at different stages of development, from ideation, to prototypes, to the final product. We had an initial group of 20 people, a mix of potential users defined by background, needs, and behavior, that we showed our paper prototypes to first. This was helpful because in the conversations with potential users we got a chance to polish our own ideas to see if people are translating what we've created to what we intended to create. Do they get the overall concept?

The second level of testing was done with a couple of different clickable prototypes. We had a diverse group of people play with the apps and talk to us about what they liked and didn't like, both about the concept and the execution.

The real test came when we actually launched the app and did a little marketing. Then, we had a much larger sample of 1,500 people using the app for a number of weeks. We did a survey online to understand why the users who were deeply engaged with the product love it and why others don't. During this testing period, we continued to learn about what features they felt are missing and what users found confusing. It was not full-blown user testing, but we were able to gain insights that were super enlightening.

However, you have to take a lot of the feedback with a grain of salt. Some people are just mean and will say, "This thing sucks. I don't know why somebody would build something like this. Nobody wants to use this." But then I had few dozen people say, "This has become my favorite app. I use it every day." The feedback that mattered was from those people who took the time to explain to us exactly what features they liked or didn't like and why.

Even when we just showed very high-level concepts of the product, we saw that a lot of people were getting what the product was and validating that they would use it the way we had intended. That was when it felt like the strategy was correct. This was crucial because we did a lot of research to understand the opportunity space and needed to know that people wanted to have this product. We had certain assumptions that the strategy was initially built on, but as we refined our ideas through the various levels of design and testing, our strategy became more and more clear. At the end, we could clearly articulate what the product that we had built is, who wants to use it, and why. And we had real data to back it up.

8. What is your secret weapon or go-to technique for devising strategies or building consensus on a shared vision?

I'm a very detail-oriented person. I have to understand the whole macro view of what else is happening in the market. So, researching the marketplace is always the first thing I do. I want to figure out who the user/target customer is, what types of products that they are using to solve similar problems. I look at every angle of competition. Sometimes, it's very predictable and sometimes it's totally outside of the industry that you expect that you are competing in. I like to understand where they're heading and how they created their UX. I want to understand their design strategy with the product and what it means for what we are trying to accomplish. Being able to share these details with my partners and team helps everyone to be well informed and make better decisions together.

Something I almost always do in every project is a simple ecosystem map (see Figure 10-7) that shows who all the players are, what they have to offer, and why people like them (what features differentiate them). It's a competitive map but in a framework that is relevant to the product I am working on.

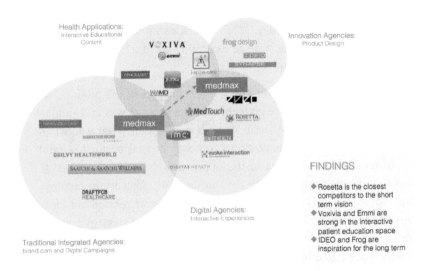

FINDINGS

◆ Rosetta is the closest competitors to the short term vision
◆ Voxivia and Emmi are strong in the interactive patient education space
◆ IDEO and Frog are inspiration for the long term

FIGURE 10-7

Ecosystem map

It's a good reference tool for everyone on the team. I want everyone to know where we are on the map and where we are going.

9. What is a business case or anecdotal story that you can share that walk us through the steps you have to go through when conducting strategy specifically for an innovative product?

In an agency environment it starts with a brief. The client usually has the basic idea of the product or service it would like to create or at least the problem that it wants to solve. Often it might have an idea for the solution without completely understanding the true source of the problem, and it needs help with really clarifying both the problem space and the opportunity. So in the agency context, we begin by downloading the knowledge from the client, synthesizing what it knows and what the market tells us, and then coming up with a clear destination and a roadmap to get us there.

In the case of a tech startup, things are a little bit more fluid and iterative. The approach is more or less the same, but less time and effort is spent on consensus building across the client's organization. More time is spent on refining and optimizing. There are less artificial time constraints, but often more resource constraints, so we must be very lean in our thinking.

In my current startup, the vision is clear and set, but the strategy has evolved and continues to evolve. Our initial vision came from us observing a certain kind of behavior that people were exhibiting around the way they were using email where email wasn't the most efficient solution. We thought something could be done about that. We didn't immediately know the perfect solution, but we had a very clearly articulated problem. We were not sure if the solution was a different kind of email app, or note-taking app, or even a task-management tool. So, step number one is to clearly identify (or make an educated hypothesis) about the opportunity space, or the problem that you are addressing for the end user. Based on this knowledge, we then form a strategy, a plan of action for the solution. In our case, we began to come up with a few different solutions that we believed were possible alternatives. But we didn't know for sure until we really began designing, and prototyping. When we understand more or less what we wanted to design, we could do a more focused competitive analysis, looking at other similar products and talking to people who used those products. And based on that knowledge we tweaked our prototypes until we basically ended up with one solid solution. The lesson is that strategy is iterative just like everything else. You come up with a hypothesis, you create a plan, and you move forward until you learn new information, reposition the hypothesis, and adjust the plan. Strategy is a living experience.

10. What are important skills or mindsets for a strategist to have? Or what makes you good at your job?

What makes me good at my job is a combination of high-level thinking and focus on details and logistics simultaneously. You have to do a lot of "homework" before coming up with a strategy that might be not so exciting. But the way you put it all together into a story that's both inspiring and practical is where the magic is. It's not always that easy. You have to have the vision. You have to see the big picture and get excited about the possibilities. But you also have to be able to communicate that to other people so that they can get behind you.

Geoff Katz

Born: St. Louis, Missouri, US

Currently resides: San Francisco, California, US

Education: BA in History from Rutgers, The State University of New Jersey

FIGURE 10-8

Geoff Katz

1. How did you become a strategist and/or get into doing strategy as part of your work?

So, I think the word "strategy" has very different meanings to different people, and you do a great job at boiling it down in the book. For me, helping people cut through the confusion, identify, and prioritize real opportunities is kind of what's at the heart of the strategy work that I've done across a number of different consumer entertainment technology platforms. I've been lucky enough to be able to work on what you can call emerging platforms time and time again. There was a moment where the Web and animated GIFs were an emerging platform—that's where we all started—and if you remember the first websites for McDonald's or Levi's from 1995, you'll know what I mean. The opportunity to try to really figure out what people *might* like to do, because in a lot of these cases the media hadn't existed previously, identify the essential components of what a UX could and should be, and then create a blueprint for how a product experience comes to market is what I've been focused on over the last 20 years.

My background and training studying the history of ideas was a perfect setup to have a strategy role in my professional life in the sense that you're learning to constantly evaluate very specific primary sources of information and then using that to inform a bigger-picture story that needs to be original, interesting, and engaging for a particular audience. I started my professional career in advertising, and the task at hand with that was communicating clearly and succinctly in 30-second chunks. I was a television-commercial producer before the Internet, so when I moved from the big ad agency world to the unfathomable depths of the Internet at Organic in 1995, I was always working to pull things into focus for our clients and lead the design and engineering teams toward goals that were able to be understood quickly and clearly actionable.

2. What does UX strategy mean to you? Is it a bogus job title?

Having worked across a range of direct-to-consumer products and B2B products, UX strategy is really an essential component of product definition. Today, there are entire disciplines that make up parts of what you or I would have normally done on any given day on and interactive media design and development project. For people getting started in UX and product design today, the opportunity to go through academic programs as an undergraduate, postgraduate, or through professional training and get deep experience with every part of the interactive product design and development process is important. That broad background is what differentiates a UX designer from a UX strategist.

Strategists needs to have a higher-level perspective and a certain confidence about where the world is headed in order to be successful. I think it really takes *will* to help people, to pull emerging opportunities into focus and to define them in a way that is actionable by a team of engineers. I've heard time and time again over my career from engineers that they "just" want to be told what to build. That doesn't mean that they're not creative people. It's that for them, without an extremely detailed level of specificity, software doesn't just "happen." Making the strategic effort to really tease out that detail and lead teams to where the world will be in 6 or 8 or 12 months and deliver a product that fits with a market at that time, is the fundamental work of a UX strategist.

I don't think the title is bogus. It *is* a new title that recognizes that there needs to be someone at every company focused like a laser on supporting the business objectives of the company from the point of view of design. By identifying product opportunities based on the evolution of technology and user behavior and driving innovation through product design you can effectively deliver a product that is fundamentally better than anything they've seen or used before and achieve product/market fit that will help your business scale. UX strategy spans across a number of previously siloed disciplines. In fact, there's evidence that leads me to believe that it's growing as a new discipline. There was a moment where UX design in general was seen as a BS title. Clients at some of the interactive design agencies I've worked for just wanted to see pixels on a page, and the way that design behaved, the way that design made an experience easier or harder for a user, and how that contributed to brand, really was an afterthought. As the world became a little more sophisticated about the UX of interacting with screens and put the user at the center of the product design process, UX as a distinct discipline emerged and has become a fundamental part of interactive product development. I think that the UX strategist is now emerging as an important role because it bridges what could be seen as really disparate and distinct silos, design, experience, and business, and that's why I don't think it's BS. I think it's incredibly important.

3. How did you learn about business strategy?

On the streets. I don't have a master's or bachelor's degree in design or business. When I was doing my formal liberal arts education, most of my classmates were aspiring to be lawyers, not MBAs. Art and design were something you did as personal expression, not as business, and the state-of-the-art technology was color Xerox. The accepted goal after four years of studying history was to take the LSATs and go to law school. An MBA was not even on my radar as an option at that time. So I moved to San Francisco, joined a band, and started making our posters. I saw the Macintosh computer having an impact on the way that print production was evolving and, taking my cues from how quickly that technology was evolving, I focused on using computers to do design. It was only in the early '90s that computers began to become a part of the creative process. Being someone who could work side by side with traditional graphic designers, art directors, commercial TV producers, and collaboratively work to bring computers into design and advertising as new tools that could unlock new business opportunities is really been something that has been fundamental to my career, since those earliest days. I think for a long time, like back in 1994 and 1995, the idea that not only the web would be ubiquitous, but it would be the primary business channels was quite hard for people to grasp. The web browser put a graphical face on the Internet that which was at the time less useful than interactive services like CompuServe (forums, email), AOL (dial-up walled garden of content), and Prodigy (ISP).

I was actually at a meeting at Netscape the day that they went public. I remember seeing someone wheeling a pallet of champagne down the hallway and knew that we were witnessing the beginning of a new world. And at the time, the Netscape guys would talk to us about how browsers would evolve (remember "frames"?) and where the Internet was headed. They were telling us that by 1997 the Internet would be a true direct-to-consumer business channel. It's hard to think back to what the Internet was in 1995, but it was anything but a business channel. It was a big experiment. It was text and hyperlinks and bad graphics. Students at UC Berkeley that I interviewed in 1995 for a project for CKS Partners about how people were using the Internet couldn't conceive of it ever being commercialized or using the Net to buy products. Jodi.org wasn't going to have a billion dollar exit. But big companies like McDonald's, Levi's, MTV, and Disney did begin using the Internet as part of a new business strategy—first as an experiment, then as a new marketing channel, and ultimately the Web and Internet-connected products have become one of the most significant forms of direct-to-consumer and B2B business communication and as a source of revenues. Especially the entertainment business, starting with music and now TV everywhere, film distribution, UGC on YouTube, and social apps: you get the drill. Business (not art) is what made the Web more than just a fad or a technology experiment. Ultimately—I hate to say it—if these efforts and these one-time experiments didn't ultimately contribute to the bottom line, they wouldn't exist. I have been lucky enough to work for some of the biggest companies in the world to be able to spend their money, or their investor's money, to prove out what works and what doesn't work in interactive media. I think once every five years or so, something crazy like Facebook comes along that has its own center of gravity and kind of pulls everybody forward. But those other four years and 364 days, we are putting one foot in front of the other, just inching out over the known horizon and trying to turn fundamental technology into killer products and build sustainable businesses.

A lot of what we do as UX strategists is informed by the work that other people are doing in parallel at a particular time. Rarely in the history of businesses has there been such a fluid landscape ahead, and the pace of change is quickening. We're still in the first couple of decades on how a globally connected media world really will affect the future of everything, not just what we view and see on our phones but the way that the world works in the future. Even this interview that we're doing right now over Skype would have been unfathomable 15 or 20 years ago. In *How We Got to Now*, Steven Johnson does a great job of explaining how small, incremental technology innovations and experiments, often performed by people who are never recognized for their contributions, can ultimately change the world for the better in ways they could have never foreseen. I'd like to think that the contributions we make as UX strategists are similar contributions that will ultimately make the world a better place.

Working in the entertainment and media business, looking at the evolution of platforms from PCs to music players, to smartphones, tablets, game consoles, new connected devices like the HoloLens or Oculus Rift, new devices like the Amazon Fire TV Stick that turn your TV screen into a whole new entertainment experience, it's a constant challenge to look out a little bit ahead of where the world is today and imagine what it's going to be like in the next few years. Just this week, Chase Carey, COO of 21st Century Fox, said in his earnings call that "the business you see today will not be the business you see in a few years." That said, the seeds of what's going to become normal human behavior really were there from the very beginning of the Internet. In 1994, at the "Information Superhighway Summit" in Los Angeles, Al Gore talked about the 500 Channel Universe and the Internet and that's the world we live in today—just add a few more zeros. Countless experiments need to happen before new technology enabled experiences become part of day-to-day behavior, and as a UX strategist, it's fun to be part of that effort. So basically, I learned business strategy from participating in all of these cross-platform product initiatives and seeing what did work and did not work with users.

4. Do you think it's helpful for UX designers who are aspiring strategists to get an MBA or have a business degree?

I think it's important for UX designers to be grounded in the reality of what it takes to be a successful company. I don't know if that really requires a business degree. I've worked with companies with thousands of employees and with companies with eight employees, and I think there's a certain value in everyone understanding the reality involved with everybody getting a paycheck every couple of weeks. That's something that really needs to be ingrained in people's mental models of why they go to work and what they do every day. There's a component of living and working in Silicon Valley in the last 20 years that kind of creates a false impression that there's an unlimited amount of money and that the next funding round will just get you through the next stretch of time until you can figure out exactly what your product needs to be and what market it serves. But, I don't think everybody's that lucky in the big, wide world. At the end of the day, you try to create a great product that people love to use, and that's a huge milestone, but it's not necessarily a business yet. Even companies like Facebook and Twitter that have built great user experiences and wildly successful products and take their companies public are under incredible pressure every quarter to meet those projected numbers, so well-designed and loved products aren't enough—you need to make money, and the more of it, the better. So, I don't think that it's possible to think about UX, product design, and UX strategy separate from the business realities of the world. I do think it's a requirement for a strategist to be grounded in basic understanding of how a business really works and scales.

5. What types of products have you done the strategy for that were the most exciting or fun to work on?

I've always had the opportunity to work on consumer-focused media and entertainment businesses, so for a kid growing up watching TV it's all fun. For me, from day one of the consumer Internet, we saw it as something that would be this kind of connected, unlimited, TV distribution platform. But, it wasn't really until consumer broadband began to happen at the end of the 1990s, when I was at Excite@Home, and moving into the 2000s, as people became familiar with how digital video would truly be under total user control on DVD and on DVRs like Microsoft's Ultimate TV and TiVo, that the dream became a daily reality for most of us. Now, with ubiquitous broadband, digital video, and a certain level of habituation around controlling media on connected devices, we finally have reached the world that I hoped we would at the very beginning of the Internet. What's been exciting and fun for me is always having the opportunity to create the first examples of what products on these new emerging platforms could be like. I love to explore how these technologies work and think about how they will make the entertainment experience better and more engaging as media moves to new platforms. There have been times that concepts and products I've worked on have washed up on the rocks of history, and there are other times they've proven to be widely adopted. I think they've all been fundamental stepping-stones to the way people use and interact with media entertainment today.

6. What are the some challenges of conducting strategy in different work environments (for example, startups versus agencies versus enterprises)?

I've had the opportunity to work at both big product companies like Excite@Home, DIRECTV, and TiVo, and also at interactive design agencies. For example, in the mid-2000s I was lucky enough to work for a while at Kevin Farnham's company Method, the brand experience design firm in San Francisco, and had the opportunity to start a media entertainment practice there that had both big entertainment product and service clients like Microsoft and Showtime Networks, and startups like Boxee.

For me, the easiest way to describe the challenges of conducting strategy in different work environments is that when you're inside of a product company, you're basically living in a world with blinders on;

your focus is 100 percent on your product and the market segment that you're competing in. Day-to-day focus is on the products that are currently in development, and all your energy goes into pushing that product development effort forward across all these different constituencies inside a company. When I was at DIRECTV, for example, they were in the business of putting satellites in space and sending video to set-top boxes in living rooms. So, the idea that we were going to create new "advanced services" that were new forms of data, and that you were going to bind that data to the satellite signal and download it to drive new user experiences, was met with a level of fear by the guys who built their careers as Hughes Corporation engineers. It was a new way to think about exploiting the platform they had developed, and their culture was one of absolutely avoiding risk. "You're going to download something that's going to turn millions of set-top boxes into bricks?" And the answer was, "Yes!" This kind of calculated risk-taking injected into a risk-averse culture at a big company is a big challenge, and it's not a surprise that it took a change in control—News Corp. bought the company and changed the culture—to create an environment where innovation could continue to flourish. The siloed nature of big corporate structures doesn't make taking risks a big part of the day-to-day. In fact, they're all there to mitigate risk and focus on maximizing profits from where the business is today. This is the innovator's dilemma, and as UX strategists, we deal with that in one way or the other every day.

When I worked at an agency, the challenge was a little bit different. You have very broad perspective. You have visibility into what a lot of companies in a broad range of industry segments are thinking about doing—and they need your help to actually get it done. The challenge in an agency environment is really trying to find a champion or advocate inside of your customer's company that can fight that good fight, given the things that are structurally inherent in corporations that I mentioned before. The tough part about that, though, is you do your work, complete your deliverable, and you walk away. Then, you work on the next project. The beautiful part of agency work is that you don't live inside of those client corporate cultures forever. The downside is that often those projects never see the light of day in the real world.

7. Have you ever conducted any form of experiments on your product or UX strategy, whether it be trying to get market validation on a value proposition or testing prototypes on target customers? How do you get closer to the truth while you are conducting strategy?

I think that that process either is or is not fundamentally baked into the culture of the place that you work at. Today, working in a 25-person venture-funded startup, we don't actually have the luxury of time to do the type of prototyping or testing on target customers that a big company has. You have to kind of posit a future where the things that we're doing are going to be wildly successful and ubiquitously deployed and ultimately enjoyed by a lot of people and keep our heads down to make that a reality. The world I worked in at TiVo was different: the corporate culture was more evolved, the user experience design group was very structured, and nothing got through to engineering or into product that hadn't gone through prototyping and UX testing. And not just in our lab in Silicon Valley. We would take new product concepts and prototypes to Cleveland and test them there. We needed to get out of the Silicon Valley "bubble" and see if we had something that resonated broadly. So in that culture, we would do extensive user and focus-group testing, roll that information back into prototypes—often we'd go through that a number of times before things got past the gate—and then you'd made it into the product. Although user-centric design is very much part of the product development process today at many of the largest and most successful companies, to me it's still seems like kind of luxury to work in an environment that fully embraces these design, prototyping, and testing best practices.

8. What is your secret weapon or go-to technique for devising strategies or building consensus on a shared vision?

I think that being able to focus on solving key business problems is core. You need to be able to clearly identify these nascent opportunities and come up with solutions that can be delivered quickly and will resonate in the marketplace, all while the landscape is rapidly changing around you. I'm working on some stuff right now around getting our television network customer's video out into big social networks like Facebook or Twitter. You see the way the world works today, and you think about the things your products can do for your customers and for consumers, and you try create products that will put your company in a place where everything comes together successfully out in the real world. But there's not really a lot of validation on it until it's out there. Maybe you nailed it. Maybe it was too late. Maybe it wasn't a great idea to begin with. I'm hopeful that the ideas from Eric Ries' Lean Startup movement—in particular the notion of defining and delivering the Minimal Viable Product—becomes a de facto part of startup and big business culture. For example, there are products I'm working on where I think we would benefit from that kind of methodology. It's just not part of the culture in every company quite yet.

9. What is a business case or anecdotal story that you can share that walks us through the steps you have to go through when conducting strategy specifically for an innovative product?

Almost all of my projects begin by a doing a technical overview and requirements analysis of a new technology platform. It is also the first opportunity to develop a clear articulation of what we see as the business opportunity. This initial work justifies dedicating resources to creating the new product or innovating on existing solutions. Because I'm not a software developer and don't have an engineering background, this is a collaborative effort with our CEO, a solutions architect, and/or senior engineer. At my current company Watchwith, this part of the product development process focuses on opportunities that are significantly ahead of where our current product management and engineering team is focused.

The technical overview sets a baseline understanding that I use to develop a creative brief (see Figure 10-9) that I use to bring the UX and visual design team into the process. While I speak with our customers to inform the creative brief, we are innovating in a space that they don't have a lot of time to think about or plan for. They are focused on supporting their business as it is today and we have an opportunity to help them see a bit over the horizon and provide a path forward. Because of where my company sits in the emerging platform media and entertainment ecosystem, we are in a position to lead the market more than responding to requests from our customers. Ultimately, we both need to unlock new sources of revenue that gives us some fundamental alignment on goals.

CONNECTED TV OVERLAY DESIGN PROJECT

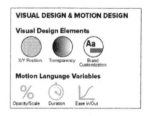

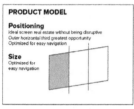

REQUIREMENTS

Technical Analysis & Requirements
Device specs provided by CE provider
Internal engineering team requirements

B2B User/Customer Observation
What do networks currently overlay?
Where does the main action take place?

B2C User/Consumer Observation
How do users currently interact with content?
What motivates/excited viewers?
How/where/why do viewers engage with programming?

RESEARCH

Best Practices
Observe other connected TV experiences
Examples include: SHO, HBO, etc.

Findings
Simple Intuitive Interaction
Content still observes 4:3 ratio
Overlays: primarily in lower right corner

CREATIVE BRIEF
Create a flexible design system for displaying events
overlaid and in sync with a television program on a tv
or set top box.

Success Criteria
Leave it on
Encourage Engagement
Flexible Solution

Design Criteria
Concise
Lightweight
Reactive

PRODUCT MODEL

Positioning
Ideal screen real estate without being disruptive
Outer horizontal third greatest opportunity
Optimized for easy navigation

Size
Optimized for
easy navigation

PRODUCT MODEL
Interface Layers

ENGAGEMENT
EVENT FEED
VIDEO

VISUAL DESIGN & MOTION DESIGN

Visual Design Elements

X/Y Position   Transparency   Brand
                              Customization

Motion Language Variables

%   Opacity/Scale   Duration   Ease In/Out

FIGURE 10-9
A creative brief

The creative brief includes a synopsis of the product goals and defines success criteria. This alignment around this creative brief document starts the conceptual investigation into product implementation options that will support our business goals. Next, we focus on defining a high-level interaction model for the product.

We've found that, at a minimum, simple PowerPoint product clicks through sequences based on wireframes really help illustrate key use-cases of the product. This step of the process where we see the UX begin to take shape is essential—wireframes alone are not enough to effectively communicate to the product and executive teams. Motion study videos are equally if not more effective as a communications tool, and when we have time and resources available, creating video is preferred.

While I speak with our customers to inform the brief, we are innovating in a space that they don't have a lot of time to think about or plan for. Because of where my company sits in the emerging platform media and entertainment ecosystem we are in a position to lead the market more than responding to asks from our customers. The creative brief and motion studies are the tools that help advance the discussion with stakeholders at the company and to build early consensus without customers and as they are reviewed/approved serve as the basis for initial development of early proof-of-concept or prototype engineering efforts and move out of my hands and into product management.

10. What are important skills or mindsets for a strategist to have? Or what makes you good at your job?

The best kind of mindset for a strategist to have is to be inquisitive and playful. Sometimes, people describe that as being clever. A belief that things *can be* different and a willingness to try—and sometimes fail—is pretty much at the core of what creative strategists, creative people in general, bring to their jobs every day. Even though the pace of our day-to-day work is daunting, great products take time to come into focus and be adopted broadly. This most often happens in very incremental steps over long periods of time. It wasn't the Apple Newton MessagePad (1993) or the Palm Pilot (1996) or the Microsoft Table PC (2001) that got to scale with consumers, it was the iPad (2010). It took DIRECTV more than 10 years (1994–2005) to get to 15 millions subscribers. The connected TV was just introduced in 2010 and won't be the dominant form of television until the end of this decade. I've been working on developing "interactive TV" products for consumers since 1994 when I created my first interactive television commercial for Levi's Youthwear and startup children's programmer daVinci Time and Space on the Time Warner Full Service Network, and I have no intention of stopping any time soon. So, I'd say having a certain type of patience is as important as having an inquisitive and playful mindset in order to be good at your job. That kind of patience comes from working to get the interactive product design process right, over and over again, every day, as we all work to invent the future together.

[11]

Dénouement

"And so, onwards...along a path of wisdom, with a hearty tread,
a hearty confidence...however you may be, be your own source of
experience. Throw off your discontent about your nature. Forgive
yourself your own self. You have it in your power to merge everything
you have lived through—false starts, errors, delusions, passions, your
loves and your hopes—into your goal, with nothing left over."
—FRIEDRICH NIETZSCHE, *HUMAN, ALL TOO HUMAN*

SOMETIMES, PRODUCTS NEVER SEE THE LIGHT OF DAY, AND TYPICALLY
never for reasons that you can expect or control. Financial crises, teams
burning out, new technologies arriving, personal motivation, broken
relationships, and more are a lot of variables beyond a UX strategy that
will come into play.

The software engineer whom you met in Chapter 1 pivoted to a B2B
model after our Landing Page experiments and attempted to negotiate
directly with insurance companies. But it was 2013, just as the entire
healthcare system in the US was restructuring to comply with the new
Affordable Care Act. When last I checked up on him, he told me how
he saw that it could take years to disrupt the process of how treatment
centers competed within a fragmented industry. There were just too
many variables out of his control that even a perfectly designed website, UX, or business strategy was not going to solve. In a heavy Russian
accent, the former chess prodigy half-jokingly told me that "I had killed
his business."

For my students, Bita and Ena, Airbnb for Weddings was their class
project, so when it over that was the end of it. They had other personal
and professional dreams to conquer. I'm sure they're rocking the world
wherever they are. (And if you'd like to develop the value proposition,
it's yours for the taking.)

For Jared, I recently spent the day with him at his Topanga Canyon home and talked about where he was with TradeYa. He's now spent four years of his life and a million dollars of investment conducting experiments to solve why bartering online is so hard. The mental model has proven tough to shift, and even with more than 80,000 users, TradeYa is averaging 10 successful transactions per day. It still has a long way to go before it successfully conquers its blue ocean of the sharing economy as Airbnb did. Nevertheless, Jared has a lot of expertise now on how to make the basics of an online barter interaction work. He knows his power users now—small businesses, independent contractors, and the burgeoning creative class of entrepreneurs.

I think it's important that we remember there are many risks in life—some professional and others personal, and often it is impossible to separate the two. Take, for instance, my maternal grandfather, Alex Zindler. He was born in 1907 in Tarnopol, Poland (now Ternopil, Ukraine). His earliest memory was watching the walls of his home crumble apart under heavy artillery during one of the many large-scale targeted attacks, or pogroms, against Jews. During one of these pogroms, his younger siblings were all killed.* His father died before he turned six. Then came World War I (1914–1918), which lasted until he was 11 years old. His country's name, the national language, and the street signs changed seven times while German, Austrian, and Russian forces surged back and forth, stamping their identity upon the town.†

In 1923, when Alex was 16, he and his mother Ronya fled Poland to avoid suffering further persecution. In search of a better life, they made their way by train to Antwerp, Belgium and boarded a ship bound for Quebec City, Canada. Tragically, though, on the way to North America, Ronya contracted cholera and died. A heartbroken Alex vividly remembered watching his mother be buried at sea.

Alex arrived in Quebec City a penniless, non–English speaking orphan with the threat of deportation back to a country he had just fled. Thankfully, a priest on board vouched for him so that he was able to stay. But Alex had to pay back the huge cost of the ship's passage to

---

*   *http://en.wikipedia.org/wiki/Ternopil*

†   *http://www.jewishvirtuallibrary.org/jsource/judaica/ejud_0002_0019_0_19604.html*

the priest, an enormous financial debt. To do that, he apprenticed as a tailor in Toronto for two years. By his late teens, he was enjoying his freedom, making lots of friends, and had taken up boxing as a hobby (Figure 11-1).

FIGURE 11-1
Photo of Alex Zindler (right) and his friend Irving Roth in 1925

For several years he practiced boxing, but a blow to his face during one of his fights caused a serious cataract to develop in one eye. After a botched surgery to repair it, Alex found himself blind in that eye with only a weak eye to get by. Many would have become discouraged or let this physical handicap limit their activites. But not Alex. He married, settled in Winnipeg, Manitoba, and had three children. To support his family, he worked with difficulty for more than 25 years as a dry cleaner presser. In 1957, at the age of 50, Alex suffered a major heart attack and became completely blind. Two years later, his wife passed away, leaving him alone to raise their youngest son.

But my Grandpa Alex didn't let these new tragedies trap him into a life of despair or failure. Instead, he faced his fear and got out of the house. Alex took mobility training so that he could travel independently by bus. He joined a blind bowling league and exercised at a gym. He encouraged his son to obtain the best education possible, because learning was everything to him.

But it was technology that gave Alex the most freedom. He was a true audiophile, buying the best possible gear for recording audio and listening to his massive record collection. He became a voracious consumer of books on tape and devoured the latest *New York Times* bestselling books.

In his 60s, through a nonprofit cooperative organization of recorder owners called the Voicespondence Club, Alex's social network expanded. Club members worldwide would use reel-to-reel tapes (and later cassette tape) to exchange stories about their daily lives, political meanderings, and even bootleg musical recordings. The club was basically the analog version of Facebook-meets-Napster. The cassette tape also was how he corresponded with my family in Los Angeles from Canada. My grandfather passed away in 1981 when he was 74. But thanks to his recordings that I heard as a child, I'll never forget his Polish accent and the uplifting stories he shared.

When you are a startup founder, product director, and even UX designer, building a digital product is a deeply personal path that can seem like a make-or-break life event. We pour our savings, health, and emotions into value propositions that we hope will change users' lives. But as inventors, we need to accept that failure, while an insurmountable barrier to some, might be an essential part of our product's journey toward success. We need to be like my grandfather—a man who did not allow the difficulties in his life to define the outcome of it. Instead, he kept pivoting, trying to live his life to the fullest, and he even found a means of using technology to do so.

Lessons to Learn

- Things don't always go as planned. We need to be agile and find new ways to move forward. Embrace life's challenges. Keep your mind active.

- Don't overlook opportunities to use everyday technologies in new and unexpected ways that can improve users' lives and help solve real problems.

- We are ultimately in charge of our lives, and we are defined by how we choose to live them. Our existence is what we make of it. DON'T WASTE IT.

[Index]

Gilt, as indirect competitors, 70–71
Google AdWords, using, 72–73
Google Analytics, 225
Google Glass, 242, 246
Gore, Al, 274
Gray, David, *Gamestorming*, 13, 135
growth hacking, 206–207
guerrilla user research
  main phases of
    about, 184–185
    analysis phase, 185, 202–204
    interview phase, 185, 198–202
    planning phase, 184–198
    Operation Silver Lake Café, 176–180
  user research vs., 180–183

H

habitual patterns, disrupting, 133
Halley, Lane, xii, 124–125
heuristic evaluation, 85
horizontal marketplace, 82, 215
Houston, Drew, value proposition of Dropbox, 154
hunches, value propositions and, 42

I

iContact, 226
Idol, Billy, Cyberpunk (CD special edition album), 121–122
indirect competitors, 70–71
influencers, UX
  cool features from, 111–113
  taking advantage of, 128–130
innovative, meaning of, 24
innovative products, conducting strategy for, 246–247
innovative services, conducting strategy for, 246–247
intelligence, competitive, 92
interactive prototypes, tools for, 171
interactive TV products, 280
interview
  problem
    conducting customer discovery using, 52–56
    in guerrilla user research, 187–189
  solution
    in guerrilla user research, 187, 189–190

interview phase, guerrilla user research
  about, 185, 198
  café etiquette, 199
  conducting interviews, 200–201
  note-taker for, 201–202
  participant compensation, 199
  preparing interview questions, 186–191
  prepping venue, 198
  recording devices in, 193
  tipping, 199
intrapreneurial, viii–ix, 29, 204
investors, wants of, 150
Invision, as tool for interactive prototypes, 171
iPad, growth of, 280

J

Johnson, Steven, 273
journey map vs. Funnel Matrix, 211–212
Joy Division, 175

K

Katz, Geoff, interview with strategist, 269–280
  on becoming a strategist, 270
  on challenges of conducting strategies, 275–276
  on creative briefs, 279
  on education of strategists, 274
  on experiments on products or UX strategy, 277
  on focusing on key business problems, 277
  on interactive TV products, 280
  on Lean Startup Movement, 278
  on learning about business strategy, 272–274
  on meaning of UX strategy, 270–271
  on skills for strategists, 280
  on technical overview, 278
Kelley, J.F., on OZ Paradigm, 158
Kempelen, Wolfgang von, creating chess-playing machine, 156
key experiences, identifying, 124–128
killer user experience design, as tenet of UX Strategy Framework

About the Author

Jaime Levy is a user experience strategist based in Los Angeles and heads the consultancy firm JLR Interactive. JLR Interactive caters to startups and enterprises, helping them transform their business concepts into sustainable and scalable online solutions.

Since the early 90s, Jaime has been creating innovative prototypes and products for distribution on disk media, mobile devices, the Web, and interactive television. She has worked for award-winning digital agencies such as Huge, Razorfish, and Schematic (now Possible) for many years, where she led the UX on projects for ABC, AOL, Dish Network, GE, iVillage, Oprah.com, and Union Bank.

She has taught UX design courses and lectured at numerous universities including Art Center of Pasadena, New York University, Royal College of Art, UCLA Extension, and currently at the University of Southern California. She speaks at design and innovation conferences worldwide and conducts public workshops and in-house training.

You can find Jaime online at *jaimelevy.com* and tweet at her @jaimerlevy.

Colophon

The animal on the cover of *UX Strategy* is a black-backed jackal (*Canis mesomelas*). The jackal is native to two areas of Africa: one region in the southernmost tip, including South Africa, Namibia, Botswana, and Zimbabwe; the other region along the east coast, including Keyna, Somalia, Djibouti, and Ethiopia.

The black-backed jackal is a very ancient species of canine, closely related to the side-striped jackal; earliest fossil carnivores can be linked to canids and date back to 38 to 56 million years ago. It is fox-like with a reddish coat and black saddle that runs from its shoulders to its tail.

It eats unprejudiciously: small to medium sized animals, plant matter, and human refuse. It is a monogamous animal; the young of a family sometimes remain to help raise new generations of pups, which allows for higher pup survival rates in this species. Mating season occurs from late May to August, gestation lasts 60 days, and pups are born between July and October, often coinciding with population peaks of prey such as vlei rats and four-striped grass mice (in the summer) and calving seasons (in the winter).

As illustrated by its eating habits, the black-backed jackal is very adaptable, and can thrive in a variety of habitats. The jackal can thrive even in deserts, as its kidneys are adapted to water deprivation. Wherever it lives, the jackal is highly territorial, using scent marking and vocalizations such as yelling, yelping, whining, growling, woofing, and cackling to advertise its presence.

The cover image is from Wood's *Animate Creation*. The cover fonts are URW Typewriter and Guardian Sans. The text font is Scala; and the heading font is Gotham.

Get even more for your money.

Join the O'Reilly Community, and register the O'Reilly books you own. It's free, and you'll get:

- $4.99 ebook upgrade offer
- 40% upgrade offer on O'Reilly print books
- Membership discounts on books and events
- Free lifetime updates to ebooks and videos
- Multiple ebook formats, DRM FREE
- Participation in the O'Reilly community
- Newsletters
- Account management
- 100% Satisfaction Guarantee

Signing up is easy:

1. Go to: oreilly.com/go/register
2. Create an O'Reilly login.
3. Provide your address.
4. Register your books.

Note: English-language books only

To order books online:
oreilly.com/store

For questions about products or an order:
orders@oreilly.com

To sign up to get topic-specific email announcements and/or news about upcoming books, conferences, special offers, and new technologies:
elists@oreilly.com

For technical questions about book content:
booktech@oreilly.com

To submit new book proposals to our editors:
proposals@oreilly.com

O'Reilly books are available in multiple DRM-free ebook formats. For more information:
oreilly.com/ebooks

O'REILLY®

©2014 O'Reilly Media, Inc. O'Reilly logo is a registered trademark of O'Reilly Media, Inc. 14373

CPSIA information can be obtained
at www.ICGtesting.com
Printed in the USA
BVOW11s0913180516

448592BV00004B/23/P

9 781449 372866